"A must read for individuals and pastors alike."
– Dwayne Barkman, retired pastor,
Warman, Saskatchewan

"I highly recommend this book."
– Lando Klassen, founder of House of James bookstore
Abbotsford, B.C.

"A sensitive and thought provoking read."
–Lorraine Dick, *Care Ministry Assistant,
Clearbrook Mennonite Brethren Church, Abbotsford, B.C.*

"A book every family and every pastor will want to possess to guide them through those times."
– *Norm Miller,
retired pastor, college president, professor, chaplain, and engineer*

"I encourage all readers to not only read these pages, but to also accept the wisdom and support they contain."
– *Scott Tolhurst, former Pastor of Clearbrook Mennonite Brethren Church, Abbotsford B.C.*

See more endorsements
at the back of the book.

Preparing to Cross the Finish Line

A Guide to Help Families, Individuals and Pastors with End-of-Life Issues and Funerals

By
Walter Wiens

Mill Lake Books

Copyright © 2022 by Walter Wiens
No part of this book may be reproduced in any form without written permission, except for brief quotations in critical reviews.

Mill Lake Books
Chilliwack, BC, Canada
https://jamescoggins.wordpress.com/mill-lake-books/

Cover design by Ryan Polinsky

Unless otherwise noted, Scripture quotations are taken from THE HOLY BIBLE, NEW INTERNATIONAL VERSION®, NIV© Copyright © 1973, 1978, 1984 by Biblica, Inc.® Used by permission. All rights reserved worldwide.

Scripture quotations marked as from The Jerusalem Bible are taken from the JERUSALEM BIBLE Copyright© 1966, 1967, 1968 by Darton, Longmand & Todd LTD and Doubleday and Co. Inc. All rights reserved.

ISBN: 978-1-7771926-9-3

Foreword

This book portrays the Christian life as a marathon, a long journey in the context of a Western, post-Christian culture. This marathon is a time in which people prepare to cross the finish line of their lives. This is a book that is thoroughly scriptural and packed with illustrations, designed to guide people through this marathon from where they are now through the challenges they will encounter as they move toward the victory ribbon.

The author, Pastor Walter Wiens, covers a wealth of life and death issues, starting from a ministry background that forms a strong foundation for this extensive and valuable document. After a pastoral ministry in Medicine Hat, Alberta, he moved on to become a chaplain at the Headingley Correctional Institution in Winnipeg, Manitoba for over thirteen years. Then he received valuable experience as a resident chaplain in Riverview Health Centre, Winnipeg, Manitoba. Since October 1, 2002, he has been the Pastor of Care Ministries in the Clearbrook Mennonite Brethren Church in Abbotsford, British Columbia, a church congregation predominantly composed of seniors. In this position, he has assisted in all levels of preparing for and officiating at more than four hundred funerals, walking with the families in their time of grief. This history of faithful ministry fully qualifies him to deliver the priceless teaching that flows through the pages of this book.

Scripturally, the marathon begins with a commitment to Christ and concludes when we come to the end of life and cross the finish life into the life beyond. Many Bible verses are used in the manuscript to provide a biblical underpinning for the subject matter.

When we are faced with our own death or the death of a loved one, there is a great need for counsel and loving guidance. When I was faced with the passing of Edna, the love of my life, my family and I became the thankful recipients of the comforting care offered by Walter and his wife Edith. As a retired pastor, it has also been my distinct privilege, not only to be an observer of Pastor Walter's ministry, but also to participate with him in conducting a fair number of funeral services. His care, compassion, and competence always came to the fore.

When death happens, there are a multitude of decisions that need to be made in a relatively short time, such as the choice of a funeral home, whether there will be a full funeral or none at all, and whether there will be a cremation or a burial. Other decisions include choosing a casket, choosing pallbearers, writing a eulogy, writing a life story, and preparing a notice for the newspaper. All of this is covered in this book.

In the course of the marathon, there might have been inner hurts and broken relationships with loved ones. These can seriously affect us at the time of a family member's death and complicate efforts to relate to one another during the planning of the funeral and during the funeral service itself. The author carefully deals with these delicate subjects at length, assuring us that healing is possible.

Most importantly, the author delves deeply into the spiritual preparation that needs to happen as we move toward the culmination of the spiritual marathon. Is there a way of finding assurance that we will actually cross the finish line to the glorious life beyond? There is a whole chapter in this book dealing with that subject, helping the reader to find assurance and peace.

Preparing to Cross the Finish Line is a book that every lay person and every member of the clergy should read in order to effectively run the Christian marathon themselves and to help others along the way.

– Art Isaac

Art Isaac served for twelve years in full-time pastorates and over twenty years in part-time ministries, as well as many years in church leadership. He is now enjoying full retirement, living with his children in Harrison Hot Springs, B.C. Art is a deeply loved mentor to the author.

Acknowledgements

As I reflect on this book, I am fully aware of my indebtedness to many people. When I begin to express thanks, I am aware that I will omit many people who had a part in the writing of this book.

I begin by expressing thanks to the many families I have had the sacred opportunity to walk with in their valley of loss and grief. Recognizing that each funeral service is a solemn journey with a family, I acknowledge that my heart has repeatedly been touched with grace and compassion.

I also wish to express my thanks and dedicate this book to the funeral directors who have partnered with me as we walked with grieving families. May God's compassion and wisdom fill and empower you to do this very important, yet often criticized, ministry for our fellow citizens.

I further wish to express my thanks particularly to several individuals who have given suggestions and helpful observations in the writing of this book in its various stages. As I recognize these people, I know I will unknowingly omit some people. Pastor Dwayne Barkman, my brother-in-law, not only provided observations on the first drafts of this book but also shared many conversations on pastoral ministry. The comments by Dwayne and his wife Irma were both instructive and encouraging. Rev. Norman Miller encouraged me to provide a broader church perspective, particularly as it pertained to funeral messages and burial words. Lando Klassen, founder of the House of James, a Christian bookstore, directed me to valuable resources, critiqued the manuscript, and encouraged me with the words that a book such as this one was much needed. When Vi Wiens became aware that I was writing this book, she stressed the value of it and encouraged me to speak with boldness and clarity in critical areas. Don Balzer, as a retired pastor, stressed the need for this book and challenged me to address some difficult areas.

It has been a sacred opportunity for my wife and me to share life with Art Isaac, and earlier with his dear wife Edna before God called her home. We value Art as a dear friend, but also as a wise spiritual father. Therefore, I have invited his input and suggestions and am grateful that he has accepted my invitation to write a Foreword to this book.

The person who has helped in ways too numerous to note in the writing of this book is David Giesbrecht. When I shared that I had a vision to write a book on helping people prepare to cross the finish line, David generously requested that he help me fulfill this vision. Over a period of more than five years, he has encouraged me to persevere, meeting regularly with me to check my progress and reading and critiquing the numerous drafts. David introduced me to Robert Martens and Jim Coggins. Robert Martens checked on the many small details that ensured the book would be presented in the best form, and Jim Coggins took the final manuscript and developed it into a book format.

I also wish to recognize Ryan Polinsky, who patiently provided numerous drafts of the book cover. Ryan, thank you for your creativity and perseverance in artistically displaying what it means to cross the finish line of life and be with Jesus.

The person who has had the greatest impact on my life, and therefore on the writing of this book, is my wife Edith. There are several areas in which I wish to express my gratitude to Edith. First, Edith has encouraged me through the numerous phases of our lives—seminary training, walking together in pastoral ministry, and particularly the times when I led families in their valleys of loss and grief. At times, I did not believe this book would ever come to completion; at those times, Edith urged that we take another vacation/study break to continue the hard work of writing. Her encouragement is a major reason this book has finally reached completion. Therefore, I gladly give my warmest thankyou to Edith, my soul mate for over 53 years. As I thank Edith, I wish to recognize with humility and deepest gratitude our children and their spouses, Andrew and Sara as well as Amy and Keith.

– Walter Wiens

Table of Contents

Preface 13

PART ONE: A GUIDE FOR FAMILIES AND INDIVIDUALS
Introduction and Overview 19
Chapter One: Being with People as They Cross the Finish Line 25
Chapter Two: The Need for a Funeral Service 29
Chapter Three: The Need to Plan a Funeral Service 33
    1. Plan as a Family
    2. Preplanning Funeral Services
    3. Preplanning while You Still Can
    4. Selecting a Funeral Home
    5. Planning Reveals Our Core Values
Chapter Four: Parts in a Funeral Service 49
    1. Naming of the Service
    2. Viewing
    3. Flowers
    4. Donations in Memory of a Loved One
    5. Obituary/Eulogy/Life Story/Tributes
    6. Children
    7. Bulletins
    8. Hymns, Spiritual Songs, and Special Music
Chapter Five: Burial Service, Interment or Committal Service 67
    1. Parts of a Burial Service
    2. Coffins
    3. Pallbearers
    4. Special Items in a Burial Service
Chapter Six: Recognizing Family Brokenness 75
Chapter Seven: Writing Our Life Story: A Personal and a Faith Legacy 79
    1. Principles and Values that Should Determine Our Approach
    2. Guidelines for Writing Life Stories
Chapter Eight: Assurance That We Will Cross the Finish Line
to Eternal Life 87
    1. A Believer in Jesus Is Assured to Cross the Finish Line
    2. A Follower of Jesus Is Assured to Cross the Finish Line
    3. Those Who Look Forward to the Prize Jesus Has for Them
        Are Assured to Cross the Finish Line.
    4. A Lover of Jesus (His Bride) Is Assured to Cross the Finish Line
Chapter Nine: Restoring Hope and Acceptance of the Present
as We Near the Finish Line 95

    1. Enjoy the Present—It Is a Gift of God
    2. Accept the Present with Gratitude
    3. Trust in God's Constant Care, Right to the End
Chapter Ten: Restoring Peace in Relationships as We Near the Finish Line 103
    1. Why Bother Restoring Broken Relationships?
    2. How Can I Have the Strength to Pursue Restoration when My Health Is Failing?
    3. Preliminary Thoughts on Restoring Relationships
    4. Classes of Broken Relationships
    5. Restoring Peace within the Family
Chapter Eleven: Running the Race and Crossing the Finish Line in Community 121
    1. An Acknowledgment that We Live in an Individualistic Society
    2. Weep with Those who Weep
    3. The Balance between Supporting and Empowering/Resourcing
    4. A Society's Care for the Weak and Vulnerable
    5. The Various Models of Living in Community
    6. Are We Our Elders' Keepers?
    7. Mentoring: Valuing the Wisdom and Blessings of Our Elderly

PART TWO: A GUIDE FOR PASTORS
Introduction and Overview 135
Chapter One: Being with People as They Cross the Finish Line 141
    1. The Hardest Climb: The Last Lap
    2. Sacred Moments
    3. The Metaphor of a Marathon
Chapter Two: Recognizing the Western, Post-Christian Culture in which We Help People Prepare to Cross the Finish Line 149
    1. The Minimal Training in Theological Institutions
    2. The Importance Placed on Funerals by Pastors
    3. Ageism
    4. Professionalism
    5. Individualism in a Spiritual Community
    6. Selfishness
    7. An Avoidance of Intense Pain and Suffering
    8. An Avoidance of Embracing the Declining Years
    9. An Avoidance of Death Itself
    10. MAiD: Medical Assistance in Dying
    11. Youth-oriented versus Intergenerational Churches
    12. Consumerism
    13. Restricting Care to Only Those in the Church Family

Chapter Three: Changes in Funeral Practices 181
    1. A Funeral or a Memorial Service?
    2. The People Present at the Cemetery
    3. An Emphasis on Joy rather than Sadness
    4. Viewing of the Body
    5. No Public Service
    6. Burial or Cremation
    7. The New Way of Death

Chapter Four: Planning the Funeral Service 193
    1. Plan Ahead
    2. Have Clear Guidelines
    3. Plan with Compassion
    4. Proceed with Gentleness
    5. Lead and Listen
    6. Plan with an Awareness of Our Own Limitations as well as
       Our Own Issues

Chapter Five: Partnering with a Funeral Home 197

Chapter Six: Components of a Funeral Service 199
    1. Naming of the Service
    2. Viewing
    3. Flowers
    4. Donations in Memory of a Loved One
    5. Obituary, Eulogy, Life Story, Words of Tribute
    6. Grieving during a Public Service
    7. Children
    8. Bulletins
    9. Hymns and Special Music

Chapter Seven: The Burial, Interment, or Committal Service 219
    1. Burial Words from a Free Church Tradition
    2. Burial Words from Other Christian Traditions
    3. Parts of a Burial Service
    4. Special Features in a Burial Service

Chapter Eight: Words of Caution 237
    1. Recognize Family Brokenness
    2. Extending Grace to Those Who Are Hurting

Chapter Nine: A Word to Fellow Pastors 243
    1. Recognizing Our Pastoral Priorities
    2. Walking with God
    3. Listening and Reconciling
    4. Leading as a Shepherd
    5. Respecting Clergy Confidentiality
    6. Representing God Faithfully and Compassionately
    7. Accepting Brokenness as Stories Are Shared Publicly

    8. Acknowledging Our Own Brokenness and Limitations
Chapter Ten: The Life Story: A Personal and Faith Legacy 253
Chapter Eleven: The Funeral Service 259
    1. A Brief History of the Christian Funeral
    2. The Essence of the Christian Funeral
    3. Funeral Manuals: Their Value and Some Reservations
    4. The Christian Funeral Service
    5. Other Ministry Areas to Remember
    6. Metaphor of a Baton or Torch
Chapter Twelve: The Funeral Message 269
    1. What Do We Not Preach on in a Funeral Message?
    2. What Do We Preach on in a Funeral Message?
    3. To Whom Do We Preach?
Chapter Thirteen: Difficult Funerals 281
    1. Preliminary Thoughts on Difficult Funerals
    2. Funerals during a Pandemic
    3. Funerals for Those Who Have Committed Suicide
    4. Funerals for Those Not in the Faith
    5. Funerals after a Lengthy and Often Painful Illness
    6. Funerals for Victims of Murder
    7. Funerals for Children
    8. Funerals when There Are Conflicting Expectations or Desires among the Grieving Family
    9. Requests from Outside Our Church
Chapter Fourteen: Assurance that We Will Cross the Finish Line 297
    1. Two Attitudes and Three Commitments
    2. Two Key Questions
    3. Two Personal Convictions
    4. Five Popular Summaries of the Core Bible Truths
    5. Six Cautions regarding these Five Four-point Summaries
    6. Assurance of Salvation?
    7. Following Jesus: An Intimate Relationship Now and Forever
    8. Two Prayers that Provide Assurance that You Will Cross the Finish Line and Be with Jesus for All Eternity
Appendices 311
    Appendix A: Writing a Personal Life Story
    Appendix B: Forms Provided by a Church
    Appendix C: Legal and Financial Matters
    Appendix D: Health Matters
    Appendix E: Necessary Information
    Appendix F: Definitions
    Appendix G: Selected Books on Aging and the End of Life
    Appendix H: Index

Preface

The Psalmist prayed that God would not cast him away and forsake him when he was old and his strength was gone. Jesus implored his closest disciples to stay with him as he knew his greatest time of need was near. These two calls for help and for support, uttered years ago by the Psalmist and by Jesus, are expressed by many older people.

> "Do not cast me away when I am old; do not forsake me when my strength is gone" (Psalm 71:9). "He (Jesus) took Peter and the two sons of Zebedee along with him, and he began to be sorrowful and troubled. Then he said to them, 'My soul is overwhelmed with sorrow to the point of death. Stay here and keep watch with me'" (Matthew 26:37-38).

This means that what I wish to address in this book is not a new phenomenon. My desire is to speak to the topic of walking with people in their final stage of life, helping them as they make key decisions. My goal is to do so from a biblical and theological framework that deals with practical issues and also speaks to our current cultural environment. I have sensed a growing conviction to write on these issues as I have walked with elderly people and their families. God has led me on a particular path in my faith journey. In this faith journey, I have perceived a sensitivity to older people and therefore how best to be present with them.

On this journey as a pastor, God has given my wife and me the privilege of walking with individuals at various stages and circumstances of life. Following a thirteen-year period of being Jesus to inmates in a correctional institution, I was a resident chaplain in the Riverview Health Centre, Winnipeg, Manitoba. This gave me a greater understanding of, and compassion for, elderly people. It gave me more familiarity with how best to walk with the residents in their final years—even months, days, and hours—of life. We sensed that God was directing our ministry focus to be with elderly people.

Therefore, the next key milestone in our lives seemed very natural. This was when my wife and I discerned God's leading to serve as a pastoral couple in a church in British Columbia. This congregation consists mostly of elderly people. Then, after serving about ten years—walking with individuals in their final years and months and planning many funerals—I again discerned God speaking to me, saying, "Walter, I have called you and your wife into this care ministry with elderly people. I want you to reflect deeper on what is involved in caring for elderly people."

In response, I did three specific things. First, I purchased and read books that dealt with elderly people. (These books are included in the resources at the end of this book.) Second, I took three summer courses at Regent College on understanding the needs of elderly people. Third, I took a vacation that was actually a study break where my goal was to read and study the broad area of serving older people.

In this vacation/study break, I read and then began writing observations and reflections on various aspects of caring for older people. After reading and reflecting for several days, I felt God's Spirit nudge me to also write down what I had learned from helping families with funerals. I had often heard from family members that they had wished that a basic manual on planning a funeral was available. When I shared the vision of this guide book, various individuals recommended that I divide this book into two sections: one for elderly people and their families, and the other for pastors who are walking with elderly people.

The initial scope of the manuscript was limited to helping people plan funerals. However, as I wrote down my experiences and read about the various facets of preparing funerals, I became aware that

> Four of the first books that informed me on the critical issues facing elderly people and challenged me to respond with a biblical perspective are:
> - Stanley Hauerwas, Carole Bailey Stoneking, Keith G. Meador, and David Cloutier, eds. *Growing Old in Christ*.
> - James M. Houston and Michael Parker. *A Vision for the Aging Church: Renewing Ministry for and by Seniors*.
> - Fred Craddock, Dale Goldsmith, and Joy V. Goldsmith. *Speaking of Dying: Recovering the Church's Voice in the Face of Death*.
> - Allen Verhey. *The Christian Art of Dying: Learning from Jesus*.

the funeral and burial are only one aspect of the final steps of our lives. I envision our lives as a marathon and our funeral and burial as marking our crossing the finish line. The title of this book expresses my goal to help people prepare to cross their finish line. But the more I reflected on the scope of the book, the more I became aware that a person's preparedness to "cross the finish line" needs to begin long before a person starts to make funeral preparations. In fact, we always need to be prepared to "cross the finish line."

This begs the questions: "What is involved in being prepared? How can I be prepared?" These questions can be answered on several levels. These levels involve relationships—with God, with people, and with ourselves. I begin with the premise that the core identity that makes us human is that we are relational beings. This means that we are fully alive and fully prepared to cross the finish line when all our relationships are right. In this book, I will touch on principles as well as practical steps that will help us in our relationships—with God, with people, and with ourselves.

> "LORD, who may dwell in your sanctuary? Who may live on your holy hill?... Who may ascend the hill of the LORD? Who may stand in his holy place?" (Psalm 15:1, 24:3). The Psalmist's answers to these questions confirm that a person's relationship with God will be evident in his character and actions.

I recognize that some people maintain that a person needs only to be in a right relationship with God to be prepared to cross the finish line. In other words, they believe that when they have made peace with God, they are then prepared to die. I am convinced that a person's right relationship with God impacts this person's relationship with other people, and certainly with himself. Therefore, the scope of this book needs to be more than what might be perceived by some people as the core requirement to be prepared to cross the finish line: stepping from life on earth to life with God in heaven.

This book is organized into two main parts along with an appendix. The first part applies to any individual who is becoming older, as well as to this person's family. The second part applies to any pastor who is walking with elderly people and is helping them, not only by preparing their funeral service, but also assisting with other major end-of-life issues.

These two major parts are made up of smaller sections or chapters. Each chapter is concluded with summary thoughts, reflections, and often a challenge, as well as a prayer. My goal is that this book will not only be a source of helpful information, but also a guide that will inspire personal reflection and action.

PART ONE:
A GUIDE FOR FAMILIES AND INDIVIDUALS

"Death be not proud, though some have called thee Mighty and dreadfull, for, thou art not soe,
For, those, whom thou think'st, thou dost overthrow,
Die not, poore death, nor yet canst thou kill mee…
One short sleep past, wee wake eternally,
And death shall be no more; death, thou shalt die."

– John Donne, "Holy Sonnet X"

Introduction and Overview

This section (Part One) is dedicated to elderly individuals and their children or friends and families. In the second section (Part Two), I have words directed specifically for pastors.

Are you an older person or senior who wants to begin writing some ideas that you wish to be part of your funeral service? Your last will and testament is in place, but do you have questions about your funeral details? Do you find yourself asking questions such as the following:
- What funeral home should I choose?
- What should I include in my life story?
- What special items would I like in my funeral service?

If you are thinking ahead to your own funeral, this book is for you.

Are you an adult son or daughter of a mother or father who has just died? I had met with an adult son and other family members to plan his mother's funeral service. As the son left our meeting, he stopped me and commented, "Before I came here to plan mother's service, I had no idea what had to be done. The church should provide a booklet on the basic things involved in planning a funeral service." Do any of the following apply to you:
- Do you wish that your elderly mother would talk to you about her funeral desires?
- Are you not sure how to bring up the topic of a parent's funeral or something else you really want to talk about?
- Do you know that you will be responsible to plan the funeral service of a loved one?

This book is for you!

Here is an overview of Part One:

Chapter One: Being with People as They Cross the Finish Line

As we begin thinking about the funeral service, there will be other matters that come to our mind. Looking at the parts involved in a funeral service might be compared to looking in a mirror. As we note the items we will take care of in the funeral, our spirit will remind us of things we believe we will want to attend to or at least things we will be prompted to consider. Recognizing that this will happen, this book is not only devoted to help you plan a funeral service. The planning for a funeral service must include more than the specific details of the service. As will become evident, we can only properly plan a funeral service when other details of life are taken care of. This book is for all of us who are in the last stage of life. Yet, since we know that none of us lives in isolation from other people, this book is also for those who walk with elderly people—parents, aunts, uncles, and friends. The book begins with a recognition that walking with people in their final moments brings about an awareness of the sacredness of life. This also means that we will want to embrace and treat the moments before and after death not only with sensitivity and compassion but also with courage and wisdom.

Chapter Two: The Need for a Funeral Service

The need for a funeral service is based on the premise that our lives and our deaths matter because we are of value. Therefore, when we cross the finish line, a funeral is needed as an occasion for grief and thanksgiving, for recognizing our loss and acknowledging God and his compassion, presence, and wisdom in our lives and the lives of our loved ones.

Chapter Three: The Need to Plan a Funeral Service

It follows naturally that there is a need to plan the funeral service. This chapter emphasizes that this planning should best be done together with the loved one and the family, so that the wishes of all are considered.

Chapter Four: Parts in a Funeral Service

Chapter Four introduced the various parts in a funeral service. This chapter begins with considering the name of the service: is it a funeral, a memorial service, or a celebration of life? Then, the chapter goes on to address items such as viewing the body, flowers, donations, music, the life story, and the bulletin.

Chapter Five: Burial Service, Interment, or Committal Service

Chapter Five presents the parts of a burial service, addressing matters such as the selection of a coffin and meaningful practices that a family might want to include in a burial service.

Chapter Six: Recognizing Family Brokenness

Chapter Six presents the likelihood and therefore the challenge that the death of a loved one and the ensuing funeral service might be an occasion that will expose family brokenness and heartache. As we become aware of this brokenness, we will not want to ignore the difficulties. But we will want to receive God's grace and also extend his grace to others with a goal of bringing healing.

Chapter Seven: Writing Our Life Story

In chapter Seven, the focus is on our life story. The purpose of a life story is that it be an honest expression of our faith journey with God. We will want to write our life story with the goal that God be glorified. We will do so by providing an open account of our brokenness and of God's faithfulness. Another goal of our life story is that those who hear and read the life story will be given hope that God can similarly be gracious to them in their failures and waywardness.

Chapter Eight: Assurance that We will Cross the Finish Line to Eternal Life

This chapter deals with being assured that when we cross the finish line, we will have eternal life. This chapter is based on the premise that being prepared to cross the finish line from this life to eternal life with Jesus for all eternity includes much more than making the funeral arrangements. We must have a restored relationship with God. This is possible only through faith expressed by obedience to Jesus. We will only have complete peace with God when we have peace with all the people he has placed next to us in our relationships.

Chapter Nine: Restoring Hope and Acceptance of the Present as We Near the Finish Line

This chapter is about the reality that, as we near the end of life, we might despair and have difficulty accepting the hard realities around us. Towards the end of life, the challenges and trials might increase. Therefore, when we are tempted to give up and despair, we need to accept what is happening because we believe our lives, with all our trials included, are lived under God. We appreciate that marathon runners can sometimes become discouraged and lose hope as they reach the end of the race. Similarly, we might have doubts about whether we will make it to the end of life. Yes, we might have peace with God, but as we come to the end of life, our sense of hope and peace might be lacking or at least diminishing. We can easily become discouraged. In this chapter, my goal is to restore hope, even when life seems to crash in with many trials and difficulties.

Chapter Ten: Restoring Peace in Relationships as We Near the Finish Line

Chapter Ten recognizes that relationships might be broken and we are called to restore them. The ultimate reason we must take the trouble to restore relationships is that God took the trouble to restore humankind to himself. As God's followers who have been reconciled to him, we should do all we can to restore relationships. The focus in this chapter is to provide direction that will help restore peace with other people. I believe we will only be fully prepared to cross the finish line when all our relationships are restored.

Chapter Eleven: Running the Race and Crossing the Finish Line in Community

Chapter Eleven looks at an aspect that is often overlooked. In the first ten chapters, we focused on the necessary preparations each of us needs to make to ensure we will cross the finish line. But, as we know from any Olympic marathon, there are many people who are supporting, encouraging, and helping each runner successfully run her or his race. This closing chapter is about the need for community as we run the last lap of life and cross the finish line. None of us is independent and self-sufficient. We need one another in all phases of life. This is especially evident in the final phase of life, our last lap in our life marathon. Even though we recognize that seniors are responsible to be prepared to cross the finish line, with all the areas that are included in that responsibility, we need to provide another emphasis. This emphasis is that the family, the church, and the community are also responsible for the welfare of seniors, particularly as they become frail and vulnerable in the last lap of the marathon of their lives.

Reflections

The metaphor of a marathon—and specifically the last phase before crossing the finish line—fits our lives. In the beginning of a marathon, the runners demonstrate strength and resolve. But as the runners near the finish line, they might be completely exhausted and even unsure whether they will be able to make it across the finish line. The spectators will cheer on the runners, encouraging them to endure and give their best. Even though the runners are frail—and some might even be so exhausted that they can barely crawl across the finish line—each runner is still cheered and valued. Yet, do we do the same for one another as we approach the end of our lives? No one would ever suggest a runner has less dignity and worth because the runner is extremely weak and can barely stumble through the last part of the race. Yet, do we give one another less dignity as we become frail and sick toward the end of our lives? As every runner in a marathon deserves recognition, so every person deserves a service of remembrance. In this book, we will reflect on how we can best honor one another as we run the marathon of life and finally cross the finish line.

Prayer
Our heavenly Father, with the psalmist David, we pray, "O LORD, you have searched us, and you know us….All the days ordained for us were written in your book before one of them came to be. How precious to us are your thoughts, O God." We honor you as our God who knows each of our days and who cares deeply for us. May our recognition of you and your love impact how we perceive our lives. Also, may this awareness of you be evident as we reflect on our lives and our loved ones' lives. May you receive all honor and praise as we reflect on our lives and then plan and provide funeral services. All honor belongs to you—in life and in death. In Jesus' name, Amen.

Chapter One
Being with People as They Cross the Finish Line

In the Introduction, I noted that our lives can be compared to a marathon that begins at birth and concludes as we cross the finish line at death. I further mentioned that there is nothing more important for any of us than to be ready for the moment when we cross the finish line.

Several times, God has graciously given me the privilege of being present at that most sacred moment when a dear person took her or his last breath. My wife Edith and I, along with her sister, stood around her father's bed as he was drawing his last breath. His spirit was with us one moment, and the next moment he was with Jesus.

Several years earlier, while I was a resident chaplain at Riverview Health Centre in Winnipeg, Manitoba, a husband requested that I stay with him as his wife neared death and to be with them as she died. Another time, a friend in Abbotsford, British Columbia, asked that Edith and I be with him as the hospital monitors showed life slowly ebbing away from his wife. On numerous occasions, we have stood with family members, holding hands, reading Bible promises, and expressing God's comfort, just hours before a loved one was called home to heaven. At other times, families have asked that we join them at the bedside of a loved one who had died.

On one particular occasion, I sensed God's Spirit directing me to visit a dying member of our church. When my wife and I entered his room, his wife was sitting next to his bed. After I took the seat beside his wife, she looked up at her husband and noted, "He just passed away." God called this elderly man home at the very minute that we walked into his room. We were able to be present to care for his wife as she faced a future without her husband, who had passed away in our presence, this time without us being aware that this was God's moment to take a saint home.

These sacred moments have changed how we perceive funerals. A close friend shared that he also has a new perception of death after he was present as his wife passed away. He wrote that his wife's passing from here to glory was the first occasion he had witnessed someone's death. It was a very sacred moment but also very traumatic, as he realized he was now alone. His life's partner was gone. (In this book I am using the word "funeral" to refer to celebration of life services, memorial services and funerals. Later, I will note the distinction between these terms.)

God has also given me the opportunity to plan and lead many funerals. Walking with families during these sacred moments has left a deep impression on my heart, and I thank God for this. I recognize these to be holy moments. Therefore, I remind myself of Paul's words to Timothy: "Do your best to present yourself to God as one approved, a workman who does not need to be ashamed and who correctly handles the word of truth" (2 Timothy 2:15). This means that even though I have planned many funerals and have also been with individuals in those sacred moments as they take their last breath, I need to realize in a greater manner than ever the solemnity of life and the seriousness of death. Therefore, in Paul's words, I want to do my best before God since I am God's workman.

Even while I accept my commitment to do my best as I write this book, I identify with the Apostle Paul's testimony, "But we have this treasure in jars of clay to show that this all-surpassing power is from God and not from us" (2 Corinthians 4:7). I use this testimony from the Apostle Paul to make clear that I am placing my frailty over against the magnificence and enormity of the topic of this book. I identify with J. Todd Billings, who recognized his inability to comprehend the subject matter in his book, *The End of the Christian Life*. He acknowledged his frailty with the words, "I write as an act of pilgrimage, I cannot possibly master the realities about which I speak in this book—the mysteries of death and new life, and his gospel among crumbling mortals….In speaking of God, I speak of One whom I cannot comprehend. As Augustine of Hippo stated boldly in the fourth century, 'If you have been able to comprehend it, you have comprehended something else instead of God'" (Billings, 17).

When I began this book, my focus was primarily on the practical steps to be followed in planning a funeral and burial service. Yet, the longer I reflect on this topic, the more I realize these practical directions can never be fully adequate nor will they ever do justice to the subject matter—being present during the final moments before death, experiencing the death of a loved one, pondering how to remember a loved one, and then preparing for this solemn moment. What began as writing a "manual" on preparing to cross the finish line has shifted to reflecting on the most sacred and solemn moments in any person's life. I trust that an awareness of the magnificence and grandeur of the topic will be evident in my writing.

Just as the Apostle Paul described humans as "jars of clay," I point to the fact that the word "humanity" has as its root in "humus," "which means "of the earth." In this book I am reflecting that we who are "of the earth" will eventually return to the earth. But we also have in us the breath of God; we are created in his image. We who are mortal will be immortal; we who are of the earth will be clothed with a heavenly body. Our "finish line" is not when we return to the earth. Our lives will continue through all eternity. This places a different perspective on being prepared for the day we cross the finish line.

Reflections

Within a span of a year, we will watch thousands of violent acts on the news. This can lead us to become callous to the finality of death and even to the tragedy of cruel acts of murder and violence. We need to stop and take a moment to consider the solemn and sacred moment when God takes breath away. Ponder these questions:

- How have I been present when a loved one passed away? What emotions did I feel?
- How have I walked with a loved one who is becoming weaker with a terminal disease?
- When an individual is near the end of life, how do I remain present with this person?

Prayer

Father God, in a world of violence and cruel and murderous deaths, may I see life and death through your lens. May I sense the preciousness of every moment. May I be grateful for all you give—for each moment of life. May I fully cherish the gift of life. In the name of Jesus, who is the resurrection and the life, Amen.

Chapter Two
The Need for a Funeral Service

Some years ago, an elderly man in our church expressed this thought: "You don't need to have any funeral service for me." This man had been active in our church; he had a loving family as well as many friends. As his death drew near, a good number of his friends had already passed away. Since I was acquainted with this man, I knew he would have felt their loss and been present at their funeral services. He was weak and frail in his last months and weeks. The family found it difficult and not easy to hear these words given right at the end of a dear husband's and father's grueling last days.

How was this family to respond to this request? Throughout his lifetime, this man had fully participated in life. His family recognized that these words were said because he was frail, full of pain, and discouraged. He spoke out of his depression and misery.

The family chose to honor his request. But they also knew their mother and the children and grandchildren would be devastated if they could not honor a dear husband, father, and grandfather. Therefore, they did not have a normal funeral service, but they had a short service as part of a reception. They had many good memories and shared them at the luncheon.

In this man's situation, his words were not consistent with the rest of his life. He had always thought of others and would do what was best for his family and friends. His final wish was therefore not in keeping with his character.

However, the trend not to have any form of a service where family, friends, and other people can gather is becoming more frequent in our Western society. A family might place a short obituary in the newspaper and then add the words, "No service by request."

We ask, "Why would individuals not desire that family and friends have a funeral service for themselves?" or "Why would a family not want to have a funeral service for one of its members—a father, a mother, a sibling, or even a child?"

Another perplexing phenomenon, at least for me, is that people will attend or watch a memorial service for a celebrity, a famous actor, or a slain police officer, but they will not plan a service where their family and friends can attend their own funeral. Does it bother us that we will watch the televised funeral of someone we don't know over TV, but we will not be able to attend a funeral of a close friend we have known for years—just because the family will not plan a service for their father or mother? What if the family of a police officer who was shot, or the family of a political leader who died while in office, stated, "No service by request." Would our response be, "That can't be done. The city or the country must provide a service for her or him"? We think it is inconceivable that a well-known politician or celebrity or slain police officer would not be given a public funeral. Yet, how can we then not provide a public funeral where others can express their love and respect for us or our loved one?

Answers to these questions need to draw us to our knees. How we view the dead, our loved ones, and our own death, is one of the greatest tests of our society—and of us individually. Thomas Lynch wrote, "A failure to deal authentically with death may have something to do with an inability to deal authentically with life" (Thomas G. Long and Thomas Lynch, *The Good Funeral*, 60).

In the first chapter, I compared our lives to a marathon. In any marathon, two things occur when a runner crosses the finish line. First, the runner will celebrate that he or she made it to the end. The celebration might be very muffled and feeble because the runner is extremely exhausted. Yet, there will be a sense of, "I made it. At times, I did not know that I could, but I finally crossed the finish line." Second, the spectators, and certainly the runner's family and friends, will celebrate that the runner crossed the finish line.

An underlying premise in this book is that our lives and our deaths matter because we matter. Crossing the finish line is an occasion to celebrate. I believe all of us should have a sense of victory and of pride in completing a long life and should want those who knew and loved us to acknowledge this. Also, since our lives matter, a natural response is that those who know us will want to stop and recognize our lives—and therefore their loss. This means that crossing the finish line is also an occasion to grieve. Funerals are the natural response we should have to the death of every person.

If there is any doubt in our minds, or in the minds of our family, whether a funeral is needed or worthwhile, may I ask the more basic question: "Do we matter? Do we matter to ourselves and to our families and friends?" The answers to these questions are an absolute and undeniable, "Yes!" Therefore, the next question is, "How do we go about planning a funeral service?"

Reflection
Have I ever thought:
- Why should my family have a funeral service for me?
- Why not just bury me and get it over with?
- Why not just burn me up and scatter my ashes?

Certainly, there will be moments when I am discouraged and feel insignificant and unimportant. However, may I always realize that I do matter.

Prayer
Father God, I turn my eyes up to you—and then I recognize my worth. May I never accept the notions that I do not matter and that a funeral is unnecessary, pointless, and an unwarranted effort and expense. May I see my worth through your eyes. In Jesus, who expressed his worth in me by being a human person and by dying for me, Amen.

Chapter Three
The Need to Plan a Funeral Service

1. Plan as a Family

From my observation, most families plan funerals together. They will do all they can to draw everyone into the planning. When they gather to plan their mother's or father's service, they listen to one another. As they plan, the passing of their parent is still very painful. The grief is deep. They gather to comfort one another. Then they meet together with their mother's or father's pastor. They listen to one another, committed to planning a service that will honor their parent, glorify God, and unite their family. Often the family members will phone, email, or text the siblings who cannot be present to help plan the service. They do their best to include all the family members in the decisions made. Those present are committed to the goal that everyone will reach agreement on all the decisions—decisions they hope will honor their parent, maintain unity, and restore broken or fragile relationships.

> **Who is Responsible?**
> Who is responsible to process the funeral details? The answer will depend on various factors. Some people are of the opinion that only immediate children should be involved in the planning of a service, along with all the details. They extend this argument to other decisions, such as the distribution of a parent's belongings. In this case, the extended family members and the in-laws are not involved in key decisions. Regardless of what decision is made, the question of who is responsible to plan a funeral needs to be answered. It is important that the answer draw the family members together rather than tear them apart.

When a family does not plan together the details involved in the funeral and the related issues at the end of life, regretful and negative consequences will occur. I cannot emphasize strongly enough that there be coordinated planning in which the desires of all the family members are considered and heard. Grieving families should listen to one another.

Sadly, I recall several painful occasions when families did not plan together, listen to each other, or attempt to bring about reconciliation and unity. On one occasion, the family had just returned from the cemetery and was assembling prior to entering the sanctuary for the memorial service. I noticed that one family member, a daughter-in-law, was distressed. I asked her what the problem was. With the family standing nearby in scattered groups, she blurted out with intense antagonism, "He (the oldest son, her brother-in-law) did it again. He always does it. As the oldest in the family, he has never considered how anyone else wants anything. This happened at the burial. This is happening in the service. He never thinks of anyone else but himself. He never asks for anyone else's opinions or desires." I knew that, as the oldest son, he was within his legal rights as the family executor. And I had just led the burial service and was about to lead the funeral service. But I had been unaware that the family members had not all been fully consulted and everyone's wishes considered. It would have been so much better and wiser if he had listened to the other family members and taken their desires into consideration.

> **The Role of Executor**
> As an executor planning a funeral, we have an option:
> • We can insist on using our authority and power; or
> • We can give priority to our family's unity and the welfare of each member.

Very likely, unless there will be a humble and complete reconciliation, this rift within the family will remain and widen. This sister-in-law might never get over the painful events at the funeral service. However, within minutes of this incident, the family would walk together for the memorial service of their mother, would sit as a unit, and would present the appearance of being a united family. This brother-in-law would talk about his mother in glowing terms as an extremely divided family listened.

I have also observed the disappointment and even resentment when some family members refuse to change their plans for the sake of the larger family. These questions, spoken or unspoken, will continue to fester underneath the surface: "Which is more important—one family member's personal priorities (such as a scheduled vacation, work, or other commitments) or setting that aside for the good of the whole family? Why did a member not make the effort and undertake the necessary travel arrangements to be at a parent's funeral?" The opposite questions are: "What will family members sacrifice for the welfare of the larger family? How important is family?"

This can go the other way as well. When a vacation plan or another important appointment has already been made and is difficult to change, those planning the service should be considerate to the people who have these significant commitments.

I remember meeting with the loved ones of a parent. They had had a very close relationship with the parent but, as stepchildren, were not involved in the funeral details. Yet they had scheduled a two-week vacation the day after their mother passed away. In this case, the family members who were the executors considered the wishes of the family members and scheduled the memorial service for after the other members returned. Being thoughtful in planning a funeral is always the best choice.

Regrettably, heartrending pain is felt when family conflict surfaces in the planning and implementing of a funeral. Hurts that are inflicted at a funeral service go deep. Families can never redo a memorial service. The person in charge of the funeral service might have gotten his or her way, and the service might have gone according to this person's plan, but the hurt and the division will only become deeper when other family members are ignored. My appeal to anyone responsible for funeral planning is: "Do not insist on your own way. If you are in charge of planning the funeral service, you also have an opportunity to bring about healing and unity. This is a time to extend grace and forgiveness. This is a time to listen and put other people's wishes before your own."

> The need to decide quickly on the date of a funeral service is taken away when the body will be embalmed or cremated. The only time there is an urgency to plan a service shortly after death is when there will be a burial service and the body will not be embalmed.

In the many funerals I have helped to plan, there is one constant challenge—the date of the service. Very likely no date will suit everyone. Planners should attempt to delay making a final decision until all the key people will have had their input. With the practices of embalming and cremation becoming more common, funerals can be delayed. However, friends and extended family members might then question why a certain date was selected, particularly when it is three or more weeks after a person died. The key issue is that the selected date was agreed on by all the family members and that the decision maintained, supported, and strengthened unity in the family.

I wish to give a final word on the importance of healing and unity within a family at the time of a funeral. The death of a loved one might not come at the right time. There may be "unfinished business" that the person whose funeral is being planned wished had been done or other people believe should have been dealt with. Family members might have similar issues—such as, feelings of regret that they did not do more. There might be regrets about missed opportunities with the loved one who passed away or unfinished business with other family members that has surfaced.

May I highlight two things: a promise as well as an appeal. The promise is that "The LORD is gracious and righteous; our God is full of compassion" (Psalm 116:5). With the Psalmist, we need to trust that our God—the God we believe in and the God of the people with whom we may have a conflict—"is full of compassion." God is aware of any "unfinished business," involving both the deceased person and the people who remain. May we hold on to God's promise and his character, understanding that the Lord is gracious. We can and must trust his grace.

The appeal is that we seek to bring about reconciliation and peace within our families. Neither we nor our loved ones will have completed everything that we or they wished. We will want to be gracious towards each other. In this regard, I am drawn to Jesus' commendation: "It will be good for that servant whose master finds him doing so when he returns" (Matthew 24:46). Jesus' approval does not depend on us having completed all our work. His approval is dependent upon our commitment to him. In other words, we may never succeed in bringing about full harmony within our families. God will bless us when we seek to bring reconciliation, when we seek to bring peace as Jesus taught in Matthew 5:9: "Blessed are the peacemakers, for they will be called the sons of God." God's blessing will rest upon us as we seek peace in our family. (The importance of recognizing conflict and striving to bring about reconciliation is dealt with in greater detail in Chapter Six, "Recognizing Family Brokenness," and Chapter Ten, "Restoring Peace in Relationships as We Near the Finish Line.")

2. Preplanning Funeral Services

Planning funeral services ahead of time is a person's expression of love to his or her family members. Before I explain the matter of planning a funeral service in further detail and explain the value of doing so, I will note an author whom I respect who takes the opposite view. Thomas G. Long argues that there is a negative element in preplanning one's funeral and suggests that all preplanning should be "held like a thistle, very gently." He is referring to items such as the hymns, the Scripture, and the choice between burial and cremation. He questions the desire to pin down the details of one's own funeral. He asks, "Why would we want to do that? Either we don't want our families making those decisions, so we decide to stay in control from beyond the grave....More commonly, we don't want to be a burden on our family. Truthfully, though, bearing one another's burdens makes us human and brings us closer to the spirit of Christ....We don't want to deprive our loved ones of the soul-making labor of fulfilling the law of Christ by bearing our burdens in a time of need" (Thomas G. Long, *Accompany Them with Singing*, 181-182).

I will not respond fully to the various parts of Thomas Long's argument except to say that when a person preplans her or his service, this person is fulfilling the law of Christ by bearing the burden of his or her children in the time of their grief and loss. In every loving family, the children will want to bear these burdens as they express their love for their parents. As I describe aspects of preplanning, it should become clear that this is usually not a matter of controlling from beyond the grave but of caring for loved ones.

I encourage children to approach their parents and bring up the topic of planning a funeral service. All the details following the death of a loved one take planning and preparation. Will the decisions be made at a time of intense loss and grief, moments after a parent has died? Or will the decisions be made, or at least contemplated, at a time when children and parents can calmly consider all the factors?

In the situation where a couple has no children, I encourage the couple to approach their siblings or close friends. If there is hesitancy on the part of an elderly couple who have no children to discuss their plan, here again it is the loving thing for those nearest to them to approach them thoughtfully. Decisions will need to be made. Will they be made according to their wishes and with their input?

This also applies to a person who is not married. I encourage this person to initiate a conversation with other family members or close friends.

A principle applies here as in all the other circumstances: to not make decisions and plans is to make a decision. The decision is that, when a person does not make any plans, the planning will be made by other people, who will need to agree on and determine core items quickly, often in a state of grief.

If you are the aging person, who will make the decisions? Possibly, you have several specific desires for your funeral. You might want favorite songs or special readings to be included in the service or printed in the bulletin. Does anyone know? Have you written these wishes down, and do your children or the people who will plan your funeral know where your wishes can be found?

I commend people who come to my office to process the various aspects of planning their own funeral service. Normally, these people have made arrangements with a funeral director. They will usually have their will in place. When their family hears that their parent has died, there will certainly be grief. But, in their emotional state of grief, the family will be much more able to cope with their grief if the parent has recorded specific requests and directives. When the parent has preplanned many details, then the grieving children simply need to implement the decisions that were made earlier. I can give many illustrations of the significance of preplanning a funeral service and recording the requests and decisions. I will give just two.

The first illustration happened when my wife and I travelled to Desert Hot Springs to spend time at a mobile home park. Most of the residents were "snowbirds." On our first day, we celebrated a memorial supper for a resident in this park. This resident had instructed her son and daughter to hold her memorial supper at a time when most of the "snowbirds" were present. The son and daughter lived a considerable distance from their mother's home. As the son shared memories about his mother, he emphasized two things. First, his mother had taken care of all the necessary details, and therefore all that he and his sister had needed to do as they came to be with their mother in her final weeks was to be present with her and show her love. He was very grateful that his mother had thought through the funeral details. Second, knowing that all the residents of this mobile home park were elderly adults, he challenged them to plan their own funeral arrangements and record their decisions and requests.

The second illustration or scenario points to what regularly occurs when I meet with a family after their parent has died. Whenever the parents have recorded the directives, including the funeral service wishes, the children express a degree of relief as they give me a page with all the details.

However, on occasion, I see grief and a sense of helplessness coming together. To illustrate, a spouse died in the hospital. My wife Edith and I were called by the family to the bedside. With the family standing around the deceased loved one, we shared in their grief and comforted them by reading a Bible passage and praying. Following this, I asked, "Can we help make plans for the service?" I followed this with, "Have you selected a funeral home?" On this occasion, the family responded, "No, we have not selected a funeral home nor made any plans." I did not probe any further, realizing that the family had likely not thought of any other matters. They could have preplanned, as the parent had been critically ill for quite a long time. This was not the time to advise the family on the need to make prearrangements. I simply said, "Can we meet? I'll help you."

The above scenario occurs on a fairly regular basis. I need to exercise compassion and patience with families who have not made any plans, even if they have journeyed with a failing parent or spouse in palliative condition for weeks. Those experiencing grief and loss do not need the added guilt that would come from being told what they should have done.

I have known children who refused to plan a parent's funeral even though it was apparent that the parent had only days left to live. The reason they gave was, "We don't want to bury mother before she is dead." Thinking through details ahead of time is not the same as wishing the person dead. Instead, it is an act of care to express love to the deceased that will include this person's wishes.

3. Preplanning while You Still Can

There are numerous contacts to make and items to consider in making funeral arrangements. These will involve the person's family, church, business associates, and friends—and a funeral director. Then, it is important that the family knows the deceased person's decisions if those have been made. (Some of these items will be explained in greater detail in the rest of this manual.)

The following are some of the decisions that need to be made:
- Writing a life story.
- Noting special things to be included in a service.
- Selecting a speaker, musicians, and people to give tributes. These should be some of the first contacts.
- Selecting favorite Bible verses to be referred to by the pastor, to be mentioned in the service, or to be printed in a funeral bulletin.
- Determining if there will be a cremation or a burial service. (The issue of cremations versus traditional burial services will be discussed later in this book.) If it is decided to have a burial service, will there be a funeral service with the body present, or will the body be buried, followed by a memorial service?
- Selecting and making arrangements with the funeral director.

Here are two illustrations of how parents planned ahead of time for their funeral service. In the first story, the father carefully and thoughtfully considered his family. In the second, the parents planned but failed to consider how the plans would impact the children.

After the death of her spouse, a widow requested that my wife and I come to her home to meet with her and the children. In this case, the husband had written out his funeral wishes and placed them in a sealed envelope. This envelope was to be opened only after he passed away. The reason we were called to the home was that the deceased husband had requested my involvement in the funeral service. The point of this story is not my involvement but the spirit in the room of the grieving family. Certainly, there was deep grief because the husband and father had just died. But there was also a feeling of comfort and hope. The man had taken a lot of time to choose his words and write down his love to his family, and also his requests, so that his grieving family would be given hope and courage to move on without him. He had processed how his death would impact his family. He cared for them. The words, possibly written months or years earlier, helped the family when they needed comfort.

In the second illustration, the parents gave specific directives for their funerals but had not thought through how these decisions would be received by the children. It became apparent that some of the instructions were felt as insensitive by the children. The children were left having to explain to their uncles, aunts, and other people what everyone recognized were not the best instructions. Family members asked the grieving children, "Did your parents really request what you are doing?" And, since the answer was, "Yes," then the next question was, "Why did your parents want that?" This second question was usually not asked, but it lingered in the minds of the relatives and friends.

My point is simply this: please think through how your decisions will affect others. Will your decisions put your children in a dilemma? Make decisions that will help in the grieving process, not hinder it.

In the first story, the father carefully thought about how he could help, by giving hope and comfort to his grieving wife and children. Family members felt honored and respected as they opened the envelope that carried his instructions. They found it easy to carry out their father's wishes because they knew these were given out of deep love for them.

In the second story, it seemed as though the parents did not realize that their directions would make things difficult and challenging for their children. Even though the children loved their parents, it was awkward and difficult to carry out their wishes. They, along with other family members, wished that the parents had not given some of the directives.

Placing final wishes in a sealed envelope might not be your preference. Your choice might be that all such plans should be discussed with the children before the parent passes away. When parents choose to give their last wishes in a sealed envelope, my concern is that these will be given to bless and provide the surviving family members with encouragement, comfort, and directions to help in their grieving. (I agree with author Thomas G. Long that this is not controlling from beyond the grave.)

a. Respecting the Parents' Plans

Before I note specific items that parents will need to consider in planning their funeral, I want to address children on how to respond to their parents' directives and wishes regarding a funeral service.

In most funerals I have observed, children will do all they can to honor their parents, specifically regarding their parents' wishes and how they will carry out the plans for their parents' funerals.

On a few occasions, I was sad as I observed that children did not honor their parents as they planned their parents' funeral service and did not carry out their parents' spoken and written requests and directions. I have listened to the life stories of dedicated believers written by their children. I know that the parents' spiritual walk and relationship to God was a very important element of their lives. But as the children developed and read their parents' life stories, there was little or no reference to the parents' faith and to their relationship to God. I consider it disrespectful for children to ignore or minimize what is most significant to their parents. On some occasions, I have heard children callously state, "We know our father would want such and such, but he is not here. Now we will arrange the service the way we want it, not as he would want it or even how he spelled it out."

I urge readers to honor the wishes of their parents when planning a funeral service, especially when the requests are clearly written out. Even when the wishes are not spelled out, the children or those responsible for the service will usually have a good idea what their mother or father would have wanted. If children are tempted to impose their personal values and belief system and ignore their mother's or father's spirituality, the time to do so is definitely not at the parent's funeral service. I cannot say this any clearer or stronger: if one's parent or loved one gave clear directions, please do all you can to carry them out. The people at a funeral service, the close friends and other family members, will recognize immediately if the children are not fulfilling the requests of their parent. Even if a child does not share the parent's values, the child should respect the parent's wishes in this, the last public and formal opportunity in which the child can honor the parent.

> **Giving Honor**
> In our Western culture, we tend to honor youth at the expense of giving seniors their due. However, children and grandchildren often express love and honor of their elders at funeral services. Two of the most inspiring examples of honor are when grandchildren create a pictorial life story accompanied with music that their grandparent loved, and when grandchildren express their love in singing a song that expresses the faith of their grandparent.

Another aspect of honoring a mother and father in how children plan the parent's funeral service is that these children are setting a precedent for their own children and grandchildren. When adult sons or daughters respect their elderly parent who has just passed away, their sensitivity will set an example for their children. How they respect or disrespect their parents will impact how their children will respect or disrespect them. Children who disrespect their parents are sowing seeds of disrespect in their own children.

God promises to bless children when they honor their parents. God declared this in the well-known Ten Commandments. The first command on how humans are to treat one another applies to the matter of respecting a parent's wishes. This command is, "Honor your father and your mother, so that you may live long in the land the LORD your God is giving you" (Exodus 20:12). The Apostle Paul included this command in a letter to Christians in these words: "Honor your father and mother—which is the first commandment with a promise—that it may go well with you and that you may enjoy long life on the earth" (Ephesians 6:2-3). Honoring a parent will include esteeming, caring for, showing respect for, and obeying. What better way to honor a parent than to carry out a parent's final wishes. The harsh reality is that the opposite is also true—God will not bless people who do not honor their parents.

Here I wish to give a word to the extended family and friends. When children have gone out of their way to honor their parents with thoughtful funeral arrangements, take the time to let these children know. Tell the children how the life story they prepared of their father, or the special arrangement of their mother's keepsakes, touched your heart.

But what do we say when we sense the children are not following their parent's requests? When is the right time to speak to children on this matter? Is there ever a good time to speak to other people, criticizing the children? Should this be at the funeral service, because that is when it happened and when everyone was together? My answer is a clear and definite "No." What will that accomplish? Certainly, a pastor needs to be sensitive even when he knows what the parent wished and when he realizes that the children have not followed the parent's request. This applies to friends and extended family members as well. No one knows all that has happened in a family. Words spoken during a time of loss can go deep. Therefore, I urge that we guard our words. It is problematic and complex to challenge behavior that we believe is not honoring to the deceased. On the other hand, maybe it is time that we, in our Western culture, speak up and lead the way in honoring our elders. An excellent time to do so is at funerals. The best response to those who don't honor their parents is to lead by example. When it is our responsibility to plan our parents' funerals, may we do our best in honoring our parents.

b. Dealing with Deep Hurts

Possibly, as you read these words about honoring your parents as you plan their funeral service, you feel deep hurts caused by your parents. Your mother or father hurt you to the core of your being. You have attempted to ignore the pain. But, as you stood at the bedside of your mother when she took her last breath, your mind was glued on a painful event that happened in your childhood or youth or even your adulthood. You wonder: how can I honor my parents when they have hurt me so deeply? This is certainly not an easy question. As you look in the mirror of your life, you feel your hurts. Answers don't come easily. (Dealing with deep hurts will be dealt with in more detail in Chapter Ten, "Restoring Peace in Relationships as We Near the Finish Line.")

4. Selecting a Funeral Home

As a pastor, I partner with various funeral homes. Families know that we as pastors connect with different funeral homes, and they often ask our opinion and advice on choosing one. The most critical thing I look for in a funeral director is empathy and compassion. Does the funeral director display a caring attitude? Will the family feel cared for in their time of need? These are critical questions. Therefore, if you are planning your own funeral or that of a loved one, may I suggest you ask other people who have bought services from a funeral home. Then contact one or more funeral homes and make your own assessment.

> **Things to Consider**
> The central focus of every funeral home should be a commitment to serve and meet the needs of the family. Thomas Lynch, a funeral director, stated that the function of a funeral home is to "serve the living by caring for the dead." (Thomas G. Long and Thomas Lynch, *The Good Funeral: D*, 81.) Other services a funeral home could provide include:
> - Contacting the newspaper
> - Contacting the cemetery
> - Being present at the memorial service
> - Being present at the burial
> - Being available for a viewing
> - Providing bereavement support after the service

I will first discuss the matter of making funeral prearrangements. Then I will share four stories. I definitely recommend that individuals make prearrangements and inform their family of these plans. However, I need to give a caution as these arrangements are made. In some instances, a family has reacted with disappointment and even surprise regarding the prearrangements that had been made. I remember a widow showing me the prearrangement form and the amounts that her deceased husband had paid for various items when he had "prearranged" his funeral. For each item, the amount paid covered only a fraction of the actual cost. No wonder the funeral director had made a sale. Yet, this husband had believed he had done the right thing and had provided his wife with a fully paid prearranged funeral.

Comparing funeral homes is similar to comparing apples and watermelons—not apples and oranges, but apples and watermelons. By this I mean that the contrast between funeral homes can be very great. The differences are on the critical issue of the level of compassion and on the items that are included. You will only find out about these differences as you ask thoughtful questions. A careful analysis will minimize surprises and disappointments.

The funeral director's purpose is to help a family in their time of grief. Part of this service will be providing products and services such as care of the body, cremation or embalmment, coffins or urns, bulletins, death certificates, burial plots, and flowers. But the focus needs to be on compassion. The family should never be left with any questions or confusion about what was paid for and what was not paid for.

As you process the matter of purchasing a pre-need contract, you will want to be clear about what is actually involved. The normal funeral contract provides the option to purchase a funeral package at today's price that will cover the expenses at the time of need when the costs will be considerably more. One criticism often leveled at a funeral contract is that it is simply an overpriced insurance policy. This might be the case with some prearranged plans offered by some funeral directors, but this is not the case with the funeral prearranged plans I am aware of. Here I need to stress the point that you need to be clear on all the details of the plans you are considering.

The following four experiences with funeral directors will help answer the question: "Did the family members feel cared for in the time of deepest need?" As you read these four stories you will want to ask yourself, "Which funeral director would I choose to provide the services for my funeral or that of a loved one?"

In the first story, an elderly woman had made the prearrangements for her sister's funeral service. She had also processed the funeral details and other concerns with my wife and me considerably earlier when another sister had died. Recognizing that, at her advanced age, she was unsure of her ability to make the best decisions, I suggested that she involve someone else who would help her walk through

> **Looking at Death**
> At times, an author will change society's perception about a whole industry. Jessica Mitford's book *The American Way of Death* (published in 1963 and revised in 1998) influenced conventional wisdom so that people believed "funeral directors are determined to sell you something you don't want for a price you can't afford, by preying on your grief and guilt." The result was that people began to believe only two questions were required: "How much did you spend? How much did you save?"—as if the math of caskets mattered most. (Thomas G. Long and Thomas Lynch, *The Good Funeral*, 68-69.) It is time we took another look at death, loss, and grief, not through the lens of a bank statement, but through the lens of compassion, love, caring, and relationships.

the details. In this regard, I encourage anyone who might feel overwhelmed with all the necessary responsibilities to meet with a trusted friend, family member, spiritual director, or pastor to seek help with walking through all the decisions. When the woman's sister died, she requested that I sit with her as she met with the funeral director to review the arrangements for the funeral. The funeral director expressed sympathy while she told the story. Only after she had shared her heart and grief did he open up the file and carefully go through all the items, ensuring that her wishes would be carried out and that there were no uncertainties.

> **Taking Care**
> "The son of a funeral director, who later also became a funeral director, heard his father say, 'Take care of the service and the sales will take care of themselves.' In describing all the exhibits at a convention attended by more than 1,200 funeral directors, this son described all 'such things as accessories only to the fundamental obligation to assist with the funeral. A death in the family was not a sales op, rather it was an opportunity to serve.'"
> (Thomas G. Long and Thomas Lynch, *The Good Funeral*, 24.)

In the second story, an elderly couple had also made the prearrangements. When one spouse died, the surviving spouse, together with all the children, met with the funeral director. The husband told me that the first thing the funeral director said as the grieving family had gathered in the funeral home was, "Now, what should we talk about?" The family members looked in shock at one another. They expected the funeral director to lead the conversation. They were in grief and needed the director to help with the details. It was not up to the family to process what needed to be done. The funeral director was responsible to ensure all the details were clear. Instead, he added an element of frustration and confusion to the family's grief.

In the third story, the viewing was early in the morning before the family left for the cemetery. After a specified time, the director placed the coffin in the funeral coach and began driving to the cemetery about twenty miles away. He did not give any instructions or directions to the family members who were also driving to the cemetery. Had the funeral director driven this route so often that he assumed the family knew the way as well? The result was that some of the family members could not keep up with the funeral coach and did not know the directions to the cemetery. But they knew that I, as pastor, was on my way to the cemetery and would know the direction, so they could follow me.

In the fourth story, the family requested that I sit with them as they met with the funeral director. In this case, the parents had made prearrangements and had decided on cremation. When the funeral director, who was new in the company, became aware that the family had not requested the funeral home's services at the cemetery, he said that it was up to the family to make arrangements with the cemetery. I was shocked when he said this. In actuality, he was stating that this funeral home would not provide the most basic and essential services. Since I had not been present when the family had made the prearrangements, I concluded that either those were the agreements that had been made or the funeral home had a new policy. I did not want to put a negative assessment on the funeral home in front of the family while they were experiencing deep grief in the loss of a husband and father. They did not need to be told that this funeral home was not providing even the most basic care. I assured the family I would help with this item. When I left the home, I contacted the cemetery directly and made the necessary arrangements. Later, the owner of that funeral home apologized to the family. His new employee had failed to provide some basic services, did not know the company policy, and certainly did not show compassion when it was needed.

These stories from different funeral homes illustrate that funeral directors are expected to care. I have heard many comments about funeral homes. Most are very affirming. Other comments illustrate that the expected service is not always provided. Since there is a wide variety in the options provided, I urge that people ask questions about the services that are available and that will be included in a pre-need contract.

One example of the services a funeral home provides is placing an obituary in the local newspaper. Funeral homes know the necessary procedure and can assist families in this matter. Some funeral homes provide this service at no additional cost. Other funeral homes do not provide this service, and in that case the family members will need to find out what is involved and make the arrangements themselves.

As you decide which funeral home to select, you will be considering people who will walk with you and your family through a most difficult time of life. This means you will expect these people to listen carefully to your concerns, feel your pain, and then do their best to meet your wishes. A funeral director cannot take away your grief and loss. But he or she can walk with you in your grief. I hear many stories about how funeral directors have assisted grieving families. Some directors will go out of their way to do whatever they can for the families.

As you make funeral prearrangements, speak with people who have had a recent funeral service. Take the time to visit several funeral homes and speak to the funeral directors in their premises. Choose the one which will best help you in your time of need.

5. Planning Reveals Our Core Values

This chapter has touched on the importance of planning ahead and some of the aspects that are included in our planning. We might know the components in planning a secure retirement or even the specific details involved in planning a funeral. We can place a price tag on the various parts involved. Wise planning is certainly necessary and prudent in all phases of life—including retirement and funerals. However, every decision involves more than a price component. It involves a value behind the decision. How we spend or invest our money exposes our values—whether we are consciously aware of them or not. We will want to examine these values. Writing this book has given me an opportunity to examine my own core values. My desire is that this will be the case with you.

> **Price versus Value**
> We might know the price of all the items involved in a funeral, but do we know the value of these items? Also, why do we do what we do and not do some other things?

Reflection #1

If I am the executor for someone who has died—and therefore have the responsibility and authority to plan the funeral—what will I be more likely to do: meet with the funeral director and plan the funeral on my own or do my utmost to involve other people, especially other family members? The reality is that planning a funeral can become complicated and even messy when more people are involved. Family members might not agree on even basic issues. How will I then extend grace as I plan the funeral with other people and listen to all their wishes?

- What have I written down about my funeral plans and where are these plans kept?
- What key people have I talked to about these plans? Who else might I need to talk with?

If I am choosing to provide my final wishes in a sealed envelope, may my desire be to consider how these wishes will be heard and received by my loved ones.

Reflection #2

If I am the daughter or the son and thinking ahead about my parent's funeral service, what are some things I will want to say that will express my gratitude and honor to them?

Reflection #3

When it comes to deciding on a funeral home:
• What is keeping me from contacting a funeral home and starting to make arrangements?
• What am I waiting for?
• If I am the executor, and the funeral arrangements have not been made, how will I consider the wishes of all the family members in the various decisions?

Prayer

Heavenly Father, with Moses, I pray: teach me to number my days aright, that I may gain a heart of wisdom. I need to recognize that I will not be here forever. My days will come to an end. May I therefore be conscious of my frailty. Certainly, this applies to all the decisions I make each day, the minor ones and the significant ones. Then give me courage to plan ahead and do so with the goal that you will be given thanks and praise throughout my life. May this be evident in the planning of my funeral service. May it be evident in my life now and in my funeral that for me to live is Christ and to die is gain. In Jesus' name, Amen.

Chapter Four
Parts of a Funeral Service

1. Naming of the Service

Traditionally, a gathering to remember a departed person has been called a "funeral service." However, when the burial precedes the service, the gathering may be called a "memorial service" or, alternatively, "a celebration of life." This last designation denotes that the family is thanking God for the life and faith of their loved one. The title "memorial service" signifies that the family is inviting those attending to thank God for their memories of a person. This includes a celebration of the life and the legacy of the loved one. The choice of what to call the service is a critical issue and might also be a sensitive matter. A family will often state they wish to name the service a "celebration of life" because the members want to celebrate the life of their loved one. However, in other instances a family might be just as emphatic that the service not be called a "celebration." I remember preparing a service with a family that had experienced a lot of pain and abuse. This family could not celebrate, nor were they ready to do so. They were not only experiencing grief but also remembering painful family experiences. There was no hesitation that the service should not be called a "celebration of life."

I invite you to consider how you wish to name your service. If at all possible, ensure that all family members agree on the nature of the service, including what it will be called.

2. Viewing

As I was discussing the various aspects of the funeral service with a family, an adult daughter commented, "My children can't stomach viewing Grandma's body. Why would we have a viewing anyway?"

a. Reasons People Do Not View the Body

There are two reasons people give for why we should not view a deceased body. The first reason is this: "I want to remember the person how she or he was when she/he was strong and healthy. I want to keep those memories."

I will respond to this first reason people give for not viewing a dead body by asking two sets of questions. My first question in response is this: Will these people not visit their friend—or even their mother—after she has had a stroke and cannot speak? Will these people not visit their parent or their child after that person has suffered severe burns and the face is disfigured? I believe that in most cases these people will visit a mother who has had a major stroke or will care for a child who is disfigured with facial burns. We would agree that when we refuse to visit a person who has a major deformity, this is an expression of insensitivity that we trust is not in any of us. When a friend has suffered a stroke or another debilitating disease, this is precisely the time we will want to come alongside this friend. At such a time of need, we should be expressing our love, our grace, our acceptance, and our compassion. We cannot abandon a person just because he or she is suffering physically and is unable to respond. We don't stop loving and caring for people when there is little dignity left. And who defines dignity, and how is dignity defined?

My second question in response to this reason is: Will the people who do not want to view a deceased body not wish to be cared for when their bodies are not perfect and beautiful, but frail, dependent, and even deformed? The answer will no doubt be a definite, "They will not want to be forsaken when their bodies seem to fail them."

> **Funeral Viewing**
> Funeral homes normally have a chapel and an adjacent room where the family and friends can gather for refreshments. When there is a viewing, the body will be in the chapel and people can then visit in the next room. One funeral director made an observation that some families gather around the coffin but other families gather as far away as possible from the body.
> • Does this indicate a person's comfort level with the ultimate issues of life and death?
> • Do I keep my distance from the coffin?
> • Why might this be?

> **Our Bodies are Important**
> "'To say that there is 'something more,' albeit unseen, is not to say that what we do see is 'something less.' The bodies of the dead are not 'just' anything or 'only' anything else....Whatever our responses to death might be...they are firstly and undeniably connected to the embodied remnant of the person who was" (Thomas G. Long and Thomas Lynch, *The Good Funeral*, 79).

The second reason some people resist having or going to a viewing is based on their theological beliefs. They state that, since the "real person" is not here anymore, no effort should be made to make the body appear pleasant or resemble how the person appeared in life. They will say, "The person—our mother, grandmother, or friend—is not here anymore. So why do we gather around the shell of a person? This is only her tent. The spirit of our mother is with Jesus—that is her real self. She is gone. She is not here."

I will respond to this reason by examining our understanding of the human body. Once we have a greater and more informed understanding of the human body, we will realize that gathering around a person's body is a natural consequence of this perception. I will begin with a Greek understanding of personhood and then go on to suggest how a society's values are measured by its treatment of a human body. Finally, I will offer a brief biblical understanding of the human body.

> **Only a Tent?**
> The Apostle Paul and the Apostle Peter described our bodies as "earthly tents" (2 Corinthians 5:1, 2 Peter 1:13). But that Jesus, the eternal Son of God, became flesh in this tent must give us a great appreciation of our "tent" (John 1:14, Philippians 2:5-11). Our body might be only a tent, but it is a phenomenal tent!

b. Understanding Personhood
i. The Greek Understanding of Personhood

Whether we realize this or not, our society is influenced by Greek philosophy, which views people in a dualistic way. This view is that human persons *have* a body. Therefore, when the body is dead, the body is of little or no consequence because the person is self-evidently separate from the body. The body is then only a shell, only a tent, that housed the real person. W. Ross Hastings argues that "we *are* an animated body, a body animated by the life or soul God has given them (not 'a body housing a soul'). After we die, when Christ returns, we will be resurrected and once again be living, integrated body-soul, whole persons" (W. Ross Hastings, *Where Do Broken Hearts Go?*, 103).

> **Understanding Viewing**
> Conscious or unconscious reasons regarding why we do or do not view the body of a deceased person:
> 1. Greek understanding of personhood.
> 2. The view a society has of personhood.
> 3. A biblical understanding of personhood.

ii. The View a Society Has of Personhood

Thomas G. Long argues convincingly that how we, as a society, treat the bodies of the dead "tells us much about what we believe about life and death, what we think of ourselves as a society. A corpse is entrusted to the care of the living for only a matter of hours or a few days, but how we carry out our responsibilities to the bodies of the dead is a strong clue as to how we will treat the bodies of the living. A culture prepared to hide the bodies of the dead as if they were an embarrassment or an insult to the living or to throw the bodies of indigent dead into a common ditch is also a society prone to cast aside its elderly, neglect its sick, leave its poor without shelter, and deprive its young of proper care" (Thomas G. Long and Thomas Lynch, *The Good Funeral*, 86-87). Long continues, "So, our deepest ethical and spiritual wisdom calls us not only to watch vigilantly over the bodies of the living but also to care tenderly for the bodies of the dead. So why don't we do it?...We are rapidly becoming the first society in the history of the world for whom the dead are no longer required—or desired—at their own funerals" (93).

Here I wish to make a comment about the presence of a coffin in a service. A generation or two ago, nearly every service was a funeral service with the body present. Currently, very few services have the body present. Has this shift been biblically and theologically driven? Are we embarrassed to have an open coffin before a service? We will normally close it during a funeral service, but what are the reasons for the shift in practice and for the present reluctance to have the body present in a service?

Before I briefly note that a biblical understanding of personhood will inform our treatment of the body, it is important to recognize that the major religious traditions will agree on this thesis: "We will learn wisdom about how to live when we care lovingly and reverently for the bodies of the dead." After presenting this thesis, Thomas G. Long gives four examples that demonstrate the common value of caring for the dead:

> **The Example of Tobit**
> Tobit wrote, "I buried, when I saw them, the bodies of my countrymen thrown over the walls of Nineveh. I also buried those who were killed by Sennacherib (for when he retreated from Judaea in disorder, after the King of heaven had punished his blasphemes, in his anger Sennacherib killed a great number of Israelites). So I stole their bodies to bury them; Sennacherib looked for them and could not find them." Tobit also recorded how he dug a grave and buried one of his people who was murdered, even though there was a price on Tobit's head for doing this earlier.(Tobit 1:17-20, 2:1-8, The Jerusalem Bible).

1. A very extensive search was made for the bodies of the people killed at Ground Zero on September 11, 2001, resulting in the final tally of 4,257 human remains.

2. Following the devastating Japanese tsunami of 2011, a retired undertaker, Atsushi Chiba, a Buddhist, attended to more than one thousand tsunami victims.

3. Tobit, a Jewish exile in Nineveh, got into serious trouble with the Assyrian authorities by giving the bodies of the dead a decent burial. Might I say that Tobit was in grave trouble for carefully placing people in a grave? Centuries earlier, Joseph gave instructions about his bones (Genesis 50:25).

4. The early Christians perplexed their Roman neighbors, who believed the body was merely a corrupted vessel, by taking on the role of undertaker, not just for the bodies of their own people but also for the bodies of impoverished Romans who otherwise would have been unceremoniously dumped into a common pit (Thomas G. Long and Thomas Lynch, *The Good Funeral*, 77, 88-91).

iii. A Biblical Understanding of Personhood

The first indication that the human body is precious is given in the creation story. In the creation account, a closing comment on the things that were created each day was, "And God saw that it was good." However, after God's creation of man and woman, we read, "God saw all that he had made, and it was very good" (Genesis 1:4, 10, 12, 18, 21, 25, 31). May I add that there can be no disagreement that God's comment about the essence of man and woman applied to the body as well as to the person's spirit.

God's assessment of his creation of human beings is certainly evident in a maternity unit in a hospital. When a mother and father see their newborn infant for the first time, they marvel at their child's beauty and how the child is designed in such a phenomenal manner. The Psalmist did not have the benefit of more recent medical and scientific studies to know how intricate the human body is, but, based on what he observed, he declared that the body is "fearfully and wonderfully made" (Psalm 139:14).

The second significant indication that the human body is precious is the undeniable miracle celebrated at Christmas time—"The Word became flesh and made his dwelling among us. We have seen his glory, the glory of the One and Only, who came from the Father, full of grace and truth" (John 1:14). The Apostle Paul declared the miracle of God taking on a human body in what is believed to be an early Christian hymn: "Who, being in very nature God, did not consider equality with God something to be grasped, but made himself nothing, taking the very nature of a servant; being made in human likeness" (Philippians 2:6, 7). If the eternal Son of

God, Jesus, God himself, took on the very nature of a person, this should settle the matter of the value of our human body.

We will agree that our bodies are beautiful. Certainly, we care for our bodies. This becomes obvious when we recognize the extraordinary care given in a burn unit of our hospitals or observe the delicate surgery required to restore a fractured and deformed face following a major accident. But does the beauty and magnificence of our bodies remain with them even after we have died? Furthermore, is there justification for all the effort a mortician takes to restore a face and make it appear beautiful and similar to the features a person had in life? This leads us back to the underlying question, "Why do we view the body of a deceased person?"

An excellent place to begin is by considering how people in the major religions treat the bodies of their people.

Even though the Hebrews had strict taboos regarding the human corpse and taught that a person became unclean through physical contact with a deceased person (Leviticus 21:11, 19:11-22), they still treated the body of a dead person with great respect. It was customary for someone in the immediate family to close the eyes of a departed parent, as Joseph carefully did for his father, Jacob (Genesis 46:4). The Hebrews washed the dead body (Acts 9:37), draped a napkin over the dead person's face (John 11:44), anointed the departed loved one with aromatic spices and wrapped him or her in linen materials.

> **Respect for the Deceased**
>
> There is a common element in major civilizations and religions in that people treat the bodies of the deceased with respect. But how the body will be treated will vary from religion to religion. Traditional Judaism rejects viewings as a person cannot and should not comfort the mourners while the dead lie before them. According to Islamic law, the body should be buried as soon after death as possible, and therefore there is no viewing. In Hinduism, viewings are allowed and usually take place before the cremation. In Buddhism, the deceased is washed and dressed in everyday clothes. Most Christian denominations allow the body to be embalmed and then viewed by loved ones. These examples from five major religions demonstrate that the body of the deceased is always treated with dignity and respect. How this is done is in keeping with the theology or beliefs of each religion. Therefore, the growing trend within Christian culture that avoids the presence of the body as an embarrassment should give us reason to pause and question our core beliefs.

An ultimate expression of treating the body of a dead person with utmost respect is noted in how people treated Jesus' body after he died. The Gospel writers describe in detail the tender care given to the body of Jesus by Joseph of Arimathea and Nicodemus. Then the writers mention the love shown by the women who purchased and prepared spices to give further care to Jesus' body. The Gospel writers stress the importance of these acts by naming the two men as well as the women involved: Mary Magdalene, Mary the mother of Jesus, Mary the mother of James, and Salome (Matthew 27:57-61, 28:1, Mark 15:40-16:3, Luke 23:50-24:3, John 19:38-20:1).

> The Bible recognized the people by name who cared for Jesus' body, as well as the expense of the materials for caring for his body. Should this not give us pause when we minimize the people who care for the bodies of our loved ones and we attempt to spend as little as possible for their care?

One principle we use to develop our interpretation of a theme or topic in the Bible is to note how many times this topic is mentioned in the Bible. When a topic is mentioned numerous times by various biblical authors throughout the Bible, then we can draw the conclusion that this is a biblical truth we need to recognize as significant. On this basis, it is noteworthy that each of the four Gospel writers mentioned the people who cared for Jesus' body by name. May we follow this example as we consider the value we place on bodies once a person is dead.

The following words point to the respect and care we need to give to a body: "Caring attentiveness to the 'mortal remains' is a token of care and respect both for the one who has died and for those who grieve. The person is dead, the body

> **How They Treated Jesus**
> In the Gospels, we notice how Jesus' enemies devalued and degraded Jesus and how his friends valued him. Judas, who betrayed Jesus, accepted the extremely low assessment that was given to Jesus by the religious leaders, that of an injured slave—30 pieces of silver, a trifling amount (Exodus 21:32, Zechariah 11:12, Matthew 26:14-16). The Roman soldiers stripped the clothing off Jesus and gambled for his inner garments, thereby giving the lowest possible value to Jesus. In contrast, Mary spent the equivalent of a year's wages to purchase perfume to anoint Jesus for his burial (Matthew 26:6-13, John 12:1-8). Then, Nicodemus paid an extravagant price to purchase seventy-five pounds of myrrh and aloes to anoint Jesus' body, and Joseph of Arimathea gave his own tomb (John 19:38-42).

will decay; relationships are broken; communities are dismembered. But the body was once—and still is—identified with the person who had died. The body was once—and still is—the medium by which we display the affection, loyalty, and honor due the person" (Allen Verhey, *The Christian Art of Dying*, 254).

It appears that viewing is becoming less common in our Western culture. The practice of viewing varies between subgroups, seeming to be more frequent in rural, conservative settings than in urban settings. A related practice that is also becoming less common is for the community to gather at a graveside service.

c. Reasons to View the Body of the Deceased

If viewing is becoming less common, we need to consider a primary question seriously: "Why do we gather at a funeral home, a church, or even a home to view a dead person?" I suggest several reasons why it is a good idea to view the body of the deceased. These reasons are not given in any order of importance.

Reasons to View the Body
- Accept the reality of death
- Honour and express gratitude
- Remember
- Take up the torch
- Support each other
- Express our trust in God in our grief
- Step out of a room without the loved one
- Proclaim our hope
- Offer a final thanksgiving for this gift of life

i. Accept the Reality of Death

By viewing the body of the deceased, we accept the fact that this person has died. The presence of the body emphasizes that the person has died. It establishes the fact of death.

ii. Honor and Express Gratitude

We gather to honor and express our gratitude to the person who has meant so much to us. We pause, reflecting on the impact this person has made in our lives.

At the funeral home, the coffin is placed in the front of the chapel, allowing people to come quietly to the coffin and reflect. If the funeral home does not have a chapel, I suggest that the coffin be placed at the front of a sanctuary. Some individuals will visit in the foyer while other people will pray and solemnly and quietly reflect on the loved one whose body is in the coffin. In some traditions, the body will be placed in a large room in the house of the deceased. Friends and family will gather to give their respect to the person.

iii. Remember

We gather to remember special moments, some painful, and many pleasant and joyful. We gather to share these memories with an intimate circle of family and close friends. I will never forget the viewing of my mother, with our daughter holding her grandpa's hand. Then, various family members stood, quietly sharing memories about Grandma. Nothing can replace the impact of gathering around a grandmother, grandfather, wife, or husband and sharing memories. We live in a culture of mostly shallow communication where we text and communicate with many people, many of whom we hardly know. And we will likely forget almost everything we text or see on Facebook. But we will never forget the emotional sharing of an uncle or a brother as we gather around a dear mother. Also, we will never forget our own words, spoken from the depth of our heart, spoken in love and gratitude. Yes, grandmother might not hear us. But our cousins and all our family will know how much we loved our grandmother or mother.

We are familiar with the fifth commandment: "Honor your father and your mother." When I observe families gathering at the coffin of a grandmother or grandfather, I come to this deep conviction: "Here is a family that is honoring its elderly parent. Here is a family that honors and cherishes one another. And God will bless this family in return."

iv. Take Up the Torch

Here I think of the metaphor of a relay race, where one runner passes the torch or baton on to the next runner. When a family gathers around the coffin of a dear grandmother, there is a sense that the family members and friends are saying, "Mother, we thank God for your legacy. We are committed to take up the torch and lift high the godly legacy you have given us." I believe that when a son or a daughter (or a friend) walks into a quiet sanctuary to view the coffin of his or her mother, he or she is often recommitting himself or herself to God and saying, "I thank God for you, Mother. I want to be like you."

v. Support Each Other

When we gather at a viewing, we are supporting one another in our grief and loss. We live in a culture that attempts to minimize pain and grief. The Apostle Paul wrote, "Rejoice with those who rejoice" but also wrote the next line, "Weep with those who weep" (Romans 12:15).

vi. Express Our Trust in God in Our Grief

When we are at a viewing, we express our trust in a compassionate God who is present in our loss. The Psalmist David wrote many more lament psalms than praise psalms. As I study the Psalms, I do not believe the worshiper's grief was immediately removed when he poured out his soul to God. I see instead a person's confidence in God. I see a person who believed God would be there in the deepest and darkest valley.

When we quote the line, "Even though I walk through the valley of the shadow of death, I will fear no evil, for you are with me; your rod and your staff, they comfort me" (Psalm 23:4), we reassure ourselves that the Lord is with us in our grief and loss. We do not have any guarantee that the Lord will immediately take us out of the "valley of the shadow of death," but we are assured that he is with us and will comfort us in the valley of death.

As I read the story of Jesus at the graveside of his friend Lazarus, I notice seven references to Jesus' deep emotions, particularly grief (John 11). Throughout Jesus' time of grief over the death of his friend, Jesus responded to Martha's and Mary's concerns and emotions with the utmost sensitivity and compassion. Another aspect to note is that even though Jesus knew he would perform the miracle of raising Lazarus to life within a few minutes, he felt the deep grief and loss that Lazarus had died.

> **Jesus' Emotions at His Friend's Death (John 11)**
> 1. Jesus was concerned about Mary and asked to see her.
> 2. Jesus saw Mary weeping.
> 3. Jesus was deeply moved in spirit and troubled.
> 4. Jesus showed concern by asking, "Where have you laid him?"
> 5. Jesus wept.
> 6. The Jews said, "See how Jesus loved Lazarus."
> 7. Jesus, once more deeply moved, came to the tomb.

Christianity does not shrink back from death. It does not force a smile to mask our grieving. Our sadness because of the loss of a dear one should be obvious. We cannot cover up grief, even though we may attempt to do so. We must come alongside one another, embracing each other in our grief. It is never appropriate to denigrate, minimize, or ignore the grieving process. Our belief in Jesus who is "the resurrection and the life" does not shield us from feeling loss when death occurs. We have heard the saying, "A grief shared is half a grief," but it is still a grief.

We cannot hold back our grief. Nor can we forsake one another in our grief. We must come to a viewing to "weep with those who weep." We must carry each other's burdens.

vii. Stepping Out of a Room without the Loved One

This reason includes all the above reasons. Some people describe this as "bringing closure." As I stood in front of the coffin of my mother with my father, my wife, and my family, I expressed a final "Goodbye." Yes, I thanked God for all that she meant to me. Yes, I was taking up the torch she had handed me throughout my life. Yes, I was supported by a loving family. But I was in deep grief because I knew this was the final time I would see her. From that time on, I could recall memories, but I could not make any more memories. Viewing was an important part of "bringing closure." However, I will qualify the phrase "bring closure" to note that I will never bring closure to grief, as some people seem to think is possible.

> **Closure**
> What some call "bringing closure" I prefer to see as stepping out of one room and stepping into another. In the one room is the loss that I grieve. At times, I will return to this room. But I am choosing to open a door into a new room, one without the loved one.

Viewing is necessary so that we can be released to move along in our grief and on to the next phase, a difficult phase which will not include our loved one. When I use the phrase, "move through our grief," I do not mean we will ever move completely out of grief. There will always be moments when we will be reminded of our loved ones, possibly at significant times of the year such as Christmas, birthdays, and anniversaries. What I mean is that we choose to move "through our grief" and not attempt to avoid it and think we can move around it.

Viewing is one aspect of closing a door so that I can open another door, stepping out of the room where my loved one remains behind and stepping into a room without a loved one. This is necessary.

viii. Proclaim Our Hope

This is the supreme principle that supports viewing. How I wish that over every coffin with a loved one's body were the words, "We Preach Christ Crucified and Risen" (1 Corinthians 15), the church motto on the wall at the front of our church sanctuary. How I wish over every coffin was a cross and a picture of an open grave.

• We gather to bow before the cross of Jesus, whose blood secured our salvation and the salvation of our loved one.
• We gather to celebrate that our loved one is alive because Jesus rose from the dead.
• We gather in grief, knowing that we will not see our loved one again here on earth.
• We gather in hope, knowing that we will see our loved one with Jesus in heaven.
• We gather in hope, knowing that Christ was crucified and Christ rose from the dead.

ix. A Final Thanksgiving for the Gift of this Life
This final reason for viewing leads into an element that is often part of a viewing—a brief meditation and a prayer. A family might request that a pastor share some Bible verses and pray. Or the family might select one of its own members to bring their hearts together under God. This will usually be a short meditation but yet a distinct word in which the family is stating, "Mother's life revolved around God. When we gather for the last time with her, we will focus on God as well as our mother."

3. Flowers

Flowers are a visual expression of our love, both for the deceased and for the family that remains behind.

Some people insist, "Why provide flowers that will perish in several days?" This argument has little validity. Should a husband excuse never giving flowers to his wife, even on their anniversary or her birthday, with the argument, "Why should I give her flowers that will perish and wilt in several days?"

Some people even assert, "Why spend money for flowers that are in memory of a person who is not able to appreciate them?" Flowers are certainly for the living, an expression of our love and support. These flowers also express our love for the dead. The flowers show how much the loved one meant to us.

This relates to the caring practice of placing flowers at the graveside of our loved one. This can be done on the anniversary of a death, on an occasion such as the birthday of the loved one, Mother's Day, or Father's Day, or whenever the family can be together.

In some cultures, the giving of flowers is a daily and regular practice that is far more prominent than for many people in our Western culture. A husband will sometimes pick up a bouquet on his way home just to express his love for his wife. He will not wait until her birthday or their anniversary. I believe we need to express our love on a regular basis and in a tangible manner. Thus, the giving of flowers at a funeral will be a natural expression of our love.

4. Donations in Memory of a Loved One

As noted above, I believe flowers should be plentiful at a funeral service. However, my viewpoint is that donations should never replace flowers—nor should flowers replace donations. I suggest that when a family is choosing to encourage people to give donations in memory of their loved one, these words be used: "Donations in memory of (name of loved one) may be given for the (name of specific ministry)."

I realize that some families do not want to highlight any specific foundation, agency, or ministry. Their loved one might have given regular contributions to a particular ministry or agency. However, the family might not choose to invite people to give to this ministry but will say instead, "Please give a donation to the agency or ministry of your choice."

I take another approach. I believe that a funeral service is an appropriate and natural setting to highlight a ministry or mission that a beloved mother believed in and supported. I will be so bold as to encourage the family to donate towards the specific ministry that their mother supported. It is good if they set the example that other people will follow.

When you select an agency or ministry, you will want to ensure this is a government-registered charity in the event that people wish to receive a donation receipt for their gift.

5. Obituary/Eulogy/Life Story/Tributes

First, we need to be clear regarding the differences between the various written or spoken items about the loved one.

a. The Obituary

An obituary is a short account of a person's life that includes key events. This is the brief write-up that will be published in a local newspaper. Such a summary informs the community that a person has passed away. A family might choose to place two notices in the paper, first a brief notice that their loved one has died and then a longer notice giving the details of the time and place of the funeral service.

b. A Life Story or Eulogy

The word, "eulogy," is a compound word consisting of "*eu*" meaning "well, good" and "*logos*" meaning "word." In other words, it is a "good word" about a loved family member or friend. I use "eulogy" and "life story" interchangeably. A life story begins with the basic facts that comprise an obituary. Then, various elements are expanded, and personal reflections and memories are added.

We all have a story. A funeral service provides an opportunity to write and then share our story. But our story is much more than "a string of biographical facts." I strongly encourage each of us write our own story. We have the opportunity to write how we wish to be remembered.

There are several questions regarding our eulogy or life story:
- Who will write our story?
- What is the purpose of our story?
- What do we want included in our written legacy?

If we neglect to record our story when we can choose what to include and still have clarity of mind, then our children will need to compose our story. Normally, children will wait until we have passed away. At that time, they will need to take care of many other funeral details and therefore will have limited time to write our story. They will also be grieving their loss. Further, if we have several children, would we prefer that one child over the other children write our story? That choice will not be ours once we are gone.

The normal practice is to write a brief story that is limited to the basic details. However, when it comes to a written life story that will be available at a funeral, I encourage individuals to take a different perspective on their life stories than what is normally the pattern. I urge this whether an individual is writing his or her own story or the children are writing the life story of a parent. Some families state that there is no purpose in having a written life story if it will be read in the service. My response is that this will give the family an ideal opportunity to provide a written legacy of their loved one, one that will be read and reread and cherished by friends and certainly by family members.

A life story might be compared to a will. In a will, a person directs a legal distribution of her/his material possessions. In a life story, a person has the opportunity to share about another part of her or his life. This is the person's spiritual and personal legacy. In a life story, a mother can leave her spiritual legacy by noting how God met and called her, listing specific landmarks on her faith journey, citing Bible verses that were special to her, and describing her relationship with God. We will never fully know how our lives impact our children and grandchildren and friends, but in our life story we can share, "This is how Jesus called me to himself. This is why I love Jesus. This is part of my journey with a faithful and forgiving God."

We return to the question, "What if the person has not written a life story?" This provides the family with an opportunity to honor their loved one. As family members write the life story of their mother, they will have a wonderful privilege to express their love. They will be able to let the other family members and their friends know who their mother really was.

I remember one family that initially saw little significance in preparing and providing a written life story. However, after I invited the members to realize the value of having a lasting written legacy, this family became inspired and committed to write the best possible life story of their mother. Their intention was to have the eulogy available for distribution at the memorial service. But the family member responsible for writing the life story kept making revisions and adding new things until late into the night before the memorial service. There were so many significant pieces the daughter wanted to include. Even though this family was unable to provide a printed life story at the time of the funeral, they later made a printed copy available to anyone who requested one.

Take the time to show your love for your mother. Your children and other family members will learn things they never knew about their grandmother. They will thank you and cherish every word, especially when you include photos with the story that show how much your mother loved her family. In our church, we gladly assist with printing the story that shows a family's love for a dear mother. Regularly, a family member, often a granddaughter, will create a thoughtful printed life story with beautiful photos. You will not be sorry you took the extra time.

c. Tributes

In addition to an obituary and a eulogy, there will often be tributes in a funeral service. A tribute consists of words of appreciation for the life and the achievements of a person. The purpose of a tribute is to share specific memories and express how the loved one left a positive impact on the speaker's life. Here I will make two suggestions that apply both to a life story and the words of tribute.

First, often every child and grandchild will want to give a personal, even a lengthy tribute. Therefore, when there are many children, with a large extended family, one recommendation is that one child speak for all her/his siblings and one grandchild speak for all the grandchildren. This also applies to the great-grandchildren. If every child and every grandchild share memories, the service can become very lengthy.

Second, some families choose to give shorter tributes during the formal funeral service and then provide the opportunity for any member of the extended family to share following the luncheon in a more informal setting.

Having given these two suggestions, I will emphasize that each family will want to do what will best express their love to the deceased in their own way. What if either the tributes given in the memorial service or the memories shared in the more informal setting become what some people will deem very lengthy? My response is that this is the only time the family is gathered to share memories at their loved one's funeral service. Do what is right and loving for you. Don't worry about what other people think regarding the length of the life story. Take all the time you need.

d. A Pictorial Life Story or a Video

Another component in many funeral services is a pictorial life story. This will include pictures of the person from birth to the final days. Whoever creates this pictorial life story should consider that this is part of the funeral service. This means the audience is not

> **Pictorial Life Story/Video**
> • Enjoy; be creative.
> • Remember the audience.
> • Label photos; not everyone knows everyone.

the same as that in an intimate family setting where everyone wants to have as many pictures as possible about themselves. I recommend that a pictorial life story not be longer than seven minutes. It is helpful to have section headings that indicate the next parts of the life to be shown. A family might select hymns or songs that their mother or father appreciated to accompany the pictures.

Some families are able to express their love for their loved one with a video. This video can be a stringing together of very short videos. Or the family might create a video just for the funeral service.

6. Children

Do we unnecessarily keep children from experiencing the loss of a grandparent or other loved one? Children have watched as a family pet, a cat or a bird, has died, or they will at least have been told the sad news that their favorite pet has died. On these occasions, we comfort our children in their grief and permit them to grieve. We take little children and show them newborn babies and want them to share our joy with them. Yet, we may hesitate to let children see the lifeless body of their grandmother, sense our deep sorrow, and reflect how this might impact them. However, as children observe the death of their grandmother and know their grandmother will never again be there for them, they must be conscious of our love and support. They must feel that we are walking with them through their own valley of the shadow of death. They might not be able to explain what they are sensing and feeling, but our desire should be that our children will experience God's love and compassion through us, their parents and their uncles and aunts in their grief.

I wish to include a testimony of a close friend who emphasized the importance of letting children be exposed to the passing of a parent. His son-in-law was only seven when his mother died of cancer. His father wanted to protect the children emotionally, and so they were not allowed to visit their mother in the hospital, nor were they allowed to attend the funeral of their mother. This had a profound effect on this man. He mentioned to his father-in-law that he would like to see his mother's grave. So, this man took his son-in-law and his wife to the cemetery. This was this son-in-law's first real opportunity to deal with his mother's death. This man hugged his father-in-law and wept for probably ten minutes and would not let go of his father-in-law. This was a very therapeutic occasion after holding his grief inside for more than forty years.

7. Bulletins

A memorial bulletin is an opportunity for the family to express affection for their loved one. A key item is the eulogy or life story. Take as much space as you wish to honor your loved one. Friends will value a printed family tree that includes children and grandchildren. If there was a special poem or a favorite Bible verse, include it. The bulletin is a short, well-defined legacy that family and friends can take home. List all the pallbearers in the bulletin. The pallbearers will then realize it is a privilege to serve and an honor to be recognized.

It is also appropriate to include a note of thanks for the love and the support expressed, an invitation to a luncheon, and an explanation regarding giving donations in memory of the loved one if this is desired.

8. Hymns, Spiritual Songs, and Special Music

As individuals prepare the various items for their memorial service, I encourage them to leave a list of the songs they want sung at their funeral service. When individuals have been blessed by special musicians, it is a good idea to write down the names of these musicians, along with the songs they request will be sung. When a funeral has been preplanned, the family and those officiating will want to honor these wishes and follow these requests. When a hymn is unfamiliar, those leading the service should make every effort to ensure the requested song is sung or at least heard or printed. The key consideration is that we do our best to follow the request of the person and not replace it with another song that is our own favorite. When no preselection of hymns has been made, those planning the service will want to select hymns that express the faith in God of the person whose service it is, at least to the best of their knowledge.

Hymns should express confidence and trust in God, acknowledge that our God is faithful, and be a witness to the hope we have in God. Our faith is rooted in a powerful and loving God who is with us now and who desires a relationship with us, his creation and his redeemed people, forever. Our faith has a future in a glorious union with our Creator and Savior.

Hymns and songs are an excellent way to remind ourselves of these truths. When we feel deep grief and possibly feel deserted and forgotten by God, hearing the old, familiar hymns is comforting because they remind us of the core truths concerning our faith in God. They acknowledge that our faith is based on a sovereign but also compassionate God. He is Lord of today, when we feel grief, but also of tomorrow, when we will be with Jesus, our Savior and our Creator. Today we can sing, "What a friend we have in Jesus." But we can also rejoice because, "There is coming a day when my Jesus I shall see." Let us never hesitate to sing songs of our faith.

When there is a soloist or a special group singing, this should not be presented as a performance in a concert. The purpose of the special music is the same as that of the songs sung by the congregation—to remind all present of our God and to express the faith and emotions of all the people in the service.

Reflection #1: Naming of the Service
　　What name do I want for my service?
• A funeral?
• A memorial service?
• A celebration of life?
Have I talked with my family about what I will name the service?

Reflection #2: Viewing
How do I feel about stopping in front of the body of a dead person? Why do I think I feel this way?

Reflection #3: Life Story
• What were some key times I sensed God's faithfulness in my life?
• If I am responsible for writinge the life story of my mother or father, what special qualities will I highlight? How do I wish that other people will remember him or her?
• When I begin reflecting on my life story, I might see this as an opportunity to take stock of where I am on my spiritual journey. What were the special times when God spoke to me and I renewed my commitment to God?
• Is God bringing to my mind relationships that need mending, phone calls that need to be made?

Prayer
Heavenly Father, with the Psalmist, I declare, "I praise you because I am fearfully and wonderfully made, your works are wonderful. I know that full well." May I respond as the Psalmist did, with praise and worship of you, my Creator. When I solemnly stand by the body of a loved one, may this draw me to you for how you have designed and created, sustained and provisioned my loved one. You have created me and everyone in a wonderful way. I give you praise. May I also treat all people with utmost respect and honor, knowing you have created all human beings. I thank you for providing me with this body, knowing there is coming a glorious day when it will be transformed to be like that of your beloved Son. In Jesus' name, Amen.

Chapter Five
Burial Service, Interment, or Committal Service

1. Parts of a Burial Service

As the term "committal service" implies, in a burial service, the body or the ashes are committed to the ground. But a Christian burial service has another, more sacred meaning of committal. We are committing or giving our loved one to our heavenly Father.

As a pastor, I will begin a burial service with a few selected words of comfort for the family. Then I focus on the hope that we who believe in Jesus have by reading Bible passages. The following verses include words of comfort appropriate for a burial service:

• 2 Corinthians 1:3: God is the Father of compassion and the God of all comfort.
• John 11:25, 26: Jesus said, "I am the resurrection and the life."
• John 14:1-6: Jesus promised that he is preparing a home for us.
• 1 Corinthians 15: Jesus' resurrection is the basis for our eternal life.
• 1 Thessalonians 4:13-18: We have the promise that Jesus will return to receive us so that "we will be with the Lord forever."
• Revelation 21:1-4, 22:1-7: We have a beautiful, eternal home in heaven.

Then the service will conclude with words of committal and a prayer.

2. Coffins

A question that is asked, if not implied, is, "Why spend money on an elaborate coffin? In fact, why bother with a coffin at all?"

The selection of a coffin, as with many other aspects of a funeral, can be approached in several ways. Often the first and most common approach is that of cost. I encourage us to look at the various parts of a funeral using other criteria than only the cost.

On some occasions, a family member, usually an elderly person who has no immediate family nearby, will request my presence when meeting with the funeral director. The topic of cremation or burial will be discussed. If the choice is made for a burial, then the next question is the type and cost of a coffin. As a pastor, my goal is to listen to the heart of the person who needs to make major decisions. Certainly, the cost is a factor. The funeral director will detail the various features of a coffin. However, there are other aspects that cannot be measured by dollars, as will be evident in the following scenarios:

- Will a grandson ever forget the time he stood between two cousins carrying the coffin of his dear grandmother?
- Will a widow ever forget the moment she placed her hand on the coffin of her husband, saying, "I love you. We'll meet again"?
- Will a granddaughter ever forget when she stood with a loving family watching her grandmother being lowered into the ground?

3. Pallbearers

There is something personal and profound that happens when a son, daughter, grandson, granddaughter, or close friend carries the coffin of a loved one. In our Western society, we have delegated most of the care of a dead body to professionals such as the mortician who cleans and prepares the body, the funeral director who makes all the arrangements, and the cemetery workers who dig the grave and then close the grave after the coffin is lowered. Then, sometime later, the family will contact a company to design and make a permanent grave marker.

This means that the only nonprofessional persons who have a direct responsibility in caring for the body are the pallbearers. They have the final honor and responsibility in the care of their loved one. The pallbearers are usually selected from among the family members for this honor. Whenever I stand with pallbearers, waiting for the final instructions from the funeral director, I sense that they feel it is a special honor and privilege to carry their loved one.

When the family has chosen cremation, I observe how carefully a child, usually the oldest, will carry the urn with the ashes of a beloved mother or grandmother. As this mother has cared for her children, often carrying them when they were tired and gently placing them in their beds, now the daughter or son has the privilege and responsibility of carrying the mother and then gently placing her ashes in her final resting place.

The decision will need to be made as to who will carry the urn and place it in the prepared hole in the cemetery. There are three options: the funeral director, who is actually then an undertaker; the pastor; or a family member. It is important that this issue be decided ahead of time. I have participated in different burial services using all three options, and there is value in each.

My preference is to invite a family member, on behalf of the family, to carry the loved one and gently place the remains to rest. This can happen in one of two ways. First, with the goal of saving money, the family will pick up the urn from the funeral home. Then, the family will take the urn to the cemetery and set it beside the hole in the ground. After words of committal and prayer, the family member will lower the urn into the hole. With this option, the pastor needs to be certain as to the exact location of the burial site. I will admit that I don't favor this first way. I prefer the second option in which the funeral director acts as a genuine "undertaker" and takes care of the details, such as leading the mourners and the pastor to the exact place in the cemetery. The urn might be given to a designated family member who will lead the family to the burial site, or the funeral director will carry the urn and place it beside the designated hole. After the words of committal and prayer, the funeral director will remove the covering, the designated family member will place the urn in the hole, and then the funeral director will replace the covering.

It is important that the names of all the pallbearers are in the bulletin. If there are more than six people whom the family desires to be pallbearers and who can all equally serve as pallbearers, one approach is to select six individuals who will carry the coffin and then have the other people walk immediately behind the coffin. The goal is to include as many people as possible or as many as the family wants. Make sure that all parts of the family are represented in the selection of pallbearers. By this I mean that if there are eight children, ensure that all children are pallbearers or, if the next generation is chosen, that each family be represented.

If, on the other hand, a family has a very small group of people who can serve as pallbearers, the pastor and funeral director will assure them that other people will be available to help. Here, as in other aspects of the funeral arrangements, the funeral director, together with the pastor, will do everything necessary to ensure a family's wishes are met.

Some families will ask elderly folks, perhaps siblings or close friends, to serve as honorary pallbearers. They will walk behind the casket and in front of the family as they are able. This is especially true for burial services for military veterans.

4. Special Items in a Burial Service

Families might add items that will make the burial service special for them. As I meet with a family, I will be sensitive to their requests and also encourage the family to show their compassion for their loved one in whatever manner they choose. Also, a pastor should speak to a family about the flow of the burial service and be clear on what will happen next. In the following directions, wherever reference is made to a coffin, the practice can apply to cremation and an urn, with some necessary adjustments and modifications. These special additions to a burial service might include:

a. Placing Flowers on a Coffin

These flowers represent a special but final interaction in the relationship between the family members and their loved one in the coffin. When family members place flowers on a coffin and then observe the coffin with their flowers lowered into the ground, there is a final but loving sense of farewell and a visible act of compassion. What better way to say, "Goodbye, until we meet again in heaven," than with a rose, a symbol of love?

b. Taking Flowers from a Coffin Spray

Taking flowers from the coffin spray and giving one flower to each family member and friend at the burial service is a thoughtful way to have each person take something home to remember their loved one by.

c. Releasing Balloons

As these balloons fly into the sky, the family reflects on how the spirit of their loved one has gone up to God. Even more, the family members are looking forward to the time when they "who are still alive and are left will be caught up together with them in the clouds to meet the Lord in the air. And so we will be with the Lord forever" (1 Thessalonians 4:17).

d. Releasing Homing Pigeons

As the pigeons are released and begin their flight "home," the family is given an unmistakable and positive illustration that the spirit of their loved one has flown "home" to be with Jesus.

e. Singing a Hymn or a Spiritual Song

A family will be drawn together, remembering their loved mother and grandmother, as the family members sing a song that was their loved one's favorite. I recommend that the words of the hymn be printed and distributed so that everyone has the words. On several occasions, a child has suggested that a song be sung and then he or another person has begun singing, but the song has faltered after the first two lines because very few people knew the words. Also, some of the children and grandchildren might not be familiar with the selected hymn or favorite song. These family members might feel left out if they cannot sing with the rest of the family. Another comment about singing as a family at the graveside: the key issue is what's in your heart, not how you sound. Yet, it is wise to have a person with a strong voice lead the singing.

f. Writing Personal Words on the Coffin

One family had selected a coffin made of light-colored wood. Every family member was given a marker with which final love notes were written about and to the loved one. As I observed this moment, I sensed the family members bonded together as they lovingly wrote about their dear loved one. Yes, the written notes were buried with the coffin, but the memories will remain engraved on the hearts of those who wrote the notes and shared the moment.

g. Covering the Coffin with Dirt

In some church traditions, this is practiced more frequently than in other church traditions. I remember several times when shovels were available and the children of the person in the coffin and also other adults would begin carefully placing dirt on the coffin. I recall a daughter state, as her siblings and other adults began pouring dirt on her mother's coffin, "Mother always covered us so tenderly with a blanket each night. Now we want to cover her as well."

Regarding the matter of covering the coffin with dirt, some funeral directors will assure the family that their beloved's coffin will be taken care of by the cemetery workers as soon as the family leaves. It is not unusual to have the cemetery workers stand just off to the side of the graveside. They are there in the event that they are needed but also to assure the family that they will take care of the next details and cover the coffin.

h. Playing a Trumpet

At either the beginning or the conclusion of a burial service, a person might play the tune of a familiar song on a trumpet. Family members will never forget hearing the trumpet play the song, "When the trumpet of the Lord shall sound, and time shall be no more," as the coffin is lowered into the grave. Those words give the assurance that, even though Mother's body will remain in the grave, Jesus will call her home to be with him. The notes of the trumpet will keep ringing in the hearts of the children, giving assurance of their mother's homegoing and their own eventual homegoing as well. If the cemetery has a small hill, an idea is to have the trumpet player stand on top of the hill.

i. Sharing Memories

Realizing that the family will never gather in this way again, at the grave of this dear loved one, means that the moment is special. Individuals will naturally reflect on their relationship with the person whose body or ashes are laid to rest. Individuals will share memories. One question is whether the sharing will be structured or informal. In a structured sharing of memories, a leader, such as a pastor or the oldest child, will invite people to share memories. These moments at the graveside will be engraved on each person's heart.

I remember one occasion when the remaining spouse and the other siblings were elderly and therefore the funeral director had provided chairs for these people. The weather was perfect, and the funeral service had already happened. The funeral director and I waited at least thirty minutes as the immediate family shared memories. We couldn't leave because the family members needed the chairs. I give this example because it shows that we ought to share memories at important times—and one of those times is when we are gathered at the gravesite of our loved ones.

j. Visiting Nearby Graves

When family members and friends have been buried in the same cemetery as the person who is being buried now, it is natural that individuals will find the grave markers of these other people. As family members then reflect at these other graves, they will sense a spirit of community.

k. Sprinkling Sand on the Casket

I don't usually sprinkle sand on the coffin at a burial service. Here, though, I want to be sensitive to the family. On several occasions as I have said the words, "Ashes to ashes (when it is a cremation), dust to dust, earth to earth," I have carefully and slowly poured sand in the form of a cross and then a heart. The family saw the heart and the cross. They knew what these meant. Possibly those two images were remembered for a longer period of time than all of my words. A heart represents the love of the person in the coffin, and the cross represents the love of God, who is present with his comfort.

Reflections
- Which of these practices would you want for yourself?
- If you were planning the parts of your own burial service, what would you want your family to do to remember you?

Prayer
Heavenly Father, gathering at a graveside is the most solemn moment I might ever experience. I will feel my mortality and finiteness. The cemetery is a clear reminder that I will not be here forever. But, as a person who believes in you, I am confident that the cemetery is not an end. It is not a final stop. Yes, it is a final resting spot for my body—but just for a time. I have the assurance that it is only a resting place, knowing that when your trumpet will sound, I will be raised to new life, and I will be with you forever. May I therefore hold on to the assurance that a cemetery is just a stop in the journey towards my eternal home, where I will be with

you forever. May this assurance be evident in my burial service. In Jesus' name, Amen.

Chapter Six
Recognizing Family Brokenness

This chapter emphasizes the need to recognize personal brokenness that results in broken relationships. I will focus on providing hope in Chapters Eight, Nine, and Ten.

When a family gathers to plan a funeral service, this special event is an opportunity for caring, remembering, and even reconciliation if necessary. There might well be hurt and unresolved issues in many families. If so, a funeral will be an occasion that will expose the family brokenness and pain. Some might wish that other family members were more pleasant and considerate. The others might wish that the first group were more sensitive and understanding. The desired outcome is that there would be reconciliation, but often that does not happen. Yet, the family need to move ahead with planning a funeral service in a limited time, hopefully with an open hand and with faces towards one another. But, regrettably, funerals are often events when our hearts are closed, we don't listen to one another, and our faces are not towards each other.

Also, the person for whose funeral the family are gathering might have caused pain. A father might not have represented God as a loving, caring Father even though he claimed to believe in God. Wishing this had not happened will not make it disappear. Hurtful memories are not magically erased at the time of a funeral service. Unkind, judgmental words always hurt. Harsh criticisms and putdowns always destroy. A daughter might have conflicted feelings as she stands by the coffin containing the body of a father who controlled and abused her emotionally, physically, and sexually and demeaned his wife, her mother, who is standing beside her. She will not only have feelings of bitterness and regret towards her father but might also have feelings of disappointment towards her mother for not protecting her from a controlling and abusive father.

The truth of the proverb, "The tongue has the power of life or death" (Proverbs 18:21), is very evident as family members recall the impact of the words of their loved one. The father's words might have destroyed the happiness and the unity of a family. Often, specific children within the family felt the deadly impact of the father's words more than other children. Yet, these family members are called to grieve over the loss of the person who inflicted pain, abuse, and even emotional death.

As a pastor, there have been times when I was aware that parents had caused pain. In one story, the rift was so deep that some of the children were forbidden to attend the funeral of the first parent. Years later, the second parent died. This same family, with all its divisions, requested that I help them process the funeral for the second parent. What should I have said to these children as they planned the funeral service for their parent? Some people will answer that in a case like this I should not bring up any difficult issues. However, my silence might also speak volumes, especially when the family knows that I, as a pastor, am aware of the hurt within the family.

Families might or might not know that the pastor is aware of their family problems. In the above situation, I was aware of the deep hurt, and the family knew that I was familiar with the family's pain and divisions. I do not believe that I, as the pastor, should open a hurtful wound. But, if the family opens the subject, I need to listen and acknowledge their hurt. I cannot undo what has happened, but I can at least listen and acknowledge their pain.

The last thing children in such a situation need to hear are admonitions that they must forgive and forget, especially if I as a pastor use Bible verses to bring home the truth. They will have heard these verses already, possibly and regrettably from the person who abused them. Instead, the family members need to be assured that I, as a pastor, accept them where they are, with all of their hurts and raw emotions. If the family members are assured of this, then they will be in a better position to accept and receive the other things I will say, both in planning the service and then at the burial service and at the funeral itself.

> **Listening and Caring**
> A carpenter uses a hammer to pound in a nail. But may Bible verses never be pounded into the hearts of hurting people. The pain and grief will only go deeper. May we instead listen and sit with people in their hurt and pain.

I have included this chapter on "Recognizing Family Brokenness" because it is a necessary reminder to me and to every family. Satan will stop at nothing; his goal is to kill and destroy. Satan does not care whether a family is in intense grief. He does not care how great the loss is. Satan's goal is to destroy families at the most vulnerable and weakest moment in their lives. Satan will do all he can to drive a wedge between family members and to widen the gulf that separates family members.

If you are in a family that is struggling with divisions and hurt at the time of grief and loss, may you feel compassion and grace from your friends and from the church. Be assured that God is gracious, no matter how insensitive people are. My prayer is that Christians will demonstrate God's compassion as well as humility and the courage to admit wrong.

At the same time, a funeral service and the other events surrounding it can be an opportunity for significant victories and personal repentance and growth. Satan knows this as well. I have observed children and grandchildren recommitting their lives to God. I have witnessed family members who have not talked for years speaking to one another on the occasion of the funeral service of a parent. These can be occasions for reconciliation and healing of fractured relationships. I was humbled as a son challenged his siblings and nieces and nephews that it was now time for them to take up the baton of faith handed to them by their parents. Satan knows that funerals can be opportunities for believers to recommit themselves to God and for wayward children and grandchildren to come home to the faith of their parents. Satan will do all he can, by any means, to thwart the gracious, merciful, and convicting moving of God's Spirit. Therefore, we must be on our knees, both as those who are grieving and also as those who lead in these services.

Reflections

As you read this chapter on the topic of family brokenness, are you thinking ahead to the funeral of a loved one, a parent, or a sibling? Do you already feel the deep emotions that may surface? My wish is that you will be assured that God will be in that valley, God will be present in that very difficult time as you feel both deep grief and unresolved negative feelings. The truth of this saying applies at all times, but especially in times of grief and loss: "Hurting people deeply hurt hurting people." May you be spared any extra hurt.

Can you visualize the contrast between a clenched fist, ready to strike, and an open hand, ready to embrace? A funeral might not be the time to resolve all misunderstandings and bitterness, but may it be a time for you to offer an open hand, ready to embrace and accept and begin the journey of reconciliation. May you feel other people offering the same towards you.

Prayer

Heavenly Father, even as I reach up to you for forgiveness and acceptance in my grief, I observe the conflict and callousness towards my brothers and sisters who are with me in our common grief. In myself, I cannot bring about reconciliation. This is a miracle that only you can perform. I open myself up to you and desire that reconciliation will begin with me. May I and my brothers and sisters come to you, Jesus, and hear your tender voice inviting me, "Come to me, you who are burdened and heavy laden, and I will give you rest." I come with my guilt and shame. I ask for forgiveness and pray for humility to reach out to those I hurt. In Jesus' name, Amen.

Chapter Seven
Writing Our Life Story: A Personal and a Faith Legacy

Planning our funeral provides us with a unique opportunity to reflect on our own life journey. As we do so, we select the details we want included. This brings up the question: "What do we want to be remembered by?" The following section applies to individuals writing their own life stories and also to children who will write the life stories of their parents.

It is one thing to emphasize the importance of developing a complete, honest, and inspiring life story and to offer guidelines for doing so. It is an altogether different matter to develop such a story for oneself. That is to say, it is easier to give principles and guidelines than to follow them. However, I have made it my goal to write my own life story, and I challenge you, who are reading this chapter, to take the time to write your own life story.

I will first give underlying principles and values that can help to determine how to approach writing a life story. This is followed by some specific guidelines that will help in writing our life stories.

1. Principles and Values that Should Determine Our Approach

We no doubt know the line, "I'm only a sinner, saved by grace." This is certainly true for each of us. But is this really how we want to be remembered?

The Psalmist David openly admitted, "For I know my transgressions, and my sin is always before me. Against you, you only have I sinned and done what is evil in your sight" (Psalm 51:3-4). The Apostle Paul confessed, "I was once a blasphemer and a persecutor and a violent man....Christ Jesus came into the world to save sinners—of whom I am the worst. But for that very reason I was shown mercy, so that in me, the worst of sinners, Christ Jesus might display his unlimited patience as an example for those who would believe on him and receive eternal life" (1 Timothy 1:13, 15-16). David and Paul openly confessed who they had been and what they had done. However, David knew that because he had confessed his sin and then received cleansing and restoration from the Lord, he was able to say, "I will teach transgressors your ways, and sinners will turn back to you" (Psalm 51:13). Paul also knew that the transformation in his life, from persecutor to preacher, would bring glory to God. This is why he concluded his brief testimony by confessing that he had been a blasphemer and persecutor but also asserting that he was now an example of God's unlimited patience with these words of praise: "Now to the King eternal, immortal, invisible, the only God, be honor and glory for ever and ever. Amen" (1 Timothy 1:17).

I mention David's and Paul's testimonies because they challenge us to examine how and for what purpose we write our life stories and how children write about their parents. As I have read the accounts of people and the stories children write about their parents, I have become troubled. I ask myself and all of us who write these accounts:
• Why does it seem that we are intent on to making ourselves appear as sinners but also as heroes and saints?
• Why do we, as children, need to make our parents appear more perfect than they were?
• Why do we avoid talking about our brokenness, our pain, our failures, and our disabilities—even and especially when these happened after we began following Jesus?

Very seldom will a family member share how a parent acknowledged a weakness or even a sin and then asked for forgiveness. I believe I have yet to see a parent write that he needed to confess to his family and then seek forgiveness from his family. If the parent did this, it would reveal that God had brought healing within the family.

Yes, we need to honor our parents. However, we should also admit that they were not perfect. Often a family will share openly in my office. They will speak of the pain and heartache felt within the family. Yet, they will be very guarded as they write their parent's life story and then share it in the service. I am not suggesting that a funeral be the occasion to bring up unresolved and painful memories. I am thankful that I have heard such hurtful words being said on only a very few occasions. But I am encouraging us to consider the example of the Psalmist who cried to God in his struggles, the example of Jeremiah who shared his questions, even his lamentations, and the example of the Apostle Paul who prayed that God would remove his "thorn in the flesh." We note:
• Lament Psalms are the most frequent of all types of Psalms.
• Jeremiah described his struggles and questions in Jeremiah 36-38 and elsewhere.

• Paul candidly acknowledged struggles with his vision and the thorn in his side (2 Corinthians 11:16-12:10).

With each of these men, we need to recognize our weakness and frailty but also God's compassion and strength.

Our reluctance to be honest makes me wonder:

• Would our life story not bring more glory to God if we shared our struggles and doubts and not only our accomplishments and victories?

• Would our children not honor their parents even more than they do now if we shared how we, their parents, were prone to fail and how we struggled yet kept on striving in our brokenness, rather than describing only our victories and achievements?

• Would such a life story not be more honest and also give us all hope—as we envision God softening our hearts as well as the hearts of the people we are concerned about?

• Would a life story that includes examples of brokenness and vulnerability not bring hope to those who follow us, in that it will show we are all broken and vulnerable, we all fail, and we all need restoration and healing?

• Would we, as those who follow Jesus, not rather strive to be those who stoop down and take a basin and wash each other's feet? (John 13) I note this for two reasons: first, many of our parents humbly followed Jesus by caring and doing the menial task; and second, this is a reason we need to honor them.

Many, if not most, of the people at a funeral service likely already know painful truths about the loved one. Questions I ask are:

• Do we need to present only the pleasant and positive experiences in our lives and in our families?

• Have we portrayed a Christianity where God cannot deal with our pain and brokenness?

• Do we honestly believe our God is the strong and faithful Good Shepherd who will never leave us, even as we stumble and fall? Do we really believe he stays with us as we live as broken people in broken families, in valleys of despair and discouragement, in valleys of death and hopelessness?

May God give us grace and humility to recognize our failures and our frailty.

The Psalmist David and the Apostle Paul shared how God transformed their lives, how God was there when they failed, and then how God turned them around, from rejecting God to repentance and recommitment to God. The prophet Malachi prophesied that a core marker of revival is that the Lord "will turn the hearts of the fathers to their children, and the hearts of the children to their fathers" (Malachi 4:6). I wish that our lives, and then our life stories, would contain many examples of such revivals in our families. May we have the humility to document how God restores and heals broken fathers, mothers, and whole families.

This brings to mind Jesus' calling of Matthew, a despised tax collector—a man the religious leaders dismissed as "a sinner." Jesus' response applies to all of us, as he said, "I desire mercy, not sacrifice. For I have not come to call the righteous, but sinners" (Matthew 9:13).

I urge all of us to become more honest and humble as we write our life stories. None of us, certainly not we who are parents, are perfect. We are not heroes, even if we are tempted to present ourselves as such. We all struggle in life.

I invite us to hear the words of W. H. Auden: "To a Christian the godlike man is not the hero who does extraordinary things, but the holy man who does good deeds" (James M. Houston, *Joyful Exiles*, 34). My appeal is that we not present ourselves as heroes. My wish is that our children will not feel pressured to present us as heroes but to celebrate the times we expressed our love of Jesus with our good deeds.

I further invite us to hear the words of creation, when God, our Creator, declared that we, his creation, are "very good." The Bible affirms the essential worth and significance of each person because we all are created in God's image. Our value does not diminish when we stumble and fall. We have incomparable worth in God's eyes, as we are created in his image and called by him to fulfill what he desires (Genesis 1:26-31, Psalm 139). My appeal is that we never diminish our value, or the value of our loved ones, but affirm their worth because it is given by God. Our worth is a given; it is no less when we fail, and no more when we have achieved great accomplishments. May none of us ever say, "I have nothing to write about my life because I accomplished nothing extraordinary."

I invite us to hear the words of Paul that we are partners with God (Philippians 1:4-6) and ambassadors for God (2 Corinthians 5:20) in the work God is doing. This applies also to our parents who were committed to be faithful, obedient servants. Most of our parents were certainly not distinguished as exceptional heroes. It is enough that they were faithful with what God had entrusted to them. My appeal is that we affirm them as faithful co-workers and partners with God. This is of far greater significance than any worldly achievement they may or may not have accomplished.

I invite us to hear the words of Micah: "He has showed you, O man, what is good. And what does the LORD require of you? To act justly and to love mercy and to walk humbly with your God" (Micah 6:8). My appeal is that we celebrate how our parents did what the Lord required and how they walked humbly before God.

I invite us to hear the words of Jesus: "Blessed are the poor in spirit...those who mourn...the meek...those who hunger and thirst for righteousness...[and] those who are persecuted because of righteousness" (Matthew 5:3-12). My appeal is that we celebrate how our parents demonstrated these godly qualities.

Even more, my appeal is that we seek to write our life stories and our parents' life stories as expressions of our faith journeys where the focus will be to honor God. When we share how God is transforming us, then God will receive the glory.

This brings in another matter. Unless we have such an approach to our life stories and our parents' life stories, unless we see our lives through the above lens, then we will have the following dilemma. We will divide humanity into sinners and saints, failures and heroes, the unknown and the celebrities—and bypass the first group and exalt the second.

> **A Suicide's Life Story**
> My invitation is that we consider how we write our life story and the stories of our loved ones. We want to do so with a sense of God's grace and compassion. May we maintain this stance even with individuals who have committed suicide. This might be seen as an extreme example, but, unless we can embrace every person with God's grace, then we will not embrace any person with God's grace—beginning with ourselves. The love of God extends to every person, even those who felt their lives were useless and took their own lives.

2. Guidelines for Writing Life Stories

We might agree that we need to write our life story while we are still able to. Or our children might recognize that they want to write a life story for their mother or father at the parent's funeral. But the question then is: "How do we go about writing a life story? What should be included?" This will be either our question or our children's question. There are resources available that help us record our life events and story. For the sake of writing a life story that will be intended for a funeral, I suggest that we see our lives in several arenas as well as several cycles.

a. Life Arenas: Family, Career, Faith, Leisure

A life story will normally begin with the person's family of origin. Then we will want to note key experiences within the family—as children, youth, adults, and retirees. We will also wish to reflect on the other three arenas: career, faith, leisure.

b. Life Cycles: Transitions and Stages

Stages are those phases in life that are linked together by transitions. Another way to understand transitions is that they are like bridges connecting stages. Some key transitions are adolescence, moving out of the home of origin, marriage, having children, mid-life decision-making, children leaving home, pre-retirement, and retirement. The ideal is to perceive these transitions as a challenge, an opportunity for growth. Richard P. Johnson explains how to write an autobiography, either an older person writing his or her own story or children helping their elderly parents write their stories. The children's goal is to help their aging parents have a more positive and meaningful attitude (Richard P. Johnson, *How to Honor Your Aging Parents*, 1999]).

As we begin writing our own autobiography or as our children begin writing our life story, it will be obvious that life has not always been as we had hoped. We will not be able to change our life history, but we can choose how we will write our life story. The ideal is that we will regularly reflect on our lives. When we write our life story, we will consciously review our lives. The concern then is: how will we review or reflect on our lives, especially when our lives contain pain and tragedy and not only pleasant and enjoyable moments? An answer is given by the Apostle Paul in his letter to the believers in Thessalonica: "Be joyful always; pray continually; give thanks in all circumstances, for this is God's will for you in Christ Jesus" (1 Thessalonians 5:16-18). If we are to have a Christian perception of our lives, we will follow these three directives given by the Apostle Paul. Paul is clear that this "is God's will for us in Christ Jesus." I will comment on each directive as it applies to our life stories.

First, we should "be joyful always." Joy is the product of seeing that God was and is in our lives. Joy is the result of knowing God's presence now and knowing that he was near in the past (Psalm 16:11, Acts 2:25).

Second, we should "give thanks in all circumstances." Gratitude is the God-lens through which we should see our lives. How we see our lives will shape our lives. We need to understand that our life is a gift, not a reward. This is especially pertinent when we look back over our lives. We are

> As we look back in life, may we:
> • be joyful always;
> • pray continually;
> • give thanks in all circumstances.
> (1 Thessalonians 5:16-18)

not the source of the things we have done or accomplished. We have been and will always be dependent on our God. Gratitude is the way to see our lives as something God has bestowed.

When we follow these two instructions by the Apostle Paul, we will become aware that we have reasons to be joyful and grateful as we write our life story. This is possible when we see God's presence in our lives. However, these two qualities do not come naturally nor easily. How can we have this perspective to see our lives as God's gift to us?

Third, I believe the answer is given by the Apostle Paul in his third directive: "pray continually." When we pray, we give ourselves the time to be in God's presence, to hear his loving voice, to feel his tender touch. As we pray, we will recognize we have much to be grateful for and many reasons to be joyful. The more we pray, the more joyful and grateful we will be.

When we take the time to be in God's presence through prayer, we will see our lives, no matter what they included, as times when God was present and therefore as full of reasons to thank God. Then, writing our life story will not be perceived as a negative chore or a duty that is required for the sake of a funeral program. We will be motivated by gratitude to God, and our stories will be filled with the sweet aroma of joy and thanksgiving.

In summary, my desire is that my life journey, when it is written, either by myself or by my children, will only glorify God and not draw attention to myself. When people look at me, or at any of us, may they see my brokenness, my stumbling, and my flaws. But may they then know that I knelt at the cross. Then, may they see me through Jesus' lens. May they see that I was continually in God's presence through prayer. May they see a joyful and a grateful spirit.

With the Apostle Paul, may this commitment be true for each of us: "For to me, to live is Christ, and to die is gain" (Philippians 1:21).

Reflections
- How do I honestly wish to be remembered—as an outstanding hero or as a humble, faithful follower of Jesus?
- What might it look like for me to come to a place where I accept my worth?
- This also applies to my loved ones: Possibly, in many people's perception, my parents are seen as failures, as people who neither succeeded nor achieved anything significant. How can I recognize their worth and have the courage to declare this publicly?
- As I reflect on my life story, are there things that I sense I would still like to do?
- The concept of a "bucket list" might come to mind—things I wish to do or places I wish to see. Often a "bucket list" is perceived as containing things people want to do for themselves. As we review our lives, my wish is that we see this list as things we want to do for other people, relationships we wish to restore, or attitudes we need to pursue. Make a (bucket) list of things such as:
    - relationships I need to restore
    - my life story that needs to be written
    - a volunteer ministry I will commit to

Prayer
Heavenly Father, as I have read this chapter on writing a life story, this has invited me to look in the mirror. I ask myself: how do I want to be remembered? I realize that I cannot undo how I have lived. But, as of this day, may my deepest desire be to simply follow Jesus closely—to hear his voice and see his eye on me. As I look back, may I have the clarity to see your faithfulness, your compassion, and your constant care. May I then write my life story so that my children and other people will also receive hope for their lives. May they see how you have been faithful to your covenant with me and that you will be faithful to your covenant with them. Then, as I look ahead in the remaining days you have for me, may I have the courage to obey, even when you lead into new paths of obedience. May I constantly renew my commitment to follow Jesus with all my heart, my mind, and my soul. In Jesus' name, Amen.

Chapter Eight
Assurance that We Will Cross the Finish Line to Eternal Life

The title of this book is taken from the Apostle Paul's reflection on his life. He looked back and with assurance declared, "I have fought the good fight, I have finished the race, I have kept the faith" (2 Timothy 4:6). I am drawing on Paul's phrase, "finished the race," for the image of "crossing the finish line."

We watch with anticipation as runners in the summer Olympic games approach the finish line. The metaphor of the twenty-six mile-marathon race fits this book. In the long marathon race, we cheer as runners endure, right to the finish line. At a funeral service, we celebrate how a loved one endured and, in the Apostle Paul's words, "finished the race and kept the faith." We also rejoice because the Lord, the righteous Judge, has "in store the crown of righteousness" for "all who have longed for his appearing" (2 Timothy 4:6-8).

It is one thing to focus on funeral services, burial services, and the important decisions that need to be made at the time of a person's death. However, it is much more important that each of us, including the person whose funeral we are celebrating, will cross the finish line from life on earth to life in heaven. By "crossing the finish line," we do not simply mean that we will take our last breath and then complete our life here on earth.

However, as with any metaphor, comparing our lives to a marathon also has shortcomings or limitations. I will answer the question, "How can I be assured I will cross the finish line?" using several additional biblical metaphors. This approach is necessary because it is biblical. The Apostle Paul, who used the

> **We will cross the finish line when we:**
> • believe in Jesus
> • follow Jesus
> • desire to be with Jesus
> • are the bride of Jesus.

marathon metaphor, also used other ways to describe the Christian life. The Bible describes the people who follow Jesus in various ways—as those who believe in Jesus, as those who follow Jesus, as those who look to the prize he has for them, as Jesus' bride, as those who are committed to do his will. As I briefly explain each, it will become clear that these are interrelated. This means that a person who believes in Jesus will follow him, love him, and serve him.

1. A Believer in Jesus is Assured to Cross the Finish Line.

We begin with the question: "Can we take for granted that everyone will cross from this life to the next in heaven?" This question can also be restated as, "Will everyone be in heaven once they die?"

Jesus spoke to the concern that not everyone will automatically cross from this life to an eternal life with God in heaven. He did so in his conversation with Nicodemus. Jesus said, "Whoever believes in him (Jesus himself) is not condemned, but whoever does not believe stands condemned already because he has not believed in the name of God's one and only Son" (John 3:18). The answer to the question, "Will everyone cross the finish line and be in heaven once they die?" is a serious and solemn "No!" Based on Jesus' words, those who believe in him will cross the finish line into heaven and be in God's eternal presence, but those who do not believe in him will not cross the finish line into heaven.

Jesus provided a solution so that everyone is able to cross the finish line. The angel Gabriel instructed Joseph to name his son Jesus because "he will save his people from their sins" (Matthew 1:21). When Jesus died on the cross, he died as the Lamb of God who took away the sin of the world (John 1:29). So, Jesus provided a solution to enable everyone to cross the finish line, but not everyone will do so. This takes us to another question: "How can *we* be assured we will cross the heavenly finish line?"

Jesus' words give us the answer: "For God so loved the world that he gave his one and only Son, that whoever believes in him shall not perish but have eternal life. For God did not send his Son into the world to condemn the world, but to save the world through him" (John 3:16-17). The essential requirement is belief in Jesus. The Apostle John emphasized the importance of belief in Jesus: "And this is the testimony: God has given us eternal life, and this life is in his Son. He who has the Son has life; he who does not have the Son of God does not have life" (1 John 5:11-12).

John also clearly stated that we can be confident we will cross the finish line: "I write these things to you who believe in the name of the Son of God so that you may know that you have eternal life" (1 John 5:13).

2. A Follower of Jesus Is Assured to Cross the Finish Line.

We have noted that the core requirement to be in heaven is belief in Jesus. But the Bible teaches that belief in Jesus is not merely an acknowledgment of various facts about Jesus. Sometimes this is described as mere "believism." A person who truly believes in Jesus will follow him in life. This becomes clear in these points:

a. Belief in Jesus Is Not Merely Familiarity with or Perception of a Fact.

James wrote, "What good is it, my brothers, if a man claims to have faith but has no deeds? Can such faith save him?...In the same way, faith by itself, if it is not accompanied by action, is dead....You believe that there is one God. Good! Even the demons believe that—and shudder" (James 2:14, 17, 19).

b. Belief in Jesus Will Be Evident in Obedience.

Jesus himself said, "Not everyone who says to me, 'Lord, Lord,' will enter the kingdom of heaven, but only he who does the will of my Father who is in heaven. Many will say to me on that day, 'Lord, Lord, did we not prophesy in your name, and in your name drive out demons and perform many miracles?' Then I will tell them plainly, 'I never knew you. Away from me, you evildoers!'" (Matthew 7:21-23).

c. Belief in Jesus Will Be Demonstrated in How We Treat Others.

Our belief in Jesus will be evident in that we will treat people as if they were Jesus. Our relationship to Jesus will be evident in how we treat the marginalized and vulnerable, the frail and the defenseless. Jesus said that when he returned in glory, he would divide people based on how they treated those who were hungry, thirsty, without clothes, sick, and in prison. (Matthew 25:31-46). James taught: "Religion that God our Father accepts as pure and faultless is this: to look after orphans and widows in their distress" (James 1:27).

d. Belief in Jesus Will Be Evident in Our Relationships.

The Apostle John wrote: "And this is his command: to believe in the name of his Son, Jesus Christ, and to love one another as he commanded us" (1 John 3:23).

e. Belief in Jesus Will Be Evident in Our Longing for His Appearance.

Those who truly believe in Jesus will display a constant expectation, anticipation, and longing for his appearance. Jesus told us: "Therefore keep watch, because you do not know the day or the hour" (Matthew 25:1-13). He also said, "Do not let your heart be troubled. Trust in God, trust also in me. In my Father's house are many rooms; if it were not so, I would have told you. I am going there to prepare a place for you. And if I go and prepare a place for you, I will come back and take you to be with me that you may be there I am. You know the way to the place where I am going" (John 14:1-4).

f. Belief in Jesus Will Be Evident in Our Waiting for the Fulfilment of His Promises.

Those who have faith in Jesus say with confidence: "I will dwell in the house of the LORD forever" (Psalm 23:6). This hinges on the relationship we have with our Lord, that he is "our Shepherd" (Psalm 23:1).

g. Belief in Jesus Will Be Evident in that We Are Following Him.

When we are followers of Jesus, it means that we have heard and accepted his invitation: "Come, follow me, and I will make you fishers of men" (Mark 1:17). This means that Jesus is the Rabbi and we are his disciples, his followers. He calls us to be with him, to follow him, to feel his heart, to know his mind, to understand and do his will, and to follow his directions in all areas of our lives.

Therefore, crossing the finish line from here to eternity means that, as we have sought to follow him here on this earth and as we have prayed that his will be done in our lives now, he is inviting us to an even greater union with him forever, where nothing will hinder our complete desire to follow him in all eternity.

3. Those Who Look Forward to the Prize Jesus Has for Them Are Assured to Cross the Finish Line.

While keeping the metaphor of a marathon, I believe we need to add another perspective to it. In a marathon, the normal concern is to run from a starting point, remain on the prescribed track, and reach the finish line. The emphasis is on the race, and usually very little mention is made of the prize for having reached the finish line. Yet, when this metaphor is applied to our lives, the focus is not merely on following some prescribed rules from birth until death, and then it is all over. In many marathons, the runners will receive some item to recognize that they have successfully completed the race. But here is where we need to add the extra element when applying the marathon metaphor to our lives. We not only run the race according to the rules Jesus gives. There is also a prize waiting for us at the other side of the finish line.

The author of the book of Hebrews wrote about this prize when he wrote that "man is destined to die once, and after that to face judgment" (Hebrews 9:27). This judgment is God's final verdict on each person. The rest of the sentence gives clarity to the issue of whether everyone who dies will be in heaven. The sentence continues: "so Christ was sacrificed once to take away the sins of many people; and he will appear a second time, not to bear sin, but to bring salvation to those who are waiting for him." The text states that Christ will bring salvation only to those "who are waiting for him." This points to the critical issue of whether a person is waiting for Jesus. This means we can say that we will cross from life on earth to life in heaven if we are waiting for Jesus. He is the ultimate prize we are longing for.

The Bible has numerous places where the prize on the other side of the finish line, the other side of death, is mentioned. These are only a sample of verses describing the major incentive and enticement God is giving us as we follow him:
- a crown that lasts forever (1 Corinthians 9:25).
- the crown of righteousness that the Lord will award (2 Timothy 4:8).
- the crown of life that God has promised to those who love him (James 1:12).
- the crown of glory that will never fade away (1 Peter 5:4).
- the right to eat from the tree of life (Revelation 2:7).
- a white stone with a new name written on it, known only to him who receives it (Revelation 2:17).

In summary, we are assured that we will cross the finish line when our goal is not the finish line but is beyond the finish line. Our goal is to be with Jesus, in the home he is now preparing for us (John 14:1-3).

Our longing to cross the finish line and be with Jesus is taken to a much higher level in the next basis of assurance.

4. A Lover of Jesus (His Bride) Will be Assured to Cross the Finish Line.

I want to conclude with another metaphor that applies to the end of life. The primary one in this book is that we are runners, striving to cross the finish line of a marathon and then receive the prize on the other side. But there are other metaphors in the Bible that are more prominent and certainly more inspiring than a marathon.

This next metaphor adds an altogether more appealing description of what it means to cross the finish line. It takes crossing the finish line to a new and exciting level. The moment of crossing the finish line is much more than a final gasp, expending the last vestige of our strength in a strenuous effort to make it. The Bible describes this moment with a much nobler image. It pictures the finish line as the beginning of a wedding celebration. This changes how we perceive ourselves here and for all eternity. Our lives are a marathon, but much more. They are meant to be a wedding preparation. Let me explain.

On Jesus' last evening with his disciples, the Thursday evening before his crucifixion, he used the following image. He pictured himself as a groom, engaged to a bride, his people. He assured the disciples, and therefore all who follow Jesus, that at this time he is building the home he wants us to live in with him. Picture this familiar passage with this understanding: "Do not let your hearts be troubled. Trust in God; trust also in me. In my Father's house are many rooms; if it were not so, I would have told you. I am going there to prepare a place for you. And if I go and prepare a place for you, I will come back and take you to be with me that you also may be where I am. You know the way to the place where I am going....I am the way and the truth and the life. No one comes to the Father except through me" (John 14:1-4, 6). This means that Jesus, as the groom, is now building a room in his Father's house for his bride. We can be assured of crossing the finish line and being with Jesus in heaven if we are his bride.

This brings us to the most critical question: "How do I know I am Jesus' bride?" The answer includes all that has been said thus far. I am assured that I am the bride of Christ if:

- I believe what the Bible says, that Jesus is the Son of God, that he is the only Savior of the world, that he came to give his life to pay for my sins, and that he rose from the dead to give me eternal life.
- I confess that I have rejected God, that I am a sinner, and that Jesus died for me.
- I believe that Jesus rose from the dead and, because of that belief, I am assured that he is now living in me. This gives me eternal life.
- I have accepted Jesus' invitation, "Come, follow me, and I will make you fishers of men." Since I have accepted Jesus' invitation to follow him, this means that I will take up my cross, I will desire to know him intimately, I will accept his teachings, and I will do what he commands.
- I believe Jesus is now preparing a room in his Father's house for me. Therefore, I am living in anticipation of the day Jesus will call me to be with him.

In the answer I have outlined to the question, "How do I know I am Jesus' bride?" I need to add this clarification to what is meant by the words "I believe." We usually think of the word "believe" as an affirmation of some mental thought. We think "head knowledge." Then, we may infer that all we need to do is accept or believe in the proofs or teachings in the Bible or the statements someone points out to us and we will be saved. Or, staying with the metaphor of the bride and the bridegroom, we conclude that we are the bride of Jesus simply because we believe specific Bible teachings. However, in the language of the Bible, and in the way Jesus and the disciples and apostles used the notion of believing, this had to do with matters of the heart and the will—trusting and surrendering oneself fully to another person. Keeping the metaphor of marriage, as a husband, I do not merely accept some truths in my head about my wife. Our relationship is much deeper. It involves our will, our emotions, our desire to be committed to one another, our commitment to love one another, and our promise to express this passionately. This certainly applies to our understanding of what it means that we are the bride and Jesus is the bridegroom.

Here I want to return to the theme of this chapter, this is, being assured that a person will cross the finish line. If you have any doubt whether you are Jesus' bride, and therefore you are unsure if you are prepared to cross the finish line when you die, the following is a second part of the answer to the question, "How do I know I am Jesus' bride?"

The answer is that you will want to do what a bride does—that is, get herself ready for her wedding. The last pages of the Bible speak about a wedding celebration that will last for all eternity. A word that is repeated is, "Come!" God's people, Jesus' bride, long for him to come. The last words that Jesus' followers say in the Bible is, "Amen. Come, Lord Jesus" (Revelation 22:17, 20). You will know, without any doubt, that you are prepared to cross the finish line when your deepest longing is, "Come, Lord Jesus!" You will know that you are prepared to die and be with Jesus when you long to be with Jesus and are living with his coming in view.

This gives us a new perception of what it means to be prepared to cross the finish line. When we cross the finish line, we enter the wedding hall to participate in the greatest wedding celebration ever.

In summary, how can I be assured I will cross the finish line to be with Jesus? As noted briefly above, the Bible provides many teachings that answer this question: To be able to cross the finish line, I will believe Jesus for who he says he is. Therefore, I will follow him in all areas of life. Further, I will look beyond the finish line to the promise that I will be with Jesus forever. And I will love him because he has chosen me to be part of his bride and I want to enjoy the wedding celebration with him.

Reflections

The most important thing in this life is that you are prepared to be with Jesus in heaven. The Bible provides many verses that explain what it means to become a follower of Jesus. My chief concern is that you have clarity on this matter, based on what the Bible states. The core issue is that you can say with confidence, "I believe in Jesus, the Son of God, and therefore I know I have eternal life." But I need to underscore that believing in Jesus is much more than head knowledge and checking a box mentally that says something such as, "Jesus is God, Jesus died for my sins, and some day I'll be with Jesus." Believing in Jesus involves trusting and surrendering our all, giving our allegiance to the kingdom of God and living out that commitment in our lives.

If there is any doubt as to whether you are prepared to die and be with Jesus, I am offering a prayer you could make your own. These words are an opportunity to express what is in your heart. Read this prayer over. If it captures where your heart and mind are right now, then make these words your prayer. May this be your prayer to God.

Prayer

Dear God: Thank you for your love for me. I have been thinking about funeral plans. But the most important thing is that I am prepared to meet you and be with you forever. Therefore, I know I must follow what is written in your Word, the Bible. The Bible says that I am a sinner—I have rejected you. I confess that I have lived in rebellion, as a sinner. The Bible also says that Jesus came for sinners like me, that he died to pay the penalty for my sins. I believe in Jesus, that what he did on the cross was for me. The Bible says that Jesus rose to new life. I believe that Jesus is now living in me. Even more, I believe Jesus is preparing a home for me in heaven. As I long for his return, I am committed to follow Jesus in everything I do and say. God, there is much more I could say, but thank you for making me your child. Even more, thank you for making me a part of the bride of Jesus. This is more than I can imagine. Thank you. Thank you, Jesus.

Chapter Nine
Restoring Hope and Acceptance of the Present as We Near the Finish Line

Being prepared to cross the finish line from this life to eternal life with Jesus for all eternity includes much more than making all the important funeral arrangements. Certainly, it is wise to plan all the many details as we look forward to the time God will call us home. The previous chapter focused on the need to be at peace with God. However, my understanding is that we will only have complete peace with God when we have peace with all the people in our relationships. Only then will we have the assurance that we will cross the finish line.

Therefore, there are three further aspects I wish to mention that are related to being prepared to cross the finish line. These three aspects are that we will restore hope and acceptance as we near the finish line, that we will restore peace in our relationships, and that we will run the race and cross the finish line in community. These are the topics of the next three chapters.

The central metaphor in this manual is that our lives are like a long marathon. In any marathon, the last section is often the most difficult, the portion of the race where the runners doubt whether they will make it to the finish line. In a marathon, the runners need to accept the challenges that come in the last few miles and even the last few feet. Similarly, we need to recognize the challenges that the final years and months in our lives present. It is of no value to refuse to recognize these challenges, to wish it was otherwise, or even to deny or ignore what is happening. In this chapter, I will note that there is an attitude that applies towards the end of life that is necessary to help us be prepared to cross the finish line. This attitude is an acceptance of the present—being at peace with the current reality of life because we believe it is lived under God.

In order to illustrate what is meant by accepting the present with all its challenges and trials, we turn to the Apostle Paul. Paul described a particular hardship he was in with these words: "We were under great pressure, far beyond our ability to endure, so that we despaired even of life" (2 Corinthians 1:8). Paul did not describe this life-threatening hardship. Later, he wrote about a time when he was "harassed at every turn—conflicts on the outside, fears within" (2 Corinthians 7:5). In our last stage of life, we might feel as the Apostle Paul felt. We could be afraid that we might not make it. Life is overwhelming, and all we seem to see are our challenges and our failures.

A personal incident in university illustrates the need to recognize what is actually happening towards the end of life. It clarifies that, with God's strength and the support of others, we can make the necessary changes and endure to the finish line. As I look back, I realize it was only a minor challenge, but it serves as an illustration that, when it seemed I was a failure and would not make it, there was still hope. I was writing my first essay in a third-year English class. When the professor returned my essay, two things jumped out. One was all the red marks on the paper (it seemed there was more red than black). The second thing was a note at the end: "Come to my office." I was extremely discouraged, but, with some hesitation, I went to see the professor. He kindly and thoroughly went through the paper, giving corrections and suggestions. His red marks were about grammar and style of writing and not the content itself. I reworked the paper, and this time there were only a few red marks. Then I wrote it a third time and received a satisfactory grade.

The comparison of the essay to the end of life is this. When we look back on our lives, certainly we will see all types of regrets, failures, missed opportunities, and broken promises. We might be filled with shame, regret, disappointment, and maybe even depression. Satan wants to paralyze us so that we see no hope, no possibility of going ahead, and no point in even attempting to go forward. We might believe we have only a few more years left, but we feel immobilized. We see only the mistakes we have made. Other people, friends as well as family members, remind us of all that we did wrong or should have done better. We hear sermons pointing to what we should aspire toward. We agree that we need to change—and we want to—yet our life appears like that essay. All we see are the red marks—failures, mistakes, shattered dreams, and broken promises. Life appears hopeless. We feel dark despair. However, just like that kind and wise professor, God both knows all our failures and desires to come alongside us and give us hope.

In this chapter I wish to point to three sources of hope. Just as a marathon runner will reach for a power drink as she comes towards the end of the marathon, take hold of these three truths.

1. Enjoy the Present—It is a Gift of God

The first source of hope might not be perceived as a source of hope. I am referring to the familiar words, "Eat, drink, and be merry." These words can be spoken with two very contrasting attitudes. We are perhaps more familiar with the first attitude than the second. The first attitude is given in the story Jesus told about a rich farmer. When this proud farmer looked over his bumper crop, he folded his hands, calculated that his barns would not store all his crops, and said to himself, "You have plenty of good things laid up for many years. Take life easy; eat, drink and be merry." God confronted this man with the words, "You fool! This very night your life will be demanded from you....This is how it will be with anyone who stores up things for himself but is not rich toward God" (Luke 12:16-21). That rich fool demonstrated greed, pride, and independence from God and from other people. The Bible is certainly not advocating this attitude.

However, the Bible encourages us to use the same words, "Eat, drink and be merry," but from a different source of strength and dependency. These same words are given by "the Teacher, son of David, king in Jerusalem" in the wisdom book of Ecclesiastes. Solomon, the acknowledged author, was able to acquire everything he desired—wisdom, pleasure, achievements, and riches. But he recognized that these were all meaningless and purposeless when they were achieved without God or without a sense of dependence on God. However, when life, with all it contains, is received as a gift from a loving God, it will bring joy. The following words contain the theme of the book of Ecclesiastes: "A man can do nothing better than to eat and drink and find satisfaction in his work. This too, I see, is from the hand of God, for without him, who can eat or find enjoyment? To the man who pleases him, God gives wisdom, knowledge and happiness, but to the sinner he gives the task of gathering and storing up wealth to hand it over to the one who pleases God" (Ecclesiastes 2:24-26). The book of Ecclesiastes contains the reflections of an old man. This is evident in the final chapter (12:1-7). Therefore, Solomon's deliberations are a necessary reminder to older people who need hope, especially when they come to the end of their lives. If you are elderly and have reached many goals and accomplished much, or if you are elderly and life has seemed to be one failure after another, hear these words again, as coming from another elderly person at the end of life: "Then I realized that it is good and proper for a man to eat and drink, and to find satisfaction in his toilsome labor under the sun during the few days of life God has given him—for this is his lot. Moreover, when God gives any man wealth and possessions, and enables him to enjoy them, to accept his lot and be happy in his work—this is a gift of God" (Ecclesiastes 5:18-19); "So I commend the enjoyment of life, because nothing is better for a man under the sun than to eat and drink and be glad. Then joy will accompany him in his work all the days of the life God has given him under the sun" (Ecclesiastes 8:15).

The first source of hope is given by an old man: "Eat, drink and be glad. Recognize that God is in control. Life is a gift from him, and he wishes the best for us." Life is a gift from God. This might be easier to accept when a person is young and healthy. But even when a person is elderly and is afflicted with pain and weakness, life is still a gift from God. Therefore, enjoy life, even with all the limitations. That is easier said than done, but take this advice from an older person like yourself—Solomon. And these are the words I, as a person in the last third of my life, want to say to myself.

2. Accept the Present with Gratitude

This second source of hope is actually another way to describe the first. When we accept life as a gift from God, then we will receive the here and now with gratitude. This might be very difficult as we become weaker and have more aches, pains, and diseases. Yet, when an attitude of gratitude has been cultivated earlier in life, this attitude will sustain us in the frailty of our final years.

I recall visiting an old gentleman. His body was filled with arthritis, he could hardly get up, and he needed assistance with the basic necessities of life. When I asked how he was, he said, "I've much to be thankful for. Better than I deserved."

> **The choice is ours:**
> • Gratitude or grumbling
> • Acceptance or resentment
> • Joy or complaining
> • Highlighting solutions or pointing at problems
> • Giving light or spreading gloom

I have been humbled and inspired by a similar attitude in other men and women, facing increasing pain, limited by disability, feeling chronic discomfort, and being extremely frail. When I approach older people, I might expect to encounter a very different attitude and brace myself to hear a litany of complaints. But they often breathe gratitude. May their gratitude inspire each of us!

May we all face the present increasing frailty with dependence on God and then with gratitude. This requires deliberate and constant thankfulness. It's not easy, but you can have this attitude.

3. Trust in God's Constant Care, Right to the End

The third source of hope is related to the first two. Since our Lord is in control, and since we have so much to thank him for, we therefore will want to trust him—even when uncertainty seems to be overwhelming us like a threatening storm.

If any of you who are reading this book are nearing the end of life and feel discouraged, hear these words by the prophet Isaiah: "I said, 'I have labored to no purpose; I have spent my strength in vain and for nothing. Yet what is due me is in the LORD's hand, and my reward is with my God.' And now the LORD says…'Though [a mother] may forget, I will not forget you! See, I have engraved you on the palms of my hands; your walls are ever before me'" (Isaiah 49:4, 15-16). We might sense that all our life work has been in vain and for nothing and that our family and friends have forsaken us. May we then hear the assurance that what is due to us is in the Lord's hand and our reward is with our God, for he has engraved us on the palms of his hands.

> What's in our hearts will give us hope: "Above all else, guard your heart, for it is the wellspring of life" (Proverbs 4:23).

As we come to what we perceive as the final lap of life, we might be filled with an assortment of negative emotions—failure, anger, shame, guilt, blaming, disappointment. Yes, we will want to name and confess these. But then I invite us to see our God, to sense his compassionate eyes on us, to experience his open embrace. He wants to walk with us even—and especially—in our frailty and weakness. He has a good life for us to enjoy even now. We know it is good because God is good. See God as gracious, with open arms. Feel God's unconditional love and embrace.

Reflections

An expression that I have found insightful over the last years of life is this: "The way I lean is how I will fall." As I examine my attitudes over against the three sources of hope, how am I leaning?

- Am I enjoying the present, recognizing it is a gift of God?
- Am I accepting the present with gratitude?
- Am I trusting in God's constant care, right to the end?

When physical and emotional challenges weigh us down, it is necessary to fill our minds with promises. The following are some promises that will give hope and peace:

- "Even to your old age and gray hairs I am he, I am he who will sustain you. I have made you and I will carry you; I will sustain you and I will rescue you" (Isaiah 46:4).
- "But now, this is what the LORD says—he who created you, O Jacob, he who formed you, O Israel: 'Fear not, for I have redeemed you; I have

summoned you by name and you are mine. When you pass through the waters, I will be with you; and when you pass through the rivers, they will not sweep over you. When you walk through the fire, you will not be burned; the flames will not set you ablaze. For I am the LORD your God, the Holy One of Israel, your savior'" (Isaiah 43:1-2).

• "Why do you say, O Jacob, and complain, O Israel, 'My way is hidden from the LORD; my cause is disregarded by my God'? Do you not know? Have you not heard? The LORD is the everlasting God, the Creator of the ends of the earth. He will not grow tired or weary, and his understanding no one can fathom. He gives strength to the weary and increases the power of the weak. Even youths grow tired and weary, and young men stumble and fall; but those who hope in the LORD will renew their strength. They will soar on wings like eagles; they will run and not grow weary, they will walk and not be faint" (Isaiah 40:27-31).

• "'I said, "You are my servant"; I have chosen you and have not rejected you. So do not fear, for I am with you; do not be dismayed, for I am your God. I will strengthen you and help you; I will uphold you with my righteous right hand....For I am the LORD, your God, who takes hold of your right hand and says to you, Do not fear; I will help you. Do not be afraid, O worm Jacob, O little Israel, for I myself will help you,' declares the LORD, your Redeemer, the Holy One of Israel" (Isaiah 41:9-10, 13-14).

• "Yet this I call to mind and therefore I have hope: Because of the LORD's great love we are not consumed, for his compassions never fail. They are new every morning; great is your faithfulness. I say to myself, 'The LORD is my portion; therefore I will wait for him.' The LORD is good to those whose hope is in him, to the one who seeks him; it is good to wait quietly for the salvation of the LORD" (Lamentations 3:21-26).

• "Come to me, all you who are weary and burdened, and I will give you rest. Take my yoke upon you and learn from me, for I am gentle and humble in heart, and you will find rest for your souls. For my yoke is easy and my burden is light" (Matthew 11:28-30).

• "Keep your lives free from the love of money and be content with what you have, because God has said, 'Never will I leave you; never will I forsake you.' So we say with confidence, 'The Lord is my helper; I will not be afraid. What can man do to me?'" (Hebrews 13:5-6).

Prayer

Heavenly Father, as I look back over my life, I have a choice—to see all the trials and challenges and complain, or to see your constant faithfulness and presence, bow with gratitude, and lift my hands in praise for your goodness. As I look at my present, I also have a choice—to utter a litany of complaints and aches and grumble, or to receive the invitation, "Eat, drink, and be merry," to accept the present with gratitude and joy. Give me grace to choose gratitude and joy, for my life is under your control. I do trust you. In Jesus' name, Amen.

Chapter Ten
Restoring Peace in Relationships as We Near the Finish Line

I want to begin this chapter with a personal comment. I am including this chapter because of a devastating burden I see when I walk with families in their grief and loss. I realize we are all prone to sin and therefore there will be brokenness and pain in our lives. But my concern is the opinion, regrettably accepted and defended strongly by many people, that they can be in a right relationship with God without concerning themselves with broken relationships they are responsible for or are in. I'll admit that this is not a prominent attitude, yet it concerns me that it exists at all. In this chapter, I want to stress that we should strive to restore relationships in all stages of life, but particularly as we become older.

As we near the finish line of life, we certainly need to be assured that we will cross the finish line and then be in Jesus' presence. Is there anything that will give us a sense of hope, that will allow us to look ahead with assurance that we will be able to celebrate and worship in the home Jesus is preparing for us? We can only have this hope when we are in a right relationship with Jesus. However, as we study the Bible, we learn that being in a right relationship with Jesus means that we will also strive to be in a right relationship with people. Jesus calls us as individuals, but he also calls us to be part of a body and a family.

Some people say that when a person has said a "sinner's prayer," this person is in a right relationship with God and is therefore prepared to cross the finish line. These people will further say that their relationship with God is independent of their relationship with other people. They say, "As long as all is right between me and God, nothing else matters." However, my understanding is that an individual is only fully prepared to cross the finish line when, to the best of this person's ability, her or his relationships are restored and this person is at peace with everyone. We hear Jesus' words, "A new command I give you: Love one another. As I have loved you, so you must love one another. By this all men will know that you are my disciples, if you love one another" (John 13:34-35). This means that a distinct mark of whether we are Jesus' followers is our love.

As we focus on the topic of restoring peace with other people as we near the finish line, two short questions need a clear, definitive answer. The questions are, "Why bother?" and "How?" The first question might be elaborated as: "Why bother restoring peace between myself and others, or between other people, when all that is left of my life is several years, months, or even days?" The second question might be elaborated as: "How can I be expected to have the strength to pursue restoration in relationships when my health is failing, and my energy is limited?"

> **A genuine follower of Jesus will**:
> • restore broken relationships
> • love other people
> • strive for peace

As you read these words on restoring peace, I am convinced that the matter of restoring relationships is of utmost urgency. I also believe that God will give the necessary strength when there is a dependence on him and a commitment to do all that is necessary to restore relationships. It comes down to the simple question: "Am I willing to do what I can to restore relationships?"

1. Why Bother Restoring Broken Relationships?

I will offer a couple of answers to this question.

a. It Matters to a Holy God.

The ultimate answer is found in the example of God. God bothered to restore humankind to himself. He was so committed to ensure that reconciliation was available that God gave what was most precious to him in order to provide reconciliation for people who were his enemies. In what is possibly the most profound and well-known Bible passage on God's love, we read about how much God gave to restore relationships: "For God so loved the world that he gave his one and only Son, that whoever believes in him shall not perish but have eternal life" (John 3:16). This passage by the Apostle Paul assures us that God not only loved us but that he loved us when we were his enemies: "For if, when we were God's enemies, we were reconciled to him through the death of his Son, how much more, having been reconciled, shall we be saved through his life!" (Romans 5:10). As we place these two passages together, we note that God, the Father of Jesus, gave what was most precious to him, his one and only Son, to reconcile his enemies to himself through the death of his Son.

The answer to the question, "Why bother to restore peace at the end of life?" is that this matters so much to God the Father that he gave what was most precious to him to achieve this reconciliation. God the Father set the example for us. When we genuinely follow Jesus, when we have received the gift of reconciliation, Jesus' complete sacrifice for us, then we will bother to be reconciled with everyone with whom we have a broken relationship.

b. It Matters to Destroyed and Broken People.

A second answer to the question "Why bother to restore a broken relationship?" is that it matters to destroyed and broken people. When a Christian leader has wronged individuals or a Christian father has abused his children, we cannot be silent. We will want to carefully, discreetly, and sensitively speak the truth. By saying nothing, for instance, to a hurting daughter, we are thereby saying that the church, and her God, does not value her. Our words and actions will—by their silence or absence or by carefully chosen words and deeds—address whether we value the dignity and worth of the person who is hurt. May God give us the wisdom and courage to do what is right.

2. How Can I Have the Strength to Pursue Restoration when My Health Is Failing?

The answer to this question is found in the answer to the first question. I will only have the necessary strength when I am rooted in God's sustaining love. This means I must see myself and those with whom I am in conflict as God saw me when he gave his ultimate sacrifice, his only Son. I and whoever I need to pursue reconciliation with are both the objects of God's love—when we were both completely undeserving of his love. Only with God's strength and love can I pursue reconciliation.

Reconciliation and the restoration of relationships is not just a nice topic. This goes to the heart of our God. Therefore, it must go to our hearts as well and move us to action. We must see people as God does—as enemies for whom he gave his best in order to make them his friends. We are called to be reconcilers—on the basis of God's calling and reconciling of us. This must be our priority as we near the finish line of our lives.

> "All this is from God, who reconciled us to himself through Christ and gave us the ministry of reconciliation: that God was reconciling the world to himself in Christ, not counting men's sins against them. And he has committed to us the message of reconciliation" (2 Corinthians 5:18-19).

I will briefly note various classes of broken and fractured relationships. Where any of these apply to you, my desire is that the guidelines will give you direction and hope to pursue reconciliation. I believe that the most important legacy any of us can leave is restored and healed relationships. The reverse is therefore also true: the most devastating legacy we can leave is a trail of broken relationships.

3. Preliminary Thoughts on Restoring Relationships

Before I describe the classes of broken and fractured relationships and what is necessary to restore relationships, I want to offer some preliminary thoughts on restoring relationships:

- **The need for sensitivity to hear God's voice.** We might believe that there are no relationships we need to restore. Satan will strive to blind us to broken relationships. David violated Bathsheba, yet was blind to his behavior until the prophet Nathan confronted him and exposed his blindness and sin.

- **The need for an attitude of brokenness.** How easily we justify our innocence in a fractured relationship. We cannot be broken before God and blame and accuse others.

- **The need to keep our focus on God.** This is critical as we consider broken relationships. Satan will want us to focus on the wrong done to us. By focusing on God, we will see as God sees. We will see the other person as God sees him or her (as he or she really is), see ourselves as we really are, and then see a path of restoration to pursue.

- **The need to recognize that we are in a spiritual war.** We are in a war, nothing less. When God's Spirit speaks to us on a specific matter, we must then move forward in obedience and faith, following God's direction.

- **The usefulness of the illustration of three chairs.** A helpful way to understand our responsibility to restore broken relationships is to imagine three chairs—one for the judge, one for an advocate (defense attorney), and one for an accuser (prosecutor). When we sit in the seat of the accuser, we are sitting where the person who has offended us is sitting. When we sit in the seat of the judge, we are taking on the role of a holy and just God. Neither of those seats is ours. We are to sit in the seat of an advocate and, with God's grace and power, seek the welfare of the person who has offended us. (This illustration is taken from material in the seminar, *Whatever It Takes*.)

4. Classes of Broken Relationships
I will now turn to the classes of broken relationships.

a. Restoring Peace when I Have Been Treated Unjustly
Jesus addressed this situation directly: "If your brother sins against you, go and show him his fault, just between the two of you. If he listens to you, you have won your brother over. But if he will not listen, take one or two others along, so that 'every matter may be established by the testimony of two or three witnesses.' If he refuses to listen to them, tell it to the church; and if he refuses to listen even to the church, treat him as you would a pagan or a tax collector" (Matthew 18:15-17).

There is an interesting sidelight to this lesson in the next story in Matthew's Gospel. Peter asked Jesus, "Lord, how many times shall I forgive my brother when he sins against me? Up to seven times?" (Matthew 18:21). We are not given Peter's motive for asking this question. More specifically, why did Peter ask Jesus this question right after Jesus had given clear instructions on how to restore a broken relationship when one person sins against another? Was Peter expressing a forgiving spirit and a commitment to restore a broken relationship? Was Peter willing to follow Jesus' guidelines and forgive a brother up to seven times? There are some possible explanations for Peter's spirit of magnanimity. The teachings of the Jewish scribes and rabbis was that a person should forgive once or twice but a third offence merited no forgiveness. The Babylonian Talmud reads, "When a man sins against another, they forgive him once, they forgive him a second time, they forgive him a third time, but the fourth time they do not forgive him." Peter was expressing a more generous spirit of forgiving than the scribes and rabbis, but his forgiveness still had a limit, albeit higher than the Jewish rabbis. (These clarifications are drawn from Bible commentaries: William Hendriksen, *New Testament Commentary*, Grand Rapids, Michigan: Baker Book House, 1973; Herschel H. Hobbs, *An Exposition of the Gospel of Matthew,* Grand Rapids, Michigan: Baker Book House, 1965; G. Campbell Morgan, *The Gospel according to Matthew*, Old Tappan, New Jersey: Fleming H. Revell Company, 1929.)

However, in Luke's Gospel, Jesus gives us an even more generous path to follow: "If your brother sins, rebuke him and if he repents, forgive him. If he sins against you seven times in a day, and seven times comes back to you, and says, 'I repent,' forgive him" (Luke 17:3-4). This means that forgiveness is to be unlimited.

Recognizing that Matthew 18:15-17 is one of the most practical guidelines Jesus gives on restoring relationships, we need to carefully study what Jesus instructed and then completely follow his directives. Jesus gave four clear steps:

1. "Go and show him his fault, just between the two of you." The goal of this step is to win the brother over.

2. "Take one or two others along." These others, along with the two people who are in a conflict, will do their best to reflect, understand, and listen—again with the goal to "win the brother over." The purpose of recruiting one or two other people is to restore the relationship.

3. "Tell it to the church." Here the conflict is addressed and reconciliation is sought afterward. This implies that the church is entrusted with the ministry of reconciling people within the church.

4. "Treat him as you would a pagan or a tax collector."

Recognizing that this last phrase might be unknown or unfamiliar, I will provide an explanation. What does it mean to treat the person who refuses to listen either to you or to the church as "a pagan or a tax collector?"

May I suggest we find our answer in two avenues: first, by looking at the context, and then, by looking at how Jesus treated pagans and tax collectors.

When we look at the context, we realize that this is the fourth step in attempting to resolve conflict. The first is by one person, the second step is with the assistance of one or two others, and the third step is by the church. All the steps have the goal to bring about reconciliation. If the goal of the first three steps is to move towards the person with the purpose to restore him, then the goal of the fourth step will be the same—to take note of the conflict and then draw the other person back into a restored relationship.

When we consider the example of Jesus, we learn how he treated pagans and tax collectors—he always sought to restore them. A key element of how Jesus treated them is that he ate with them. When we eat with a person, we are committed to be on the same level, to open ourselves to the other person even when we disagree—with the goal to value the person and connect with him or her.

Luke records a story to show how Jesus welcomed and embraced sinners. Tax collectors and sinners gathered around Jesus and wanted to listen to him. Jesus then told three parables to make it perfectly clear how he was treating pagans and tax collectors: first, as a shepherd who sought the one lost sheep until he found it; second, as a woman who swept her house until she found a lost coin; third, as a forgiving father who embraced the prodigal son and restored him into the family. Following each parable is a statement of rejoicing—the first two about the exuberant rejoicing in heaven and the third describing the family celebration over the son who was dead and is alive, who was lost and is found (Luke 15:1-32).

Another story that explains how to treat people as a pagan and a tax collector is in Genesis 3. Immediately after Adam and Eve rejected God and despised his command, he came looking for them (Genesis 3:1-21). To treat a person as a pagan or a tax collector includes both a recognition that the person has estranged/separated himself from us (is lost) and a commitment to draw him back, to look for him until he is found and restored.

There are three further Bible principles regarding restoring relationships in Jesus' teaching in Matthew 18:

1. Our words have authority. In Matthew 18:18, Jesus said, "Whatever you bind on earth will be bound in heaven and whatever you loose on earth will be loosed in heaven."

2. God is present as we reconcile people to ourselves. In Matthew 18:19-20, Jesus said, "Again I tell you that if two of you on earth agree about anything you ask for, it will be done for you by my Father in heaven. For where two or three come together in my name, there am I with them." Normally we quote this passage, especially the last line, "to assure ourselves that God is present, even in the smallest gathering. However, the interpretation from the context eliminates any reference to the small numbers of people gathered. The context means that the number refers to those who come together to seek healing, restoration, and reconciliation. Therefore, the assurance is that God is present especially when two or three witnesses come together in an effort to bring about reconciliation. Reconciliation is of such a high priority that God ensures his presence when people are committed to it. In fact, this is the only place in the Bible where God assures us of his presence when believers gather in a small number. Jesus commits to be present with us when we take seriously the mission of reconciliation because this is his mission. We are on holy ground—with God's presence among us—as we seek to do his mission, bringing peace where there is conflict and healing where there is disease.

3. Be lavish in forgiving. Peter heard Jesus teach that reconciliation and forgiveness is a core practice for believers. Then he followed up the teaching with the valid and relevant question, "Lord, how many times shall I forgive my brother when he sins against me? Up to seven times?" (Matthew 18:21). We don't know what prompted Peter's question. Was he simply wanting information? Or did he want to present himself as a very forgiving person? Jesus' response referred back to Lamech, who bragged to his two wives, "Adah and Zillah, listen to me; wives of Lamech, hear my words. I have killed a man for wounding me, a young man for injuring me. If Cain is avenged seven times, then Lamech seventy-seven times"

(Genesis 4:23-24). Jesus' answer to Peter's question about forgiveness is a counterpart to Lamech's vicious announcement of personal revenge. Even as Lamech announced ferocious, brutal, and multiplied personal revenge, so Jesus instructed equal, if not greater, personal forgiveness. As Lamech was committed to repeated vicious revenge, so we who follow Christ should be committed to lavish and generous forgiveness.

b. Restoring Peace when People Believe They Have Been Treated Unjustly

When a person believes he or she has been wronged, this conclusion might be drawn from inaccurate or partial information. Or their information might be accurate, but their conclusion distorted. Either way, they hurt, and their understanding is darkened. They judge by assumption, appearance, and hearsay. They see themselves as victims and not responsible for their responses, for their part in a broken relationship, for their actions, for their perceptions, or for their duty to restore the relationship. Proverbs 18:19 says, "An offended brother is more unyielding than a fortified city, and disputes are like the barred gates of a citadel."

I don't have any quick and easy answer or formula to explain how to follow Jesus' way to restore peace when a person believes he or she has been treated unjustly. However, may I offer some direction in this difficult subject:

i. If you are uncertain about what actually happened, wait and check your own heart first. I confess I have not always done this. However, as I have checked my own heart, I have often sensed God's Spirit directing me to leave the situation in his hands. I found this instruction to be helpful: "It is mine to avenge; I will repay....The LORD will judge his people and have compassion on his servants" (Deuteronomy 32:35–36).

ii. God promises that he will maintain justice and avenge when necessary. Both the Apostle Paul and the author of Hebrews point to this truth (Romans 12:17-21, Hebrews 10:30-31). I take assurance that the passage in Deuteronomy brings together two commitments on God's part. First, he will avenge and do as he sees fit. Second, he will have compassion on his servants. We rest in the assurance that God is not only fair but is also compassionate.

iii. Seek God's help. The Psalmist's prayer is a helpful corrective: "Search me, O God, and know my heart; test me and know my anxious thoughts. See if there is any offensive way in me, and lead me in the way everlasting" (Psalm 139:23-24).

iv. Take responsibility. A verse that speaks directly to what might be happening in the soil of my heart when I am offended or believe I am offended (believe I have been treated unjustly) is: "Make every effort to live in peace with all men and to be holy; without holiness no one will see the Lord. See to it that no one misses the grace of God and that no bitter root grows up to cause trouble and defile many" (Hebrews 12:14-15). This verse implies that I am responsible for the soil of my heart, and since this is the case, when bitterness is growing, then I need to search my heart.

v. Don't be hasty. Is it necessary to speak to a person who I believe has offended me? Maybe I'm just timid when I suggest that we should lean towards hesitation before taking action. My hesitancy is based on these two factors. First, I want to follow Jesus' instructions when there are clear offences (Matthew 18:15-17). Second, I want to search my own heart, check the condition of the soil of my heart, give the concern to God, and extend grace. Since we live in a fallen world, we will offend and be offended constantly. Then there will be times when we are not certain whether either has happened. Possibly the best approach is to leave these uncertain times to God and check the soil in our hearts. Even better, we should till into our soil the character qualities in the Beatitudes, beginning with "Blessed are the merciful." I am in enormous need of mercy—may I extend it in equal abundance.

c. Restoring Peace when I Have Treated Another Person Unjustly

The matter of maintaining right relationships and restoring broken relationships is a core element in the Christian faith. This is much more than a responsibility or commandment for those who claim to follow Jesus. The very *essence* of the Christian message is reconciliation and restored relationships. The centrality of right relationships is based on who our God is and on the unity within the Trinity. Jesus' prayer is that the unity between him and his Father would also be between himself and his followers and *among* his followers (John 17:11, 20-24).

Further, we will not be able to worship God when we have a broken relationship with another person. Jesus taught the seriousness of offences when he said, "If you are offering your gift at the altar and there remember that your brother has something against you, leave your gift there in front of the altar. First go and be reconciled to your brother; then come and offer your gift. Settle matters quickly with your adversary who is taking you to court" (Matthew 5:23-25).

The seriousness of mending relationships was also stressed by the Apostle Paul when he wrote, "If it is possible, as much as depends on you, live at peace with everyone" (Romans 12:18).

How do we approach people we have offended? To make this more personal, I will change the question into the singular: How do I approach a person I have offended? I must begin the journey of reconciliation as one who has been reconciled and whose very nature is birthed and based in a God whose nature is one of peace and making peace. Therefore, I will come with humility, dependence on God, and vulnerability, not demanding anything.

- I always begin with the premise that I am responsible for what I have done, never trying to give any explanations or justifications.
- I will not seek to justify or explain my motives. Even if the other person says that I am selfish, inconsiderate, proud, rude, harsh, and arrogant and states this is the reason I am seeking reconciliation, I will only assure the person of my responsibility for my actions and attitude and my desire for reconciliation.
- I will not insist that I am right, thereby implying the other person is wrong.
- Instead, I will listen. I will seek both to hear and then to understand the other person. I will hear how this person understands my words and senses my motives. I will remain silent until the person has said all that he wants to say. Even then I will ask, "Do I understand this is what you are saying?" If I don't agree with the other person's understanding of what I said or did, the key is to respect this. Then, I will request that he forgives me for offending him. I will commit to search my motives and leave the relationship in God's hand.

> **Our Intentions, Their Actions**
> Often we judge ourselves by our intentions and judge everyone else by their actions. (John Bevere, *Bait of Satan*, 243.)

- I will never say, "If I have offended you, please forgive me." The bottom line of this statement is: "It is your fault that you are offended. I never meant to offend you, and since you are offended, that is your problem."
- I will say, "Where I have wronged you, please forgive me."

Following these steps is among the hardest things we can ever do or say. But, when we genuinely follow our God, who reconciled the world through the death of his Son, then we will take any action required to seek reconciliation. Restoring peace is at the heart of God. May this also be at the core of our heart.

d. Restoring Peace when There Is Discord between Other People

Our goal of reconciliation applies not only for ourselves but also for other people. Sometimes we are aware of a conflict between people and one or both of these people is becoming weaker and may only have a limited number of months or even days left. This becomes more critical and personal when there is conflict between members of our own family. Do we simply let it be, or do we get down on our knees, pray for godly wisdom, grace, and courage, and then take the bold step to urge those family members who are in conflict to restore their relationship?

One evidence that we are genuine followers of Jesus is that we will be peacemakers, as is manifest in Jesus' Beatitude: "Blessed are the peacemakers, for they will be called sons of God" (Matthew 5:9). Are we tempted to see the struggles in our neighborhoods, our cities, and even our world and respond, "During my life, I have been involved in many things, but now, in retirement and towards the end of life, I need to let others be involved. My time was then, not anymore"? As we become frail and struggle with a lot of pain, do we have a sense that we should withdraw from our involvements? We might rationalize it this way: "What can I do, now that I am old and feeble? Why should I concern myself with the issues around me?"

The answer to these questions is that, as followers of Jesus, we have his nature, and we will therefore seek to be peacemakers, no matter what age we are or even how frail we are. Actually, our life experiences should have sensitized us so that we are more capable to be reconcilers and peacemakers now than when we were younger and possibly more impulsive and demanding. May God give us

> Is it possible to approach this matter from another vantage point? Imagine that we have had a difficult and broken relationship with someone for many years and have an inner longing to be restored. But we are becoming weaker and do not know how to begin the process of reconciliation. Would we not wish that a peacemaker would help us to restore the relationship?

courage to become involved and engaged in the ministry of reconciliation. This is at the core of who we are.

e. Restoring Peace with Those Who Have Died

This applies when those who have offended us have died, as well as when we have offended someone and this person has died. The sobering reality is that this happens all too frequently. How do we find an answer and restoration—or is this not possible?

We know that the person who has offended us and is now dead will not come and ask for forgiveness. Does this mean we need to live with bitterness? Also, we know that when we have offended someone and this person has passed away, we likewise cannot seek forgiveness from him. Does this mean we need to live with regret? To varying degrees both scenarios are present with each of us. The reason is that we are continuously offending and being offended against.

An answer regarding the matter of restoring peace with those who have died involves a discussion on the topic of forgiveness. I believe that reconciliation is critical all the time, but there is a degree of urgency when we are placing this concern in the context of the final stages of life. (In the Appendix, there is a short list of books on reconciliation and forgiveness.)

I see reconciliation as part of a healing process. This healing process involves the following elements: confession, forgiveness, reconciliation, and then healing. The ideal is that all four of these elements will happen. When a wrong has occurred, a person will confess his wrong, the confession will be accepted, and forgiveness will be extended. This results in a reconciliation of the two parties, and then healing can begin. The critical question when we are speaking to the issue of restoring peace with those who have died is: "Can there be forgiveness when there is no confession?" We know the ideal is that all four elements will be included, but a dead person cannot confess. Nor can we confess to a dead person.

May I suggest that our answer is in Jesus' example. On the cross, he declared, "Father, forgive them, for they do not know what they are doing" (Luke 23:34). As we follow the crucifixion story, we see that the people he was referring to had not confessed what they were doing, nor were they reconciled. If Jesus had waited until his enemies felt some guilt or shame for their words or actions, he would never have forgiven them. Jesus' example demonstrates that total forgiveness must take place in the heart. If I have a genuine heart experience of forgiveness, I will not be devastated if there is no reconciliation. If those who hurt me don't want to be reconciled and be in a mended relationship with me, it isn't my problem because I have forgiven them and released them. I will feel hurt and wish it was otherwise, but I will have released them in my heart.

I believe this is how we can find an answer regarding someone who has offended us and has died. With this understanding of forgiveness, a person can achieve inner peace even when forgiving someone who has died. This person cannot confess to us, but we can still forgive, we can still free that person from what they did against us. This also applies in a situation where a person who is still living refuses to confess. The same principle applies. It is also then in our power and it is our responsibility to forgive.

The above explanation speaks to the situation where a person who has offended us has died. I have the ability and responsibility to forgive him and thereby release him of any wrong he has done to me. But what about the situation where I have offended a person who has died? The Holy Spirit convicts me of the wrong I have done, but I cannot go to this person and confess my wrong. Do I live with this turmoil and guilt in my heart?

I believe an answer can be found when we consider the core essence of sin. Sin, wickedness, and iniquity are first and foremost attitudes and actions against God. Our sinful attitude towards God is demonstrated in wrong and destructive behavior towards people. David understood this when he confessed, "*Against you, you only*, have I sinned and done what is evil in your sight, so that you are proved right when you speak and justified when you judge" (Psalm 51:4, emphasis added). When the prophet Nathan confronted David of the sin of adultery, David confessed to Nathan, "I have sinned against the LORD" (2 Samuel 12:13).

There are several other stories that reinforce this understanding that sin is primarily against God:

- When Abraham and Sarah moved into the region of Gerar, Abimelech, the king of Gerar, took Sarah. God spoke to Abimelech in a dream, saying, "I know you did this with a clear conscience, and so I have kept you from sinning *against me*" (Genesis 20:6, emphasis added).
- Joseph was responsible for Potiphar's household. When Potiphar's wife made an immoral advance on Joseph, he responded, "How then could I do such a wicked thing and sin *against God*?" (Genesis 39:6-10, emphasis added).
- When the prodigal son came to his senses he formulated his confession, which included these words: "Father, I have sinned *against heaven* and against you" (Luke 15:17-21, emphasis added).

With the understanding that sin at its core is a heart attitude towards God that is demonstrated in behavior towards people, I see a way forward when I know that I have offended a person who is now dead. Instead of going to that person who is dead (which I cannot do), I can and will go to God, confess my sin, and ask for forgiveness. Here, as in all incidents of sin, the instruction given by the Apostle John applies: "If we confess our sins, he is faithful and just and will forgive us our sins and purify us from all unrighteousness" (1 John 1:9).

5. Restoring Peace within the Family

I have presented five classes of broken relationships and have provided a brief direction to help restore peace in each area. In actual fact, all five of these classes of broken relationships are demonstrated in families. This becomes evident when families come to plan a funeral service for their loved ones. There is a phenomenal contrast between walking with a family where I have sensed the beloved mother or father was committed to having positive relationships and being at peace with all people within the family and beyond, and walking with a family where there was discord, animosity, and division. I believe the topic of restoring peace within the family deserves special attention, and therefore I will focus specifically on this critical issue in this separate section. Having said this, the principles in the first five classes apply to the family as well.

I will begin the discussion of restoring peace within the family with several questions. I invite you to ask these of yourself:

1. When I look at my family—my uncles and aunts, my brothers and sisters—is there a sense of unity and harmony or a sense of conflict and avoidance? Or were there other ways we related?

2. When I look back at my family experience when I was a child and young person, was there joy and grace or fear and criticism, or were there other emotions within my family?

3. From my parents, did I sense affirmation and blessings or judgement and put downs? Were there any other feelings?

4. Can I think about or talk about how serious I feel about having all my relationships mended within my family?

5. Why is it necessary or important to attempt to restore relationships?

6. What legacy do I wish to give my children?

7. How have I attempted to bring about peace within my family?

8. How do I respond when I observe character flaws and sinful behavior in my children that I observed were in my parents? Do I respond with anger, fear, repentance, or some other reaction?

a. The Nature of Forgiveness

The matter of broken relationships within a family is so very "close to home"—it is actually at home—that it is difficult to face these issues and respond in a wise and effective manner. Often parents deal with broken relationships in their family of origin by modeling the same brokenness—and their children learn to deal with brokenness in the same way as they were taught. Then, this behavior will continue from generation to generation unless a new approach is taken. To break this destructive mode of family relationships, it is necessary to recognize it for what it is. It is impossible to fully explain this in a short space, but I wish to point to some ways that I trust will bring about reconciliation and peace within a family.

i. Forgive or Excuse

We begin with the two approaches to deal with family discord: forgiving or excusing. This image helps me understand what is necessary to bring peace within a family. Imagine the family you are in now as a room filled with discord, fear, non-affirmation, a judgmental spirit, and even abuse and violence. You desperately want out of this room. You see two doors. One is marked "Confess and Forgive," and the second is marked "Excuse." The only door that will break the generational curse is the door marked "Confess and Forgive." If a family member walks through the door marked "Excuse," this person will step into an identical room of broken relationships.

ii. Confess and Forgive

Making a decision to forgive and actually forgiving are two different things. Forgiveness must be grounded in truth. We can only forgive to the degree that we know the extent of the damage inflicted. We will not forgive when we minimize, deny, or ignore the damage done. To forgive, we first need to feel the pain of the wound and know the consequence of the injury.

iii. Forgive

Forgiveness means to first, recognize the extent of the damage done to us, and second, hand over to God the right to stand in judgment.

iv. Excuse

To excuse is to overlook and make allowances for bad behavior. When we excuse, we take the focus from where it belongs, on the transgressor, and place it somewhere else. For example, we can take the focus away from the transgressor and place it on our society or on our family history or even on ourselves, the victim. Here we, as children, take the blame for our parents' violence.

Here are some excuses offered for parental malpractice:
- My parents really had a hard time growing up.
- They did the best they could.
- They were really struggling when I was a child.
- My dad spent long hours at work trying to help the family survive.
- Trying to avoid the mistakes of their own parents, they swung too far the opposite way.
- Worrying about money made them angry, but they were trying to make our life better than the one they had.
- They did not know any better.
- They were sickly.
- It was the culture that shaped them.
- It will not do any good to stir this up.
- I can cope with my parents' shortcomings.
- In many ways, he was a good father.
- My parents didn't become Christians until later.
- If they knew the impact of their sin on me, it would destroy them.
- It's okay because I have broad shoulders and I can carry it.
- It's no big deal because I am not worth it anyway.

(Trevor Walters, *EAS Syndrome*, 80-81.)

b. Giving and Receiving a Blessing

A related issue to broken relationships within a family is "blessing." This is not a separate and unconnected issue. The way God has designed a family is that parents are to be the avenue through which God extends his blessings, pouring them onto the children within the family.

The example of God, the Father, will demonstrate and help to explain this. After Jesus' baptism we read, "He saw heaven being torn open and the Spirit descending on him like a dove. And a voice came from heaven: 'You are my Son, whom I love; with you I am well pleased'" (Mark 1:10-11). Trevor Walters explains: "Jesus' Father's blessing enveloped Jesus before Jesus could ever have done anything to earn it....His Father's blessing was totally grace-based. It wasn't in the least dependent on any past achievement or any expectation of future performance" (Trevor Walters, *EAS Syndrome*, 20).

Where is the connection between "blessing" and resolving family brokenness? We begin with the plan God has for parents, especially fathers. Generally, children draw their perception of God, the Father, from their earthly father. God has designed it that children are to be blessed—affirmed for who they are, not because of what they have done or what they might do in the future—and this blessing will come primarily through the father.

How does a father pass on God's blessing to his children? The father will first need to receive the blessing of the heavenly Father. Using the image of soil, the father will need to have soft and rich soil so that God's Spirit will produce the fruit of the Spirit. The father's fruit of the Spirit (described by the Apostle Paul in Galatians 5:22-26) will be received by a child as a blessing and an affirmation. Paul's description of the fruit of the Spirit is followed by a brief comment that applies to the matter of family unity or discord. A father will either live in such a manner that his life will show the fruit of the Spirit, or his life will exhibit the deeds of the sinful nature. A child will feel the father's blessings, as evidenced by the fruit of the Spirit, or the father's lack of affirmation, as evidenced by the three final actions listed by Paul: being conceited, provoking, and envying.

c. Sour Grapes or Delicious Fruit?

At times, we might believe a family's dysfunction and brokenness is so major that it is futile to attempt to work towards any resolution. We cannot see any change possible. We despair that the brokenness that has been handed down through generations will continue like a mighty waterfall for the next many generations. We might even refer to the biblical proverb: "The fathers have eaten sour grapes and the children's teeth are set on edge" (Jeremiah 31:29, expanded and interpreted in

Ezekiel 18:1-32). The Israelites used this proverb as a form of self-pity, fatalism, and despair. They claimed that they were not responsible for their own behavior and that any ill effect on themselves was inevitable. They based this claim on a false interpretation and application of Exodus 20:5 and Numbers 14:18. There it states that a man's sins can have a negative effect on his descendants. However, this does not take away from the fact that every person is responsible for his own behavior. Ezekiel's teaching on this topic concludes with, "For I take no pleasure in the death of anyone, declares the Sovereign LORD. Repent and live!" (Ezekiel 18:32). The application for our topic—resolving division within the family—is that our gracious God calls us to repentance and to new life. Then the father and family will produce, not sour grapes, but delicious fruit for their children and grandchildren.

Reflection #1

Why is it that so many families, even Christian families, not only have significant divisions among their various members, but that there seems to be no urgency among them to restore relationships even as individuals come to the last months of life?

Reflection #2

Do I feel an urgency to restore a broken relationship—whether this is between myself and someone else or between two other people?

If so, what will I base reconciliation on? Do I really believe that God, through Jesus, has given me the ministry of reconciliation?

How will I commit to restoring relationships:
- with those who have done me wrong?
- with those I have wronged?
- with those who have died?
- among other people when I sense discord among family members?

How will I do what I can to restore friendship and peace?

Prayer:

Heavenly Father, this chapter has been difficult. As I look back, I wish that things had been different. There was pain, a spirit of fear—certainly not affirmation—in the family in which I grew up. I did not feel blessed or valued for who I was. Today I look up to you, seeking your affirmation and love, but also seeking the necessary courage to make wise decisions. I know I will need help. May I reach out, accepting the help I need so that your blessings will flow in me and then through me to my children and through them to my grandchildren. May I hear your reassuring words, "You are my child, whom I love; with you I am well pleased." May I then say the same to my children, with your power and grace. In Jesus' name, Amen.

Chapter Eleven
Running the Race and Crossing the Finish Line in Community

We have heard the proverb, "It takes a village to raise a child." Society will rally around a newborn child and support the parents. The grandmother will come, often from a long distance, and give needed help, even when there is a normal birth and the child is healthy. In some societies, a mother is expected to bring her newborn child and move back to her parents' and grandparents' neighborhood. The extended family will then be involved in the care and the upbringing of the child.

We also recognize the need to have a stable home for teenagers. When a home is dysfunctional, the child is moved into a foster home, according to government guidelines that seek to provide the best possible environment for children and teenagers.

And, when a man and woman commit themselves to one another for life in marriage, the families and friends will again gather to give their support and blessing.

These three examples demonstrate that a common feature in any stable society is a strong interconnectedness among the citizens. In such a society, all members watch out for each other. This sense of community will be evident across generations, so that children feel loved by their grandparents and youth are considerate of the elderly. The members of such a society lean into each other, instead of distancing themselves. They embrace each other instead of turning away from one another. A society in which individuals are isolated or feel shunned and marginalized will disintegrate.

As we return to the metaphor of a marathon, I want to add another element. This element is that every runner needs the help of other people in order to successfully cross the finish line. Before a runner enters a marathon, she will consult a trainer or medical person to ensure she is in proper physical condition to be able to complete the long marathon. Individuals will prepare the track so that it will be safe for the runners. Along the marathon path will be medical stations, as well as people who have fresh water for the runners. These support systems are more frequent and critical the closer a runner approaches the finish line.

The application to the subject of preparing to cross the finish line in life is this: as in a marathon where a runner needs other people, so each one of us needs support and help throughout the various stages of our life. But this help is most critical when we become frail and vulnerable towards the end of our lives, as we strain to run the last lap of the marathon of life.

The emphasis throughout this book is that each person is responsible to be prepared to cross the finish line. However, it is necessary to add another emphasis—on the significance and responsibility of the community in helping to ensure that we will successfully cross the finish line. The sober reality is that we cannot finish well on our own. We need one another.

There are several principles that are crucial if the elderly are to be cared for in a healthy and supportive community and are able to cross their finish line with hope, courage, the necessary strength, and the endurance they will need.

1. An Acknowledgement that We Live in an Individualistic Society

Various sayings point out our Western society's spirit of individualistic pride, including "If it is to be, it's up to me" and "I did it my way." In a memorial service, we may hear words of acclamation such as "What an accomplishment," "He did it all by himself," and "He certainly had many achievements and successes." When individuals are in their youth or young adulthood, they might believe they can make it on their own. Our Western society promotes individualism, admires self-made, independent people, and places on a pedestal those who seemed to make it on their own. Yet at no stage in life is a person ever independent.

This spirit of individualism is of particular significance as a person becomes older. Earlier in life, when a person was stronger, he might have assumed he was self-sufficient and did not need anyone else. But when a person becomes older and weaker, the myth of being independent needs to be acknowledged for what it is—a myth and a falsehood. Yet, how often older men and women want to assume they can function alone without any support. This is unrealistic, and it puts unnecessary stress on their families and close friends.

When a person becomes weaker in advancing years, a difficult balance or tension needs to be faced. This tension is between giving a person control over his own decisions and confronting him when he is unrealistic in what he believes he can do. His spirit of independence needs to be addressed, faced, and even challenged.

2. Weep with Those who Weep

After a memorial service, a friend of the family approached me and said, "What is wrong with all of us? No one cried. No one showed any emotions. Did no one love our dear friend? Did none of the family members really love their mother and grandmother?"

Christians in Western churches will certainly not be accused of wailing, tearing their clothes, and throwing dust and ashes into the air, which are common expressions of grief in some other cultures. But have we drifted too far to the other extreme? If we genuinely love our mother, or whomever we are conducting the funeral service for, and know that we will never again see her on earth, then this should be evident in our deep sorrow.

I recall hearing the testimony of a widow whose husband was murdered while they were missionaries. At that time, I was just beginning my pastoral ministry, having conducted only one or two funerals. But I sensed something was not fitting as I listened to her testimony. This widow had been asked to be a key speaker in our church's missions event. Instead of an expression of deep grief over the murder of her husband, she only talked of how God was with her. Certainly, I rejoiced that God was with her and that she felt God's presence and compassion in the tragic murder of her husband. But why did she, a Christian leader, not even hint at the loss and the grief I expected her to be experiencing—not only over losing her husband but also over having to relinquish the vision of being a missionary with him? Why did she need to be silent about her pain? Did she have any feelings of anger and frustration, or even doubt about God's ways? Why did it seem that the whole congregation, except for me, did not see that something was not authentic? Those were the questions I felt in my heart.

The words written by the preacher in Ecclesiastes 3:1-8 are regularly spoken at funeral services. They begin, "There is a time for everything, and a season for every activity under heaven." Then the preacher lists a series of "opposites." The two opposites that apply to a funeral service are "weeping and laughing" and "mourning and dancing." I cannot go into detail on the subject of grief, loss, and mourning—this would require more space than I have here. But I have experienced how this passage has been misinterpreted and misused so that grieving people have been left without hope and without comfort.

First, this text can be used in such a way as to leave grieving people with no hope. The text can be seen to mean that we have little or no capacity to change the situations that happen to us and to others. The interpretation is that God's timing is perfect and therefore we are not to interfere. This interpretation includes the premise that sometimes God provides painful occasions for weeping and mourning and at other times he gives us pleasant experiences for laughing and dancing. In my opinion, this is an improper reading of the text. The message of the whole book of Ecclesiastes, including the words on the opposites that life presents, is that God is infinitely concerned for the world but is also sovereign. Life is made up of both of these contrasts. These are givens. The preacher is not thereby implying that both are good, merely that both just *are*. Furthermore, the book teaches that when good or bad, painful or pleasant experiences happen, God is still in control. Therefore, we are called to trust God and submit to him, as expressed in the final words of the book, "Here is the conclusion of the matter: Fear God and keep his commandments, for this is the whole duty of man" (Ecclesiastes 12:13). Applying this specifically to valleys of pain, grief, and loss, the message is that we can trust God—even when we do not understand and cannot make sense of our tragedy. As we hold on to God in our grief, we believe he walks with us in our valley of death. This gives us hope, knowing God is present even—and especially—in the darkest valley of absolute loss and uncontrolled grief.

The passage in Ecclesiastes that lists the opposites has also been misused in another manner that leaves people without comfort. I recall a phone call from a close friend of a grieving widow. The caller requested that I visit this widow, whose husband had passed away several years earlier. The reason this close friend wanted me to go to the widow and speak to her was, "She has grieved long enough. She needs to get over it and get on with life." This friend thought that I, as the pastor, could coerce this widow to cease grieving. Possibly the friend of this widow had heard some preacher read Ecclesiastes 3:1-8 and then admonish the audience, "People, there was a time to weep and a time to mourn. But that time is long past. Now is a time to laugh and to dance." Some preachers even go so far as to point to admonitions such as, "Be joyful always, pray continually; give thanks in all circumstances" (1 Thessalonians 5:16-18) and then tell people that they should not grieve or weep. This is an absolute misuse of Scripture. It insults those who are grieving and shows an ignorance of human nature.

Jesus' words apply here: "Blessed are those who mourn, for they will be comforted" (Matthew 5:4). Jesus did not promise, "Blessed are those who refrain from mourning." Keeping a stiff upper lip in a time of sorrow and forcing ourselves not to break down when sharing a tribute to a dear mother might be good stoicism, but it is certainly not good Christianity. God created us with the full range of emotions, and we are meant to experience them all. Jesus promised, "The thief comes only to steal and kill and destroy; I have come that they may have life and have it to the full" (John 10:10). But how do we apply that verse? Have we defined the "life to the full" that Jesus came to give as a life in which all our wants are met and we feel pleasant and joyful all the time? A study of the 150 Psalms shows that the largest group of psalms are lament psalms. In these lament psalms, the Psalmist cried out to the Lord, trusting in the Lord's constant presence, goodness, and power. The Psalmist believed that the Lord is always present and that he will hear and will answer. I believe we will readily agree that the Psalmists who expressed these laments had a deep trust in the Lord. The Psalmists who lamented and cried out to the Lord lived life to the full, even in their distress and loss. Therefore, we can state that the full life that Jesus has come to give will include extreme grief.

Family, it is right that you express grief and sorrow, even to the point of sobbing and being unable to continue speaking when you share deeply about a dear mother. I remember several times that the following would happen. A family member, usually a son, would share a moving tribute about his mother. Then he would come to me after the service and say, "I was so afraid that I would begin sobbing and just bawl like a little baby. I am so glad I was able to control myself." How I wished that this son did not feel such pressure to remain calm. I wish that son had known that when he grieved, he could let it show.

Jesus wept with the two sisters Mary and Martha at the death of their brother Lazarus. Paul described God as "the Father of compassion and the God of all comfort, who comforts us in all our troubles, so that we can comfort those in any trouble with the comfort we ourselves have received from God" (2 Corinthians 1:3). Our grief is an expression of our emotions, demonstrating that we have lost someone who is precious.

I have expanded on the aspect of "weeping with those who weep" because I believe it is an important reminder, particularly in our Western society where we attempt to control our grief.

Another reason I have expanded on the need to "weep with those who weep" is because this applies particularly to older adults. As a person reaches the last years of her life, she will have an accumulation of loss after loss. These are only some of them: the loss of children as they left home, the loss of a career, the loss of health, the loss of dignity if the bodily functions cannot be controlled, the loss of a spouse, the loss of friends. Therefore, it is critical that family and friends will support this elderly person. May we never express thoughts such as, "I know what it is like, and I understand you." May none of us hesitate to sit with those who are grieving. May we let them bawl, even uncontrollably. May we simply be present—just sit and listen, and maybe just sit.

3. The Balance between Supporting and Empowering/Resourcing

We need to empower and resource people so that they are prepared to run the final part of their marathon of life and successfully cross the finish line. We also need to recognize that their community—their family and close friends—will have a major bearing on their failure or success in their last years.

The Apostle Paul pointed to the balance between supporting and empowering when he instructed Christians to "carry each other's burden, and in this way you will fulfill the law of Christ" and also taught, "Each one should carry his own load" (Galatians 6:2, 5). In other words, the community, the church, and the family are responsible to support the elderly people in their midst. At the same time, these elderly people are responsible for doing what they can do.

The following is an example of this balance. We encourage individuals to plan ahead and make certain their pension plans and medical insurance will sustain them in their final years. However, we must admit that many people who have been living under the poverty line all their lives have not been able to put aside savings for their retirement, much less the years when they need major medical care. This means that we, as members of a church, will think of those who are frail in their final years. As citizens in our country, we need to speak up and advocate that scarce resources will be allocated to help the frail elderly.

4. A Society's Care for the Weak and Vulnerable

It is well documented that a society can be measured by how it treats those members who are frail and weak. This also applies to a religion and a value system. The Apostle James defined the essence of pure religion with these words: "Religion that God our Father accepts as pure and faultless is this: to look after orphans and widows in their distress and to keep oneself from being polluted by the world" (James 1:27). Jesus stressed the importance of caring for those in need, noting that when we do so, we are in fact doing this for him: "Whatever you did for one of the least of these brothers of mine, you did for me" (Matthew 25:31-40). We, who claim to follow Jesus, will want to commit our time, examine our priorities, reallocate our resources, and advocate that the frail and elderly will be cared for.

In the Jewish culture of the first century, the oldest son was responsible for the care of his mother if his father had passed away. We are familiar with Jesus' sensitive and compassionate words, spoken when he was suffering unimaginable pain and loss as he was hanging on the cross. To his mother Jesus said, "Dear woman, here is your son." To the beloved disciple John he said, "Here is your mother" (John 19:26-27). With those words, John was given responsibility for Jesus' mother. We know that at the time of Jesus' crucifixion, his brothers did not believe in him even though they were among the believers after Jesus' ascension (John 7:5, Acts1:14).

As those who follow Jesus, we need to accept our responsibility to care for our elderly, not only within our churches, but also within our neighborhoods and cities. In summary, caring for, walking with, and being present with the weak and vulnerable in the last years of their lives is at the core of our Christian faith. May the way we fulfill this responsibility be compelling evidence of our faith in God.

5. The Various Models of Living in Community

Care for our frail elderly is a key component of a stable and whole society. There are various models of how we can provide a caring environment for our elderly. For most of society's history, frail seniors were cared for within their own families and in the community. This is still the practice in many Eastern cultures. A fairly recent phenomenon is the building of care homes for the elderly. These care homes often have several levels of support—from minimal assistance through partial support to full support.

However, a harsh reality, at least in our Canadian society, is that there are not enough financial resources to build care homes for all of our seniors, even if we agreed that this is the best way to care for our elderly. Also, the villages or communities for seniors offering the various levels of care are limited to only a small segment of our society who can afford this avenue of care. Having noted this, our Canadian health system provides subsidized complex care for the individuals with the greatest need. However, there are several major issues involved.

- Awareness of the available care resources needs greater attention. Elderly people, along with their families, need clear directions on how to "navigate the health care system." All too often, older adults and their families do not know how to take the next steps—from living at home to receiving support at home to independent living in a seniors' facility and then to the various levels of complex care.
- Individuals with limited financial resources have challenges navigating the transitions from being fully independent to needing full care.
- The models of support should be appropriate to the people involved. In other words, what might fit some cultural groups will not fit other groups. We will want to ensure that every senior is cared for in a way that is most desirable to her or him, even though the model of care will vary.

6. Are We Our Elders' Keepers?

After Cain, in a spirit of jealousy and anger, killed his brother Abel, God confronted Cain with the question, "Where is your brother Abel?" We know the callous response by Cain: "I don't know. Am I my brother's keeper?" (Genesis 4:1-12). As families, as neighborhoods, as church congregations, and as citizens of our country, we have a responsibility to know where our elderly people are and what their needs are. This means we need to listen to them, sit with them, and hear what they desire. We are our elders' keepers.

I recall a conversation about the ministries churches were providing for seniors. A denominational leader and pastor gave this comment, "Our focus and energy is on the next generation—on the children and youth. The seniors are capable of caring for themselves, and therefore the church should not provide any ministry for them." Regrettably, this attitude is very familiar and widely accepted among Western evangelical churches.

Another example is a senior pastor of a church who characterized his seniors as being in the categories: no go, slow go, and fast go. Those categorized as "no go" tended to be frail, demented, and dependent upon others, while those categorized as "fast go" were strong and independent. Those who were characterized as "slow go" were somewhere in between. James M. Houston and Michael Parker responded to this regrettable caricature of our elders with, "The church should ask the hard question: what value to society is a 'no go'?" And they say we should answer confidently: "An incontinent, dependent person suffering from late-stage Alzheimer's disease provides the person's family and church with one of life's most important lessons. This is an opportunity to learn how to love a person unconditionally, without any expectation of something in return."

If the church continues to relegate its responsibilities toward its senior members to other institutions in society and fails to recognize the gifts that lie within those members, it will become like salt that has lost its taste, its purpose, and its capacity to preserve that which is good, and it will have lost its capacity to light the way. Houston and Parker conclude: "The aging church is not an accident. It is God himself who has granted longer life for his purposes, and we believe that elders hold the keys to solving many, if not most, of society's problems" (Houston and Parker, *A Vision for the Aging Church*, 31-33).

The early church recognized its responsibility to care for the frail elderly. Here are three examples of how the early church cared for dependent and weak seniors:

• Specific steps were taken by the Twelve to ensure that widows from the Grecian Jews would receive daily food (Acts 6:1-7).

• The Apostle Paul instructed Timothy to "Give proper recognition to those widows who are really in need" (1 Timothy 5:3).

• James, the brother of Jesus, described the religion that God our Father accepts as pure and faultless is one that "looks after orphans and widows in their distress" (James 1:27).

In summary, we, as families, as churches, and as a society, are our elders' keepers, especially as they near the finish line of their lives.

7. Mentoring: Valuing the Wisdom and Blessings of Our Elderly

The first six sections of this chapter discussed various expressions of walking with and caring for the elderly. In various degrees, these sections described what the family, the church, and society should do for the elderly.

This seventh section replaces what we do "to" and "for" the elderly with what is done "with" or "by" the elderly, what we receive "from" the elderly. Regrettably, there is a pervasive belief that seniors are a group that need help and that ministries and services should be directed "to" and "for" them. This view is prominent within most Western congregations and government agencies. Yet possibly one of the greatest gifts that can be bestowed on our elderly people is welcoming the gifts that they can bestow on the rest of society. However, little effort is made in the areas of consulting them, seeking their advice, working with them, affirming them, appreciating them, and requesting what they can provide.

In the last lap of a marathon race, the runner's focus and energy are directed towards completing the marathon. But, in the marathon of life, God has so designed society that that those in the last lap have more to do than simply ensuring that they themselves make it across the finish line. God has so designed us that we will want to help other people in life. This is the reason he has placed us within families and in communities. Possibly one of the greatest things that will motivate our elderly people is if we acknowledge their worth. Their value is a given, but it is often not affirmed nor appreciated.

The Apostle Paul unashamedly instructed the Corinthian believers, "Even though you have ten thousand guardians in Christ, you do not have many fathers, for in Christ Jesus I became your father through the gospel. Therefore, I urge you to imitate me" (1 Corinthians 4:15–16). On the basis of Paul's maturity and long-time relationship with the believers, he was able to urge them to imitate him.

The Apostle John addressed the older men in the church with these words: "I write to you, fathers, because you have known him who is from the beginning" (1 John 2:13–14). He recognized that they had known Jesus for a long time, and he instructed these older men, believers and followers of Jesus for many years, to recognize the rich gift of their experiences and wisdom. They were to draw on this wealth of wisdom and life experiences and use it to inspire and guide those who were younger in their life and in their faith journey.

When we consider Old Testament society, we recognize that God provided several groups to give leadership and direction. We normally think of the priests and the prophets, but there was another class of people who were an important part of Israelite society—the "wise men" or "sages." A reference to these three classes of people is given by those who opposed Jeremiah when they said, "Come, let's make plans against Jeremiah; for the teaching of the law by the priest will not be lost, nor will counsel from *the wise*, nor the word from the prophets" (Jeremiah 18:18, emphasis added).

In one of Ezekiel's words of prophecy, there is a sense of hopelessness and despair. The reason for the calamity is the people's conduct. As a consequence, there would be no guidance from God and no direction from the elders. Ezekiel prophesied, "Calamity upon calamity will come, and rumor upon rumor. They will try to get a vision from the prophet; the teaching of the law by the priest will be lost, as will the *counsel of the elders*" (Ezekiel 7:26, emphasis added).

The point is that God led his people through three groups—prophets, priests, and elders. The thrust of the Wisdom books of Proverbs and Ecclesiastes is words of wisdom from a father to his son. In Bible times, God provided "sages," "elders," and "wise men and women" as a critical class of leaders to guide his people. Similarly, in our modern world, God has given us elders, both women and men, to guide us as well. We need to affirm and hear the words of these elders because they have words of wisdom from God.

Today, we regrettably hear older people say that they have no value—or, at least, they feel that way. In Israelite society and in the early church, the assumption was that older people had value because they were older. It is no coincidence that an elderly couple, Zechariah and Elizabeth, were the first to hear about the conception of Jesus, the Messiah (Luke 1:35-56). It is also no coincidence that God so directed it that two elderly people, Simeon and Anna, were the first to see the baby Jesus in the temple and bless him and his parents (Luke 2:25-38).

The best hope for our country, our churches, and our families is to return to the biblical model and affirm the role and contributions of the elderly. "When one thinks of elders, one should not think of frail, dependent people. On the contrary, the hope of our nation and perhaps of the world rests on the shoulders of those who comprise the aging church. The most frail and physically dependent person may also be the most ardent prayer warrior or the most wise or courageous member of a congregation" (James M. Houston and Michael Parker, *A Vision for the Aging Church*, 124).

Reflections

Recognizing the wisdom seniors provide requires a response:
- As a senior: How do I show courage to accept my responsibility?

- As a non-senior: How do I humbly show that I receive the wisdom of seniors?

Prayer
Heavenly Father, as I come towards the end of my life, I look back with deep gratitude, remembering all the times you have carried me. You have been faithful, no matter what I was experiencing. Further, as I look back, I am also keenly aware that many people have walked with me. At times, I have felt alone, but in those times you provided family, friends, and the church, who lifted me and cared for me. And this is also the case now. I am not walking alone. At times, it feels that way. But you place caring people around me. I value them, and I want them to know how much they mean to me. Thank you for expressing your love through your people. This gives me hope. In Jesus' name, Amen.

PART TWO: A GUIDE FOR PASTORS

The Funeral Director

The midnight hour, the darkest hour,
That human grief must know,
Sends forth its hurried summons;
Asks me to come – I go.
I know not when the bell may toll,
I know not where the blow may fall,
All I know is I must go
In answer to the call.
Perhaps a friend, perhaps unknown,
'Tis fate that turns the wheel.
The tangled skeins of human life
Wind slowly on the reel.
And I am the funeral director,
Cold blooded, you'll hear them say:
Trained to the shock, And chill of death,
With a heart that's cold and grey.
Trained, that is what they call it,
How little they know the rest.
I am but human and know the sorrow
That aches beneath the throbbing breast.

– Anonymous
Posted in the Western Canada
Development Museum, Saskatoon.
Used by permission.

Introduction and Overview

"Dad, what do I do? How do you plan a funeral?" This was the gist of an urgent phone call I received from our son Andrew. As the pastor of a church, Andrew had wondered when this day would come, and now he was responsible for planning his first funeral. At the time I received this call, I had been a pastor for a long time and had helped with more than three hundred funerals. Andrew represents the many pastors who have never received any formal training in conducting funerals but who are about to lead their first funeral service. They need to help families deal with their grief and then plan the burial and funeral services.

This guide is dedicated to pastors such as Andrew, whom God has called to walk with families in their time of loss and grief. If you are a pastor who lacks confidence in the area of planning funerals, this book is for you. You might have attended numerous funerals. You might remember a particular funeral message and appreciated the encouraging and comforting

> **Dealing with Death**
> The initial conception of this book was developed in the context of a congregation with mostly older adults. Yet my intent is not that the focus or application of this book should be limited to older persons. Will the content of this book also be relevant to the death of infants, young children, or younger adults in the prime of life? My answer is "Yes." As pastors, we will need to prayerfully, compassionately, and humbly seek to speak God's truth and share his heart in each specific situation.

words that the pastor said. On the other hand, you might remember a different funeral, where you sensed that the sermon or the minister's words were insensitive or even inappropriate. You might be asking yourself, "What would have been a more appropriate message? What might I have said to the grieving family? What might God want me to say to the people at a funeral?" Possibly you are in your first pastorate and are wondering when you will be called on to conduct your first funeral. Or you might be in a church where you lead only two or three funerals a year and you have never taken the time to focus on how best to walk with a family in their time of loss and grief. With each funeral, you dread the responsibility to help another family in their grief. Your sense of inadequacy overwhelms you in this area of ministry. You honestly wonder if you have anything significant to offer the family. Or you might have conducted several hundred funerals but are still open to reflecting on how you are doing and wondering whether there might be a better way than you are now offering. If you are in any of these situations, I am dedicating this guide to you. My goal is to help you as you shepherd individuals in the last years of their lives and as you walk with their loved ones in a time of grief.

In this guide, I address items from a practical point of view as well as from an ideological, biblical, and theological perspective. I combine stories and illustrations with principles so that it will become clear that what we do is based on our theological foundation. How we relate to a family in their time of grief is based on what we believe about issues such as death, grief, heaven, salvation, caregiving, and even funeral homes. Another way to put this is that "life" and "truth" are not independent and separate identities. What happens in our lives, in this case in the midst of loss and grief, is never separated from our theological beliefs and our interpretation of the Bible. This applies both to us as pastors and to the grieving families who come to us.

The metaphor of an iceberg illustrates this principle. The grieving family's feelings and how we walk with them in their grief are like the small, visible, above-the-water part of the iceberg. But this visible part is connected to a much larger part beneath the surface—our own experiences and our beliefs about critical life and death issues. Therefore, my goal is to provide practical ideas and suggestions, but also to invite you, as a fellow pastor, to examine your beliefs and values. This latter work is essential, so that when you walk with a grieving family, they will have a sense that you are speaking from the heart of our God, who is the Father of compassion and the God of all comfort (2 Corinthians 1:3). As pastors, we don't primarily need a manual on funerals, even though we can benefit from one. Instead, what we need above all is a renewed and transformed theology in critical areas that will compel us to change how we serve during the time of a funeral.

The initial goal of this book was to help ordinary people plan their funerals or the funerals of their loved ones. With this in mind, Part One of this book was addressed to the people preparing funerals. This part, Part Two, is for us as pastors, who help people prepare funerals. However, as I reflected on the topic of preparing funerals, I came to the realization that a funeral is not an isolated event. Everything that has happened in an individual's life has a bearing on her or his funeral. In a corresponding sense, everything that the grieving people bring with them to a time of loss will significantly shape their response to their loss and grief. Therefore, when a loved one dies, our work as pastors is never as straightforward as preparing a funeral. Our work involves many issues leading towards the end of life and preparing to cross the finish line from this life to the next. This means that our responsibility as pastors is not limited to helping individuals prepare funeral services and walking with them in their time of grief. We are called to help people be prepared to cross the finish line of life. A biblical understanding of this theme will necessarily include the various aspects that are involved in being prepared to cross the finish line. These are elaborated in the chapters of this book.

Following is an overview of Part Two.

Chapter One: Being with People as They Cross the Finish Line

This book begins with a recognition that being with people as they take their last breath will have a deep impact on each of us. As we recognize the sacredness of the moment a person crosses the finish line, we will want to do all we can to help people be prepared for this moment. We will also want to walk with their loved ones as they grieve their loss and at the same time celebrate precious memories.

Chapter Two: Recognizing the Western, Post-Christian Culture in Which We Help People Prepare to Cross the Finish Line

In this chapter I outline thirteen attributes of the current cultural and religious environment in which we are called to provide care for people at the end of life, as well as for their loved ones. As we help people prepare their funerals and process end-of-life issues, it is important to recognize that we do so in the context of a Western culture whose values are often opposed to biblical and Judeo-Christian values.

> What is the greatest point of contrast between a Christian and a secular approach to dying and death?

Chapter Three: Changes in Funeral Practices

This chapter outlines several key changes in recent years, which suggest profound changes in the understanding of death. Increasingly, people are avoiding burial services, viewing the body, and even having a funeral at all. This "new way of death" reveals a society with no hope.

Chapter Four: Planning the Funeral Service

This chapter deals with planning a funeral service with a family. I emphasize that when we plan the service with a family, we need to hold two goals in balance. One goal is to express compassion and sympathy with those who are grieving, and the other is to ensure that the service will be planned in the best possible manner.

Chapter Five: Partnering with a Funeral Home
This chapter deals with the significant matter of partnering with a funeral home. it is important that a family's needs and requests are met regardless of which funeral home is selected.

Chapter Five: Components of a Funeral Service
This chapter offers guidelines on the various parts of a funeral service, such as the name of the service, the viewing, flowers, donations, the eulogy, bulletins, and hymns.

Chapter Seven: The Burial, Interment, or Committal Service
This chapter provides guidelines for the burial service, including choosing appropriate words of committal. I also touch on issues such as the coffin and pallbearers and offer specific suggestions that a family might request.

Chapter Eight: Words of Caution
Here I present a word of caution, urging us to be extra sensitive and understanding, realizing that the loss and grief that occur when a loved one dies may be compounded by brokenness within the family.

Chapter Nine: A Word to Fellow Pastors
This chapter is an appeal to pastors to recognize the distinct responsibility and the opportunity God is entrusting us with. I also raise the concern that we must recognize our own limitations and be aware of our own issues.

Chapter Ten: The Life Story: A Personal and Faith Legacy
This chapter invites us to examine how we view the obituary or life story of a person—seeing it not merely as a list of details about a person but as a testimony of how God was transforming that person's life. It is a story of God's grace, forgiveness, and faithfulness—no matter who the person is or how the person died.

Chapter Eleven: The Funeral Service
This chapter includes discussion of the history of the Christian funeral, the essence of the Christian funeral, and the value of funeral manuals, and what makes a funeral Christian.

Chapter Twelve: The Funeral Message
This chapter gives guidelines for the funeral message, discussing what we should not preach on and then what we should preach on.

Chapter Thirteen: Difficult Funerals
Realizing that we will be asked to provide funeral services for followers of Jesus and for other people who were not following Jesus, I will give counsel for both situations. I will also speak to other difficult situations, such as a death resulting from a crime or accident, suicide, and the death of a child.

Chapter Fourteen: Assurance that We Will Cross the Finish Line
This chapter focuses on the most important question we will face in this life: "How can I have assurance that I will be with God once I have crossed the finish line of life?"

Reflections
• Can you recall a time when you attended a funeral service and you responded, "The pastor spoke words of hope and compassion. This is what I wish to say at a funeral"?
• Can you recall a time when you were at a funeral service and you left in despair—or even anger—feeling that the words spoken did not give the assurance that God is compassionate and caring?
• If you could improve one thing in a funeral service, what might this be?
• What does a pastor who believes in the Bible have to offer a grieving family that a person who does not follow God cannot offer?
• What is the primary thing you will say to the loved ones in their time of grief?

Prayer
Heavenly Father, we come to you as the Giver of life and the Sustainer of life, but also as the One who takes away life through death. We know that you care for and walk with us in all phases of life. As those who are called to care for people, we have the special opportunity and responsibility to care for people in their final years. We have a sacred ministry to care for a family in their time of loss and grief. May we truly represent you, the Father of compassion and the God of all comfort. As you carry us with gentle hands, may we likewise carry those you have entrusted to us, especially as they walk in their last years of life. We are committed to fulfill your mission. Give us grace to do so. Further, as we reflect on our responsibility to walk with a family in their grief, may we begin by looking up to you. May we sense that your tender eyes observe the pain and loss in every one of your creations. As we remember that your Son cried out on

the cross, "My God, my God, why have you forsaken me?" we recognize that you were deeply aware of your own loss. Therefore, we can be confident that you fully sense the loss of every person who comes to us. May our eyes feel your compassion. Fill our hearts with your sympathy as we encounter the loss before us. Give us grace to receive and share your compassion and grace. In Jesus' gracious name, Amen.

Chapter One
Being with People as They Cross the Finish Line

This book uses the metaphor of a long marathon with a particular focus on the final meters as the runner crosses the finish line. A sports coach will observe that many runners begin a race with intensity, but only a select few will cross the finish line. A coach's goal is to ensure that the runners he is responsible for will endure right to the end of the race. As pastors, we have the God-given responsibility to ensure that the people he has placed in our care will cross their finish line of life with joy and confidence. Another way to describe our mission is to inspire, motivate, and equip older adults to make their final years their best possible years.

The Apostle Paul visualized his death as "crossing the finish line." When he sensed that his final days on earth were limited, he wrote to Timothy, "The time has come for my departure. I have fought the good fight, I have finished the race, I have kept the faith. Now there is in store for me the crown of righteousness, which the Lord, the righteous Judge, will award to me on that day—and not only to me, but also to all who have longed for his appearing" (2 Timothy 4:6-8). In this testimony, Paul could honestly state that he had diligently and faithfully exerted himself in the Christian fight and race and had conscientiously observed all the rules God had given him. Now he was ready for the moment when God would take him across the finish line. Was there a sense that Paul was fearing the final moments before his death? Even though he could look back on a life characterized

> **The Importance of Our Prayers**
> "The dying should receive not just our sympathy and our prayers for healing but also our prayers for courage as they witness and serve, even as they depend on others. The dying are still athletes running the race" (J. Todd Billings, *The End of the Christian Life*, 68).

by obedience and commitment to God, was he concerned about the next weeks and days leading to his death? We do not know. But we know that for many of us the final years, months, and days of life might be the most difficult, calling for an extra level of commitment, focus, and discipline, as well as support from other people.

1. The Hardest Climb: The Last Lap

Frequently we hear yearnings such as these expressed: "I wish God would call me home in my sleep. If I could only go to sleep here on earth and wake up in heaven. I wish I would not need to struggle in the last months, days, and hours of life."

On several occasions, my mother expressed this sentiment in her native German in her last years, usually with a tone of despair: "*Sterben ist nicht so leicht*" ("Dying is not that easy").

The phrase "crossing the finish line" is taken from the metaphor of an Olympic marathon, where a large crowd is cheering a runner who seems to sprint effortlessly across the finish line. That may be how it appears from the top bleachers, several hundred feet from the exhausted runners. The reality is that the runner is expending his last ounce of energy, and every step is filled with extreme pain.

The following description of the last years, months, and days might be more the norm than the exception: "There is no point in imagining old age, especially in its last years, to be easy, nor should we expect that many of us will have a lot of 'golden years.' From what I have observed, what lies ahead is more like a rock-climbing expedition, straight up a rock face, and then slipping and sliding down through the shale on the other side to the place of our 'crossing over'" (Maxine Hancock, "Aging as a Stage of the Heroic Pilgrimage of Faith: Some Literary and Theological Lenses for 'Re-Visioning Age'," *Crux*, Spring 2011, Vol. 47, No. 1, 2).

2. Sacred Moments

God has graciously given me the privilege of observing that most sacred moment when a dear person takes her or his last breath. My wife Edith and I, along with her sister, stood around their father's bed as we saw him take his last breath. His spirit was with us one moment, and the next moment he was with Jesus. Several years earlier, while I was a resident chaplain at Riverview Health Centre in Winnipeg,

> **No one Deserves to Die Alone.** The sacredness of being with a dying person is undisputed and undeniable. Therefore, can there be a justifiable reason a person is not given the comfort and compassion of having a loved one present when she or he dies? Is there any valid reason a loved one cannot be present when a loved one dies?

Manitoba, a husband requested that I stand with him as we waited for his wife to take her last breath. A dear friend in Abbotsford, British Columbia, asked that Edith and I be with him as we watched the monitors that showed how life was slowly ebbing away from his dear wife.

On numerous occasions, Edith and I have stood with family members, holding hands, reading Bible promises, and expressing God's comfort, just hours before a loved one was called home to heaven. On other occasions, the family has asked that we come to the bedside of a loved one who had just passed away. We have been present just before a person crossed the finish line, when a person crossed the finish line, and immediately after a person crossed the finish line. These sacred moments have changed not only how I perceive funerals but also how I hold other values in life. My desire is that I will permit the sacredness of watching a person cross the finish line to deeply touch my soul. As pastors, may you also let the enormity of this sacred moment soften, inspire, and challenge your heart.

In this book, I am using the word "funeral" to refer to celebration of life services and memorial services, as well as funerals. Later, I will note the distinction between these.

A range of experiences have profoundly impacted my perception of funerals. The first set of experiences are the many funerals I have participated in as well as planned. I cannot use the words "attended" and certainly not "observed" when it comes to a funeral service. Being present at a funeral is not the same as being present at or attending a sports event or hearing a public speech. I can be present at a public event, but my attendance normally has little impact on me, certainly not the impact that a funeral service has.

Here I must make a qualification. When I observe how engaged and involved spectators are at a sports event, I realize they are fully committed to sports teams and professional entertainment. At times, their motivation in life, their attitudes, and their behavior are based on the success or failure of their sports hero. However, there is something very different that happens at a funeral service. When I am present at a funeral, God's gentle Holy Spirit speaks to my heart. I am not a spectator who is merely attending an event. I am confident that no one can attend a funeral without being touched, either with God's comfort or by his conviction. I believe we do not leave a funeral service the same as we came.

God has given me the opportunity to plan and lead many funerals. The first funerals I conducted were as a pastor in Medicine Hat, Alberta. Later, when I was a prison chaplain in Winnipeg, God called me to conduct funerals of former inmates and prison officers, as well as inmates' children and their family members. Following that time, I also led funeral services as a resident chaplain in a health center in Winnipeg. Then, as Pastor of Care Ministries at our church in British Columbia, I have had the opportunity to meet with many grieving families for more than twenty years, hearing their loss, feeling their grief, and planning their funeral services. Walking with families in these sacred moments has left a deep impact on my heart, for which I thank God.

> **Words of Wisdom**
> "A good name is better than fine perfume, and the day of death better than the day of birth. It is better to go to the house of mourning than to go to a house of feasting, for death is the destiny of every man; the living should take this to heart. Sorrow is better than laughter, because a sad face is good for the heart. The heart of the wise is in the house of mourning, but the heart of fools is in the house of pleasure" (Ecclesiastes 7:1-4).

As well, the experiences of other people regarding death and funerals have deeply impacted me. Here I begin with the people I walk with in funerals. But I also include the many people I am learning from as I read books and articles on the topics of aging, dying, and funerals. As a pastor who accompanies many families as they plan the funeral service of a loved one, I recognize these as sacred moments. Therefore, I need to remind myself of Paul's words to Timothy: "Do your best to present yourself to God as one approved, a workman who does not need to be ashamed and who correctly handles the word of truth" (2 Timothy 2:15). This means that, even after I have planned many funerals, I need to realize that each funeral is unique. It is the only one for this precious person, involving this person's family members and friends. Therefore, in Paul's words, I need to do my best before God, since I am God's workman, and I need to "correctly handle the word of truth." This is why I am committed to learning from other people about the sacred topic of funerals. This is why I invite you to review and examine how you walk with families in these sacred moments.

We can also learn a great deal from the Bible, from church history, and from various church traditions on how to approach death and how to conduct funerals. In our Western world, we often avoid talking about dying and might attempt to make every aspect of a funeral as easy and painless as possible. The books I have read (many of them listed in the bibliography at the end of this book) show that there is a better, more biblical and Christian view of death and funerals than we in our contemporary Western society have become used to. There are also several books listed there on the "new American way of death," reimagining death ceremonies for home funerals and green burials. It is wise to know the cultural and spiritual context we are in as we develop a biblical and pastoral approach to helping families plan funerals and resourcing them as they deal with other end-of-life issues.

We cannot and we will never fully understand all that happens at the moment of death and in the moments leading up to it. But we need to hear the words of Solomon: "He has also set eternity in the hearts of men, yet they cannot fathom what God has done from beginning to end" (Ecclesiastes 3:11). The wisdom of Solomon teaches us that we must approach planning a funeral with a sense of wonder, knowing that we cannot fathom all that God is doing.

In this book, I will share personal reflections and observations about funerals and other end-of-life issues. My desire is that these observations will be more than ideas that come from my experience and that you can choose to accept or to reject. My prayer is that you will hear and receive them as coming from my heart because walking with families in their grief and loss must always be a matter of "God's heart touching families' hearts through our hearts." I realize that how God's Spirit touches an individual's heart does not depend on us. Yet, may we never go through the various parts of a funeral or burial service as a series of repeated and well-known items in a routine that we simply check off. May we always examine our own hearts, listen to what God is saying to us, and then, with a sensitized heart, pray that God will touch the people involved as God is touching us.

I am combining stories with reflections, realizing that real life stories are what we remember. At times, these experiences will be painful, and at times they will be pleasant. At times, we will want to forget our memories of funerals because they were hurtful. At other times, we will want to relive funerals because these memories encourage us, comfort us, and give us hope. By combining stories with reflections, it is my desire to help us recognize that there are better, more God-like, more life-giving ways of responding in a time of grief and death than we might have experienced. There is a better way to traverse the valley of the shadow of death than we are familiar with.

As a pastor, my goal is to help you, a fellow pastor, prepare a funeral in the critical time of grief and loss. My desire is that these words will also help other individuals who are preparing a funeral service. But, in order to help individuals and families in this time, I trust that you will realize that this topic includes much more than planning the funeral service.

3. The Metaphor of a Marathon

An added note comes from the metaphor of a marathon. A marathon does not begin in the last moments before individuals cross the finish line. Their ability to cross the finish line depends not only on how they exert themselves during the long marathon. It also includes their preparation in the days before the marathon. We know that marathon runners will do all they can to be in the best possible physical condition. Their ability to cross the finish line depends on factors other than just giving their best in the last meters of the race. I am including this added note because a person's preparation for crossing the finish line of life does not begin just days or even months before a person's death. In order to successfully cross from life to death, we need to begin years and even decades before our death. This is especially so as we cannot predict beforehand the timing of our death. Therefore, we must be in a spirit of constant preparedness all the time.

There is a further observation to be drawn from the metaphor of a marathon. A marathon runner will either be encouraged and assisted by other people or hindered by them. Similarly, in our spiritual marathon, each of us will be encouraged and assisted by other people or hindered by them in our ability to cross the finish line. I recognize that we live in an individualistic society where we are often told that we are the masters of our own success or failure. But, as with all the components of life, we are responsible for our own beliefs, values, decisions, and actions, and we are also dependent on what happens to us. This means that even as we must do all that we can to be prepared to cross the finish line, we must be aware that we are always impacted by what other people do.

> **Honor to Our Bodies**
> "The stakes are high here. I am persuaded that in this, our moment in history, we are going through one of those periodic upheavals in the ways we care (or don't) for the dead that are inevitable signs of an upheaval in the ways we care (or don't) for the living. To put it bluntly, a society that has forgotten how to honor the bodies of those who have departed is more inclined to neglect, even torture, the bodies of those still living" (Thomas G. Long, *Accompany Them with Singing*, 7).

Reflections

Preparation involves what I need to do in the last weeks and months before my funeral. However, realizing that I do not know when this will be, I need to be in a constant state of preparedness.
• What does it look like to be in a constant state of preparedness?
• What are some values in our society that help a person to be in a state of preparedness for the end of life?
• What are some values in our society that push against being prepared?
• What is my view as a pastor concerning what it means to ensure a person is prepared to die? If I envision a continuum of what is necessary to ensure a person is prepared to die, do I have a narrow and limited view or a broader view of what is necessary to be prepared to die? At the one end of the continuum is the need to present the gospel, and at the other

end are items such as mending relationships and thus fully following Jesus. As a pastor, where is my responsibility? How will I show that I am open to doing more than simply presenting the gospel?

• What are my values that I believe will ensure that I am prepared to cross the finish line? How do these values and beliefs motivate me to ensure that other people are prepared as well?

Prayer

Father, with Moses, we pray, "Teach us to number our days aright, that we may gain a heart of wisdom" (Psalm 90:12). May I recognize how brief my life is. Therefore, may I accept each day as a gift from you. As I reflect on preparing funerals, may I do so with a sense of humility, recognizing my inability to fully comprehend life and certainly not death. I pray for your wisdom and compassion as I walk with grieving families. I pray for grace to do so. Amen.

Chapter Two
Recognizing the Western, Post-Christian Culture in which We Help People Prepare to Cross the Finish Line

You might never have planned a funeral service. You might even hope that you will never be called upon to conduct a funeral service. This is certainly not an attitude I would wish a pastor to have, but, it is understandable considering our Western societal values. This is why I want to begin by addressing what I describe as "the spirit of our age," a Western societal culture that does not focus on nor appreciate the best end-of-life principles and certainly not those that apply to a good Christian funeral. At times, these cultural values are exhibited in our churches' values as well.

In keeping with the metaphor of a marathon, just as there is a lot of enthusiasm at the start of a marathon, our Western society celebrates the beginning of life and youth. But our society does not

> **Critical or Compassionate, Judgmental or Concerned**
> As we look at and assess the characteristics of our society, what emotions stir in our hearts? Do we callously dismiss and judge, or do we have a sense of compassion for our neighbors? When the prophet Jeremiah witnessed the desolation of his people due to their sinful attitudes and actions, he responded with empathy: "Since my people are crushed, I am crushed; I mourn, and horror grips me" (Jeremiah 8:21, also 13:17). May we be fully aware but also deeply compassionate.

have an equal focus on what happens at the end of the race of life. This is not the case with Eastern societies, where the cultural value is to honor older people and therefore also the concerns involved at the end of life.

As a pastor, you might wonder why you find it difficult to walk with a family in grief and plan a funeral service. A partial answer lies in the fact that funerals are connected to other beliefs and societal values, many that we may not be conscious of. As we recognize these values, we will realize that we are living in a particular culture or *Zeitgeist*. You might have your own observations that show that our society does not place importance on being prepared for the end of life and therefore does not put a high value on funerals. I will briefly highlight thirteen characteristics in our Western culture that I believe speak against the values associated with positive end-of-life concerns and funerals.

1. The Minimal Training in Theological Institutions

During my seminary education, I do not remember any specific training in the area of funerals. I deeply respect the excellent teaching and mentoring provided by committed and competent professors. They were outstanding in both their competence and their character. The caliber of teaching in biblical languages, theology, Bible, and church history was exceptional. Yet I do not remember extensive classes preparing us for the practical areas of pastoral ministry such as planning funerals, marriage preparation, and leading worship services.

When I note the absence of training regarding funerals, I am referring to two areas, one focused on the funeral arrangements for the loved one and the other focused on helping families during their time of loss. The first area includes practical matters such as planning and leading the funeral service, writing a life story (eulogy), selecting and working with a funeral home, and planning and leading the burial service. The second area concerns the biblical and theological foundation that will train the pastor in how to approach funerals as well as end-of-life issues.

I recognize that there has been a significant shift in recent years. An example is that the primary seminary for my denomination, Mennonite Brethren Biblical Seminary, teaches strategically about grief, loss, and funeral planning. These topics are covered in a comprehensive course on Grief, Change, and Loss. Grief and loss are covered in a Pastoral Counselling course, and funeral planning is covered in a Pastoral Formation course. Furthermore, when I recently wrote to several other seminaries, I became aware that many of them are now offering foundational, biblical, and theological teaching in areas such as grief and loss, as well as practical teaching on issues such as planning funerals. I strongly commend this emphasis on providing a biblical foundation for practical areas, including specifically walking with families in the time of grief.

2. The Importance Placed on Funerals by Pastors

I recall a fellow pastor commenting about a young pastor who was new in the ministry and was busy in church work. This younger pastor was contacted by a local funeral home to conduct a funeral service for someone in the community who was not part of this pastor's church family. The older pastor said the younger pastor "should clearly state that he has no time and is not able to conduct the funeral. He should tell the funeral director to get someone else to conduct the funeral service." I find it incomprehensible that an older pastor would counsel a younger pastor not to provide this critical ministry to individuals at a time of loss and grief. Is there a better and more natural time to provide comfort and express God's love than at the time of death?

Pastors have many areas of responsibility and a limited time to complete them. Some of these areas have a higher priority than others. Is there a consensus that funerals are not a high priority? Do we, as pastors, give the impression that funerals have little importance and are a burdensome task to be avoided if at all possible? Do we demonstrate a belief that we should spend as little time as possible on a funeral and then get back to what we consider more important aspects of ministry? I trust not.

3. Ageism

Ageism (also spelled "agism") is stereotyping and discriminating against individuals or groups on the basis of their age. This may be casual or systemic. The term was coined in 1969 by Robert Neil Butler to describe discrimination against seniors. It is patterned on sexism and racism (Robert Butler, *Growing Old in America: Why Survive?*, New York: Harper and Row, 1975, referenced in James M. Houston an Michael Parker, *A Vision for the Aging Church*, 112). Our Western culture has identified racism and sexism as serious forms of discrimination and is taking steps to address the beliefs, attitudes, and behaviors involved. Regretfully, ageism remains a significant problem, not only in Western society at large but also in our Western churches. Ageism "is a self-defeating societal ill that has many forms of expression. Simply stated, it is the presence of negative stereotypes, incorrect assumptions and distorted characterizations about older people and their capacities" (James M. Houston and Michael Parker, *A Vision for the Aging Church*, 30).

One reason churches, denominations, and seminaries fail to give proper attention and provide ministries geared for the elderly is that we accept aging myths. This is true in a broad and general sense. However, as

I note several of the most frequently circulated and accepted myths in our Western society, I invite you to reflect on whether you personally identify with any of them. Recognizing that these myths are possibly accepted by some of us who are pastors, I will briefly respond to each myth. Even if these myths are not accepted by us who are pastors, these myths are certainly prevalent within our churches.

Myth #1: To be old is to be sick.

Older people suffer from what geriatricians label chronic, long-term diseases, such as arthritis, diabetes, hypertension, heart disease, and vision and hearing problems. Yet, in general terms, they are experiencing less disability than ever before.

Myth #2: You can't teach an old dog new tricks.

This myth implies that older persons are unable to be lifelong learners. There are at least three responses to this myth.

First, seniors have an advantage over youth because their experience compensates for the ability of youth to learn more quickly.

Second, our society is based on an age-graded model that assumes there are three distinct periods of life: education, work, and retirement. The premise is that learning occurs primarily in the first two periods. This premise, largely accepted by Western churches, needs to be reviewed. Opportunities and programs need to be developed that are based on different attitudes about the elderly and that will be geared towards them.

Third, we must be sensitive to the reality of dementia, particularly Alzheimer's disease. Then, we will be both compassionate and informed as we walk with people who have dementia and their families and friends. However, our fears about dementia should not be the basis for prejudging all older adults as unable to be lifelong learners.

Myth #3: The horse is out of the barn.

This myth states that it is too late to reduce the risk of disease and the disability that are the result of earlier unhealthy behaviors. However, it is never too late to make healthy lifestyle changes. When these changes are made, even after years of unhealthy life choices, lost functions can be recovered, and the risk of disease can be reduced.

Myth # 4: The secret of successful aging is to choose your parents wisely.

It is often thought that how long people live and how healthy they are in their later years is largely determined by genetics (heredity). In reality, the role of genetics in longevity is mostly associated with lifestyle, in that people will have similar lifestyle characteristics, such as eating and exercise habits, within a family. As we become older, the influence of genetics becomes less important, and lifestyle becomes more important.

Myth #5: The lights might be on, but the voltage is low.

This myth implies that older people suffer from inadequate physical and mental capacities, including sexual ones. Our response has three parts: intimacy in late life is very real, health conditions do have an impact, and affectionate physical contact will change as people become older.

Myth #6: The elderly don't pull their own weight.

This myth implies that the elderly do not carry their fair share of society's workload. Regrettably, this myth is widespread within the Western church culture. The premise is that elderly people are a drain on society and even on the church. Much can be said to refute this myth. We begin with the reality that even though the elderly might not do what they did during their employment years, they can still contribute significantly as volunteers.

Also, this myth defines a person's contribution by comparison with what that person formerly did—the person's contribution and value are dismissed based on the fact he can't do the same things he did before. The response is that we need to reassess how we assign meaning to work and to people. We should not characterize people by their disabilities but by their abilities, recognizing that those will change with time.

This sixth myth must be challenged by another perspective. This is that we need to review our starting point of what defines worth. As those who have a Judeo-Christian belief system, we begin with the premise that all people have value because they are created in the image of God. This is a given. We begin with who we are—not with what we can or cannot contribute, as defined by a society or a church culture.

These six ageism myths are discussed and refuted more fully in James M. Houston and Michael Parker, *A Vision for the Aging Church*, 111-119. I invite you, as a fellow pastor, to examine your beliefs. Are you propagating these negative stereotypes and incorrect assumptions about older people and their capacities? I believe there is a direct correlation between how we view our elderly people and how we provide care for them in their last decades, years, months, and days and also how we then minister at the time of their funerals. Any tinge of ageism will be evident in how we prepare and conduct funerals. This will also impact how we prioritize our ministry as it involves the elderly.

4. Professionalism

The proverb, "A heart can speak to a heart, but a head will only speak to a head," gives me a helpful and valuable perspective when I sit with a grieving family and plan the funeral of their loved one. They will have broken hearts, unresolved issues, and unspoken regrets as they face their loss. They need a listening ear, a sensitive touch, and thoughtful words coming from my caring heart. The last thing a grieving family needs is a professional analysis of their grief and then a polished program. Admittedly, pastors often feel compelled to provide such a service. Might I ask, "Where does this pressure come from? Does it come from within ourselves, from our own selfish desire to impress the people who will come to a funeral service?"

As an aside, consider the root meaning of the word, "profession." To "profess" means to declare openly and freely our deepest conviction. We "profess" what we believe at the core of our being. I trust that each of us pastors, at the core of our being, desires to express God's heart to those who are grieving. Therefore, our "pastoral professionalism" should be about speaking God's truth and sharing his love and compassion because this is what we are about at our deepest level. Does our professionalism need to be redefined from providing a polished performance to being "Immanuel," God with us, to the people in grief? What a grieving family needs, and what we as pastors must provide, is our presence, expressing God's heart through our hearts. Certainly, we will want to do this with excellence. But our priority should be to walk with people and speak from our hearts to their hearts.

In this regard, I wish to direct a passionate word of encouragement to any pastor who might feel intimidated and inadequate in leading a funeral service. The Apostle Paul explained that we have different gifts and that these are all given by the Holy Spirit. In the lists of gifts (Romans 12:6-8, 1 Corinthians 12:1-11), two gifts apply especially during a time of grief and loss. As you care for the next grieving family, hear the Apostle Paul say, "If it is encouraging, let him encourage…if it is showing mercy, let him do it cheerfully" (Romans 12:8). Grieving families need our heartfelt

---

Speaking with Confidence and Humility

When confronted by jealous rivals, Moses responded with, "Are you jealous for my sake? I wish that all the LORD's people were prophets and that the LORD would put his Spirit on them!" (Numbers 11:29-30). The Apostle Paul wrote, "Therefore, since we have such a hope, we are very bold" (2 Corinthians 3:12). May we speak and live with confidence and humility, recognizing that our identity and authority are in Christ and that God's Spirit empowers us.

encouragement, genuine mercy, and profound compassion. Open your heart to God's heart of compassion, and then embrace grieving individuals with God's love, expressed through your heart, your mouth, and your hands.

Having emphasized the importance of compassion, I am not saying that we offer a mediocre or second-rate effort. Whenever we serve, we want to do so with excellence. The Psalmist urged those who praised the Lord to "play skilfully" (Psalm 33:3). In providing directives on how to be a pastor, the Apostle Paul instructed Timothy, "Do your best to present yourself to God as one approved, as a workman who does not need to be ashamed" (2 Timothy 2:15). This means that when families come to us in their loss and grief, we will walk with them, both compassionately and skilfully, leading them through their dark valley, and expressing the hope and light we have in our God. Then, when they recall the funeral and burial service, may they remember God's compassion through us.

5. Individualism in a Spiritual Community

The essence of genuine Christianity is that it is lived in community. Our relationship with God is personal but always lived out in community with other people. Further, our primary self-identity includes several core elements. The first is that we are created by God (Genesis 1:26-27, Psalm 4:8). The second is that we are created to be in relationships. The Apostle Paul used the metaphor of a body to express the dependence and commitment people have for each other, each contributing something unique (1 Corinthians 12). This means that no one should die alone nor should grieving individuals be alone. We are created to be in community at all times and particularly in times of loss.

> **Privatized and Individualized Christianity**
> The recent packaged approach to become a Christian presented in many evangelical circles usually concludes with a person praying to receive Jesus. The person is guaranteed forgiveness, inner happiness, and peace. The link with the Christian community is not crucial. When people are instructed to commit to a church, they might object that this is not necessary and does not fit with the Christianity that they were given and that is presented in many churches. As a consequence, there is little motivation to see the value of a church body and therefore to grieve with other people in the church, in the neighborhood, or even in extended family.

Throughout most of church history until very recently, the whole community came together when there was a death. The people in the community and the church would surround and embrace a grieving family at a wake or a viewing, a funeral service, a burial service, and then a time of visiting around a luncheon (brought by everyone from the community). The community came together to embrace and carry a grieving family as it "walked through the valley of the shadow of death." It is not inaccurate to say that the community grieved with the family because the loss was everyone's loss, not only the family's loss. It is a sad commentary on a society and even a church when this element of community and grieving together is absent.

How a death is announced and made public is an indication that our society has changed from one where the community is central to one where the individual is the focus. Two centuries ago, the news of a death would be announced to the whole community by the tolling of a church bell. Today, when a person dies in a hospital, there will usually be a policy, written or assumed and followed, on who reports a death and to whom. Another example is the change in announcing a death in the public media. Consider the following illustrations:

a. Radio. A station in southern Manitoba has a daily feature called "Funeral Announcements." My recollection is that other public radio stations provided similar funeral announcements—until about fifty years ago.

b. Newspapers. In the past, death announcements (obituaries) were published in local newspapers as a public service. Now the cost has increased significantly. In a recent discussion, a funeral director told me that the cost seems equal to that charged for advertisements. Some families tell me the cost is such that they choose to have either a very condensed death announcement or none at all.

c. Religious periodicals. In the past, most denominational periodicals would set aside significant space for life stories. How many denominational papers include a section for obituaries or remembering individuals today?

d. Email and Facebook. Modern media such as email and Facebook are now often used to announce a death.

One element contributing to the fact that the community is not coming together when a member passes away is that the significance of the funeral has changed. This is expressed by David Moller in these words: "The funeral has lost its value as an established and prominent and community ritual. The funeral has become a rite of individual expression—a personalized response to the death of a significant other." (David Wendell Moller, *Confronting Death: Values, Institutions, and Human Mortality*, New York: Oxford University Press, 1996, 240, quoted by Thomas G. Long, *Accompany Them with Singing*, 133-134). This means that, with the breakdown of the old infrastructure of community support at the death of a person in the community, most people now come to a funeral to show support for those who have lost a loved one. When there is a funeral service for an individual who has very few surviving family members or friends, there will likely be few people at this person's funeral.

I will give one example to illustrate the phenomenon that the community does not come together as in the past. An elderly lady passed away. Her sister-in-law was convinced that people came to church funerals just for the luncheon meal. I assured her that this was not the case, but she did not believe me. She insisted that the service be in the small chapel in the care home and the luncheon in the common room in the condo where this person had lived. This sister-in-law planned it so that only the people she wanted to attend would be able to attend this funeral and luncheon. Close friends were hurt by the restriction on who was invited to grieve and show compassion.

Philippe Aries describes practices that were "the normal and generally understood rituals that Christians performed for a thousand years throughout Western Christianity": "Shutters were closed and other visible signals outside the house alerted neighbors to what was happening inside. Candles were lit; prayers said; and clergy visited and performed their rites to bind the wounds of the mourning. Neighbors and relatives visited, and when death occurred tolling bells marked the significant loss of a member of the community. The body or coffin was displayed outside, or later just a notice hung from the door of the house, and in came the neighborhood. They brought food or simply their best wishes, and the bereaved began their reintegration into the community without their loved one....There was safety and comfort in numbers; no one was left to grieve alone" (Philippe Aries, *The Hour of Our Death*, Oxford University Press, 1991, 559-560, quoted by Rob Moll, *The Art of Dying*, 65-66).

Our Western culture has adopted a new rule, as Ella Wheeler Wilcox put it: "Laugh and the world laughs with you. Weep and you weep alone" (Ella Wilcox, "Solitude," quoted by Allen Verhey, *The Christian Art of Dying*, 334). Has this expression, "Weep and you weep alone," taken an additional step? Is it evident when a grieving family chooses not to weep publicly and does not seem to want the community to know about its grief? Is it demonstrated in the increasingly common note at the end of an obituary: "No service by request"? Did this person live by himself or herself, in isolation from everyone? The answer will usually be "No." The person who is described in the obituary likely was very much part of the community and might have had many friends. Yet, somehow the family members do not want to share their grief and loss and be comforted by their extended family and friends—at a time when they need these family members and friends the most. Often there are family members and friends who want to come alongside those grieving. Why have so many accepted the belief and practice that they can grieve alone and that this will be good for them?

Throughout all of Western Christianity until recently, "no one was left to grieve alone," but there is now a shift to where the opposite is accepted. And this cultural value is becoming evident within the church. Friends might want to embrace their grieving friends and be present at a burial service, but we in the church are adapting to the cultural values of the world around us and refusing to let friends embrace us when we need them the most. Henri Nouwen wrote this about his response to the news that his friend "Moe" (Maurice Gould) had died: "I knew at once that I must return to Toronto [from Freiburg, Germany] as soon as possible to be with Moe's family and many friends and to experience with them the sorrow of his leaving, as well as the joy of his fifty-eight fulfilling years of life" (Henri Nouwen, *Our Greatest Gift*, xii).

In our Western culture, there is a new norm of skimming over death and grief as quickly as possible so we can get on with our lives. We need to ask, "Why don't we want to sit with our friends and family, share their grief, and comfort them with our embrace? Why don't we want them to sit with us in our grief and loss?" Our response to death exposes our individualistic and isolated lives, existing without the support of community.

As pastors, we have the opportunity first to model community and then to encourage grieving families to think beyond their immediate concerns and include the church family and the broader community in their grief. How we approach a funeral and decide whether it is a private or a public event brings in considerations that apply to all of life. We have heard the expression, "It takes a village to raise a child." The reality is that we need one another in all stages of life—certainly during the first months of our lives, and in the final months as well. Grief and loss, as well as the other major concerns in growing older, are not things we must, or can, carry on our own or even within our nuclear family. We need our extended family, the church family, the "village" God has placed us in.

6. Selfishness

You might wonder why I include this as one of the traits of our Western society and ask how it might apply to how we approach funerals. One element of our sense of individualism is that we consider only ourselves and not the community. In most societies—and in the past in our Western society—when a person planned a funeral service for a loved one, this person would consider the wishes of the deceased and of those still living. Today in our Western society, there is a growing acceptance that the people planning the funeral should consider only their own wishes and not those of the deceased. Some people take this to the next step and argue that the people who make the funeral arrangements should ignore and even reject pressure from other people. The following are several examples in which the person planning the funeral considered only his or her own wishes and needs and not those of the extended family, the community, the friends of the deceased person, nor the church.

> Restricting who can be present at a funeral is unmistakably not how God has designed the church and the family.

In the first story, an elderly church member died. When the family prepared the memorial luncheon in our church, they invited only a few people. When close friends came who were not on the list, they were told they could not be present at the memorial and could not express their compassion and love. I expressed concern about this exclusion of close friends, but I was told this was acceptable because the family makes the decision.

In the second story, a father and mother were faithful members of our church. When the one parent died, the children deliberately did not contact our church and instead had a service in the local funeral home. The surviving spouse, who had minimal dementia at the time, did not know why the church did not honor her deceased spouse and provide a church service. This story illustrates the dilemma that children face when they have different spiritual convictions than their parents and then have the responsibility to plan a parent's funeral service, not wanting to follow a structure and beliefs that they do not adhere to.

I realize that it is not easy to address difficult conflicts, resolve complex issues, heal, and forgive in the short days between when a person dies and the funeral service. My concern is with the decision to put aside the values of the parents and plan the service according to values that conflict with the parent's spiritual values. This decision to set aside the values of the parents in a time of grief is increasingly promoted by people who guide families in planning a funeral. Doug Manning presents himself as an expert who has helped many families in their grief and in funeral preparation. He states that a person who is planning a funeral has only one question: "What would please you?" He writes further that a funeral should accomplish two things and only two things: "First, it should memorialize your loved one. Second, it should comfort you. Whatever arrangements accomplish those two things are right. All else is secondary.

That may sound harsh and selfish, but in reality, it is neither. To have people force their will upon you at this time is harsh and selfish. You have the right to arrange the funeral as you feel it should be in your God-given privilege....If done in an effort to follow how the person to be memorialized would want it, then it is not your gift to that person. It is just you following out some vague plan. Most of the time there is no detailed plan to follow—only general assumptions with no real guidelines" (Doug Manning, *Don't Take My Grief Away from Me*, 8-9).

I wish to respond to Doug Manning's question, "What would please you?" on two levels.

First, the answers he gives to this question completely miss the target of what a Christian funeral should be. He says that "memorializing your loved one" can be done by "showing photos of the deceased, reading poetry loved by the dead person, and having a few warm and sometimes lighthearted remembrances." In this way, the person becomes a celebrity with an hour of fame (this is further explained by Thomas G. Long, *Accompany Them with Singing*, 136-137). In contrast, a Christian funeral will invite remembrance of the person but place the focus on God, his grace, his faithfulness, and his mercy. A Christian funeral can't include only a story of a person, no matter who the person is. Ultimately, it is only God's story that will give hope.

Second, I want to address the issue of whose desires are met in a funeral. When a person planning a funeral follows the wishes of a loved one on how she or he wants to be memorialized, why is this not the planner's gift to the deceased person and the deceased person's family? Also, when a person has provided written directions, this is certainly not "some vague plan" but guidelines family members should value and should want to follow. At other times, there might not be written directives, but those who plan the funeral usually have a good idea what the loved one would have desired. Even Doug Manning's chapter on "What about a Minister?" begins with the premise that the memorial service is all about the one who plans it. The first words are, "Once again—how do you want the funeral to be done? That question should determine your choice of a minister. It should also determine your choice

> **Understanding Death**
> Is death an enemy to avoid or a friend to embrace—or both? Death disrupts relationships and destroys dreams, but death also opens the way to eternal life. For Christians, death is both a completion to this life and a violent catastrophe; we therefore sing in both the major key of hope and praise and the minor key of loss and grief. Both views are explained by J. Todd Billings, *The End of the Christian Life*.

of whether or not a minister is used" (Doug Manning, *Don't Take My Grief Away from Me*, 12).

I am surprised that a person who "devotes his time to writing, counseling and leading seminars in the areas of grief and elder care" has accepted the premise that the only person who matters is the person who plans the service and not the person who has died nor the loved ones who are grieving. This "expert" has simply applied our selfish societal value to the specific area of funerals. When I observe the direction and emphasis of many memorial services, I realize that he is not alone in his views. As pastors, I trust that we have not accepted the premise that the only person who really matters at a memorial service is the person who is planning the service. Does this mean that the service is actually not a memorial of the loved one—because the focus is really not on the loved one but on one of the people attending? Again, I trust not. A core premise I hold is that if a funeral is a Christian funeral, then the focus must and will be on God, who in his grace, faithfulness, and compassion has been with the person whose life we are remembering.

7. An Avoidance of Intense Pain and Suffering

The core values and beliefs we hold are exposed in times of joy, pleasure, and plenty, as well as in times of pain, loss, and grief. Is one of our societal beliefs the idea that suffering, disease, loss, and grief are to be avoided or at least minimized? Further, is there an underlying premise to this belief that suffering, disease, loss, and grief are bad? Is this related to our avoidance of the symbol of ultimate pain—death? An instance where our answers might be revealed is in the debate on how we respond to the decision on maintaining life when the so-called "quality of life" is no longer present in a person. Specifically, the public controversy about euthanasia, PAS (Physician Assisted Suicide), or MAiD (Medical Assistance in Dying) might be on a family's mind as they plan the funeral of an elderly parent.

Consider the following situation. A brother and a sister have had a heated discussion about euthanasia for their ailing mother. The government has passed a bill permitting PAS or MAiD under strict controls. The brother has pressured his sister into requesting euthanasia for their mother. Now this sister comes to your office, not only with intense grief and loss over the death of her mother, but also with bitter hatred towards her brother for pressuring her against her will. This angry and grieving sister and this estranged brother need to plan their mother's funeral service, process many decisions, and somehow reach agreement on their decisions.

With the advancements of modern medicine, we, as pastors, need not only to be aware of the issues families are facing but also of the emotional and relational pain and the pressure put on the families. May we never offer easy and superficial answers. May we instead walk with families, embracing broken families in times of disability, increasing dependency, loss, and grief.

8. An Avoidance of Embracing the Declining Years

I believe our hesitancy to walk with people in their grief and through a funeral is connected to another avoidance. Do we avoid walking with people in failing health when they are becoming weaker and when they are more dependent on other people? Have we divided our lives between productive and unproductive years, between a period when we can contribute and a period when we cannot contribute, at least according to society's values; and between a period when we can think creatively and a period when we are sliding into dementia? Are we making these divisions because we have not accepted our own mortality?

> **Health Span**
> A person's "health span" is the length of time the person is healthy, not just alive. This new phrase was added to the Miriam-Webster dictionary in March, 2018. How do we walk with people who are beyond their "health span" but possibly have many years left in their "life span"?

Another reason we might avoid embracing elderly people is that we place ourselves and other people into these three groups: independent, interdependent, and dependent. However, even though we might look up to people who claim to be independent and self-sufficient and we strive to be the same, no individual is ever completely independent. We are created to be interdependent and dependent on one another.

However, increasingly, as seniors enter declining health, they might feel useless and worthless and even a drain and a burden on their family and on society. In their despair, they might ask, "What can I do now that I can't do what I used to do? Why am I still here? All my friends are making all sorts of plans, but I have no future anymore. Why is God keeping me alive?"

Do we, as pastors, find it difficult to walk with people during their declining years, beyond their "health span"? Do we change the topic when these people share about their approaching frailty and death? Our answers will expose how we feel about walking with people in their declining years and then providing adequately for their funeral service.

There are several indications or tests we will want to reflect on that will show whether we are prepared to walk with people in their frailty.

1. How do we respond to our own frailty? If we are not prepared to face our own disability and dependence on other people, we will have little to offer people as they face their frailty and helplessness.

2. How do we define and measure our value and our worth? Do we only feel good about ourselves when we can succeed and contribute? What do we base our worth on—our accomplishments and successes? Is our worth not given—because of who God is and our relationship with him? Our worth cannot be taken away, no matter what we can do or cannot do.

3. What is our response to "humor" about seniors, specifically as it relates to dementia? Check your response to jokes about dementia. Why are these jokes seemingly widely acceptable in our society and even spoken by preachers? Reflect on how a person with dementia, no matter how minimal, or a person with a family member who has dementia, will feel about these jokes. Do we make jokes about disabilities or frailties in other areas—such as, cancer, arthritis, heart disease, or high blood pressure? Why not in these other areas when we are prone to use humor in regard to dementia?

> **Walking with Frailty**
> I am prepared to walk with people in their frailty when I:
> • accept and value my disability.
> • accept my worth as a given because I am created by God.
> • check my humor about seniors and confront all jokes about dementia.
> • have a clear understanding about the "quality of life" and "health span."

Examples of insensitive "humor" often occur when stories are shared in the "open mic" time, as participants list numerous instances when the deceased was forgetful. We might justify these by labeling them "senior moments." However, the spontaneous laughter, with an undertone of embarrassment, suggests that the humor is neither honoring to the deceased person nor accepted without a sense of shame by those who joined in with laughter. On the other hand, I wish to point to an example of the opposite of insensitive humor. This occurred in a memorial service for a deceased person who displayed major dementia for approximately the last ten years. In the service, there was no insensitive hint of the beloved's dementia, only an honoring of a godly and loving mother and grandmother. There was ample material for humor associated with dementia in the person's life, but none of these embarrassing moments was spoken about—the words spoken displayed only respect and honor.

4. ***What do we define as "quality of life"?*** How do we respond to the difficult decisions when someone does not have a "quality of life" or is beyond his or her "health span"?

9. An Avoidance of Death Itself

We cannot and will not prepare for something we avoid. If we find ourselves changing the subject when a person mentions that we need to prepare for our own passing and that of our loved ones, then we will want to examine our hearts. Why do we avoid preparing for an event that will inevitably happen?

In all stages of life and not only in our "declining years," we need to change the question from, "How much can we do and contribute in the time we are given?" to "How are we preparing ourselves for our death?" and "How am I living fully in the moment?"

> **Consistency?**
> Our societal values are not always consistent. On the one hand, we avoid planning our own funeral and even choose not to have a funeral. On the other hand, our society is death-giving when it legitimizes abortion in the beginning of life and euthanasia at the end of it—choosing to call one a woman's choice and the other Medical Assistance in Dying. As a society, we both avoid death ("Let's not talk about planning Mom's funeral," and "No funeral service by request") and yet embrace death (abortion and MAiD). Consistency is not necessary, but inconsistency should give us pause for reflection.

After I met with a grieving husband and his children to plan his wife's funeral, the oldest son told me with intense emotions, "For eighty-five years, Mom taught us how to live. Now, for the last five months, Mom taught us how to die." This godly saint had been given a diagnosis of terminal cancer. She continued to live with a deep trust in God, assured that God loved her and her family as they walked together through the valley of the shadow of death. She did not hesitate to talk about her death.

Where might we place ourselves on the continuum of preparing for our own death or ignoring death by keeping busy and occupied elsewhere? As pastors, are we helping our congregation anticipate a healthy death? Again, I need to emphasize that the topic of death is not an isolated topic but one that impacts how we respond to other critical issues. How we lean into and

> **Making Sense, Giving Hope**
> Are we attempting to make sense of life without recognizing the Giver of Life? Are we attempting to make sense of death without having any hope beyond death?

embrace the difficult and challenging issue of death will determine how we embrace all other difficult yet core areas of life.

When church members become weaker and believe they cannot contribute to the church ministry, at least as they once could and as they would like to do, do we answer with the common response: "God still has a ministry for you, and that is to pray. At least, you can pray"? Certainly, we need to affirm the vital ministry of prayer, but is that all there is to consider? I firmly believe we, who claim to believe in a crucified and risen Savior, need to look ahead towards our own death. At the same time, we also want to affirm the last years and months as very significant. Only as we genuinely model what we believe will we legitimately and with integrity be able to help fellow believers look ahead to their own passing. Only then will we be alive in the core of our souls and minister from our relationship with God.

> **A Modern Challenge**
> "Western culture can indeed become death-giving when it legitimizes abortion at the beginning of life and euthanasia at the end of it all. Ignoring our seniors takes the first step in that direction" (James M. Houston and Michael Parker, *A Vision for the Aging Church*, 107).

The Apostle Paul articulated the purpose of living in his well-known words, "For to me to live is Christ and to die is gain" (Philippians 1:21). Jesus Christ was the source and secret of Paul's life and joy, even in prison when his ministry was greatly restricted and he could not do the things he had done in his earlier life. Paul did not avoid death, because his life was centered in his relationship with Jesus. This was demonstrated in how he faced his changing ministry.

Quite different are the stories of ten dying pastors documented in "The Dying Pastor: Everyone Knew, but No One Would Talk about It," the first chapter of the book *Speaking of Dying*. Not only were their end-of-life days lived out "on the job," but their suffering in the grip of terminal illnesses was lived out in full view of their death-denying congregations. In none of these instances did the dying pastor or her or his congregation respond to terminal illness by facing dying head-on. Reference was made to Elizabeth Kubler-Ross's five-stage process of responding to death: denial, anger, bargaining, depression, and acceptance. In the case of these ten dying pastors, the most prominent response to the news of terminal death was denial, given in the form of silence (Fred Craddock et al., *Speaking of Dying*, xviii, 8-16, 44). If asked, these ten pastors would no doubt have stated that their goal in life was similar to the Apostle Paul's purpose in life and death. Yet, might their insistence on serving as a pastor even with a terminal illness suggest that they were avoiding death?

What ultimately brings us, as pastors, purpose and fulfilment? This will have a bearing on how we serve families who are dealing with loss and how we walk with people who are facing death.

10. MAiD: Medical Assistance in Dying

Medical Assistance in Dying (suicide assisted by medical professionals) has been legalized in Canada and some US states. How we approach and deal with end-of-life issues will naturally have a bearing on funerals. The reason is that a funeral provides

> **End-of-Life Issues**
> Our thinking and conclusions surrounding MAiD will have a bearing on other end-of-life issues, including how we approach funerals.

an opportunity to consider the essence of life and the value of life. Furthermore, any discussion surrounding MAiD will be influenced by our understanding of who we are and of the essence of life. Therefore, it is appropriate to consider the topic of MAiD as we reflect on funerals, even if this reflection is very brief.

The need to face the ultimate realities of life appears more apparent when a person is in the ICU unit, the palliative care unit, or even in a hospice than it does when a person is in the prime of life with no apparent weakness, disease, or disability. However, a conversation on end-of-life issues, including palliative care, euthanasia, and MAiD, is best done when there is no sense of urgency or stress.

We bring our deepest values to any significant decisions we make. Our conversations and also our decisions surrounding end-of-life issues will expose these core values. We do well to hear the exhortation of the "words of the Teacher, son of David, king in Jerusalem": "Remember your Creator in the days of your youth, before the days of trouble come and the years approach when you will say, 'I find no pleasure in them….Remember him—before the silver cord is severed, or the golden bowl is broken; before the pitcher is shattered at the spring, or the wheel broken at the well, and the dust returns to the ground it came from, and the spirit returns to God who gave it" (Ecclesiastes 1:1, 12:1, 6-7). The exhortation of the Teacher is to remember our Creator. This exhortation to remember is given twice—in the time of youth before troubles come and in the time of frailty and the final stages of life. The issue before us is to consider what is involved in "remembering our Creator" and specifically doing so at the end of life. I believe there are several aspects to consider and that these should provide the basis for our understanding of issues surrounding MAiD.

a. Remember Your Creator throughout Life

We are to remember our Creator at all stages of life—in our youth and in our waning days as we anticipate returning to dust and to our Creator, that is, in our strength and in our frailty. These comparisons have been made and are helpful: we do not put on a seatbelt after we are in an accident, nor do we run into a burning house with a smoke detector. Similarly, conversations and decisions about end-of-life choices need to be made before we are in the hospice with possibly only a few days of life remaining.

b. The Sanctity of Human Life

The sanctity of human life is derived from our Creator. In the Mennonite Brethren Confession of Faith (the denomination in which I serve) there is an unambiguous and clear statement regarding the end of life and death: "God values human life highly. Ultimate decisions regarding life and death belong to God. Therefore, we hold that procedures designed to take life, including abortion, euthanasia, and assisted suicide, are an affront to God's sovereignty. We esteem the life-sustaining findings of medical science, but recognize that there are limits to the value of seeking to sustain life indefinitely. In all complex ethical decisions regarding life and death, we seek to offer hope and healing, support and counsel in the context of the Christian community" (Article 14). We hold to the biblical doctrine of the *imago Dei*. This means that since we are created "in the image of God," we have intrinsic value. The essence of life is not measured by a person's ability to contribute, to think, and to provide. It is not taken away by what some people describe as diminished usefulness or increased disabilities. Instead, our essence is a given because it is derived from our Creator.

c. Individuals in Community

Individuals live in community—the communities of family, of friendships, and of faith. The profound medical advancements of recent years have certainly provided an opportunity to provide services that were not possible for most of history, even in the recent past. Yet, even when we consider how beneficial these medical advancements are for a patient, it is helpful to remember that the primary relationship this person has is still to her/his Creator, and then also to the person's three primary communities—faith, family, and friendships. However, when the critical decisions about MAiD are made, the patient is often isolated and cut off from these three primary communities. Stated another way, a concern I present is that a person's final important decisions in life might be made with individuals who have not known this person before this critical time and who have no connection with this person's primary relationships. I suggest that this is both an ethical and a moral issue. Why do medical people have this significant power and influence when they do not know the individual as deeply as do other people who who have a strong bond to the individual, have known this person for many years, and will feel the loss of this person's death?

An example of the shift away from living our final days within our community is that in the 1940s most Americans died in their own homes, yet by the 1980s just seventeen percent died in their homes (J. Todd Billings, *The End of the Christian Life*, 31). Today, most individuals in our Western society will die in a hospital, in a care home, or in a hospice. The added grief in the time of the COVID-19 pandemic has been that the immediate family has often been excluded from being with their loved one in the person's last weeks, days, and hours.

> **The Transition**
> "At the door of death, doctors have replaced pastors, and the ventilator has replaced the prayer book." J. Todd Billings, *The End of the Christian Life*, 114.

Having noted the important role that family, friends, and the faith community have at the end of life, I wish to make two observations. First, it is a sad commentary on our society when an individual might not have any of these sources of support in the critical final days of life. Second, this is an opportunity for the key people in a person's life—the children, close friends, and religious leaders—to enter into the challenging and difficult final journey with a frail person and to do so with understanding and grace.

d. The Basis of Authority

When we remember our Creator, we remind ourselves of who has the ultimate authority over our lives. It is our Creator. If we do not begin with our Creator as the basis of authority on the core issues of life, then we will grasp for any other basis of authority.

e. An Opportunity to Examine Our Core Beliefs and Values

The conversation surrounding MAiD provides an opportunity to examine our core beliefs and assumptions. Do we assume that since God loves us, he will provide a life of pleasure that is without pain and disabilities? Further, do we assume that our God will provide all of this until the moment we die? Taking this a step further, do we assume, as Job's three friends did, that when we are blameless and upright, we will not suffer great calamity as Job did? Further, when we suffer pain, do we have the authority to shorten our pain, or do we at least assume that long suffering and sickness are not a normal part of life? Those who accept the prosperity gospel believe that God owes them a long and prosperous life. As those who claim to believe in God, we have an opportunity to examine our assumptions about life.

The conversation surrounding MAiD is also an invitation for society to examine its assumptions and central values. I believe our society should be concerned about our core values when eighty-four percent of Canadians are in agreement with this statement: "A doctor should be able to help end someone's life if the person is a competent adult who is terminally ill, suffering unbearably, and repeatedly asks for assistance to die" (Gloria Woodland, "Ministry amid Competing Values: Pastoral Care and Medical Assistance in Dying," *Direction*, Fall 2018, Vol. 47, No. 2, 142-153). Is it fair to say that the majority of Canadians assume that life owes them a pain-free existence and that when this is not possible, they have the authority to choose to end their lives? Should it be of concern that society's belief regarding MAiD is the church's reality as well? Does this demonstrate that the people who claim to follow God have very similar assumptions about the essence of life? The answers to these questions will lead to an examination of our assumptions and core beliefs.

> **A Major Shift**
> When the prophet Jeremiah saw the desperate condition of his people he asked, "Is there no balm in Gilead? Is there no physician there? Why then is there no healing for the wound of my people?" (Jeremiah 8:21-22). As Jeremiah witnessed the plight of his fellow citizens, he was crushed, he mourned, and horror gripped him. What stirs in our hearts when we observe how our society has rejected the "balm in Gilead" for "religious practices customized for each person"?

Another conversation surrounding MAiD concerns the meaning of spirituality and spiritual care. I recall the shift in the title of those who provided spiritual care in hospitals and prisons from "chaplain" to "director of spiritual care." The earlier title carried with it the assumption that the chaplain provided her or his spiritual ministry by virtue of a relationship with the Judeo-Christian God, the ultimate Shepherd. The chaplain was required to be credentialed or ordained by the person's religious affiliation. The basis of spiritual care, often referred to as pastoral care, was drawn from the authority of the Bible.

J. Todd Billings describes the present-day care that is provided to dying individuals with these words: "Today, doctors, social workers, and advertising campaigns advise cancer patients to embrace spirituality in the face of biological death. As far as I can tell, 'spirituality' in this context refers to a set of prayers or religious practices customized for each person; it's a means to our own preferred end, whether that's becoming calm, finding peace, or discovering meaning. It's a bit like getting to choose our favorite shovel to dig ourselves out of the pit of Sheol, where our lives are increasingly cut off from the living—even seemingly cut off from God. We are told that if we focus on each day and on what is in our control, we will make our way out of Sheol and perhaps achieve 'a good death'" (J. Todd Billings, *The End of the Christian Life*, 25-26).

Another assumption we need to examine concerns the roles of the various relationships we have in life. As noted above, we live in three primary communities, or spheres of relationships, these being with our Creator, with our family, and with our friends. Other relationships are also critical, such as those involving our education, our employment, our civic responsibilities, and our medical care. The concern is when individuals in one area, such as the medical sphere, make it difficult for the people from the other primary areas, such as the family and religious leaders, to be meaningfully involved, particularly at a person's end of life—or even exclude them altogether.

We need to hear the summons of the Psalmist that we invite our Lord to help us know our end and to know how fleeting our lives are (Psalm 139:4-5). Decisions surrounding MAiD invite us to accept our mortality, to realize that our life never has revolved around us nor ever will. Our lives always revolve around an almighty and faithful God, whom we can never fully understand but whom we can always trust and worship, a God who always loves us (Romans 8:38-39).

> **A Contrast**
> The accounts of Abraham's and Jacob's deaths have a quality of peace and calmness about them. This is evident in phrases such as "Abraham breathed his last and died at a good old age, an old man and full of years" and "When Jacob had finished giving instructions to his sons, he drew his feet up into the bed, breathed his last and was gathered to his people" (Genesis 25:8, 49:33). How might these accounts of the death of Old Testament followers of God inform our discussion surrounding MAiD and end-of-life issues?

f. An Historical Perspective

We acknowledge that a long-accepted tradition or belief system might be examined and found wanting. We can give examples such as accepting slavery or withholding the right to vote from segments of a society. Yet, as we discuss the topic of MAiD, it is well to examine both the historical Judeo-Christian tradition and the morals and laws of nations. I believe the evidence will show that the beliefs underlying MAiD have neither been present in the historical Judeo-Christian tradition nor evident in the laws of most civilizations. Should this not give us pause to consider the wisdom of laws promoting MAiD? Another concern to be noted is that, in the short period of only a decade or so since MAiD was first legalized in parts of North America, the safeguards and restrictions surrounding euthanasia and MAiD have changed considerably. Are the safeguards like moving goalposts in a football game—what was originally a very small target is constantly expanding? Again, is this an invitation to examine what is happening from an historical perspective.

h. An Attitude of Humility and Grace

Recognizing the complexity of the issues surrounding the end of life, we must proceed with humility and grace. When an individual or a faith group has a different position than ours, this need not imply that this individual or faith group does not recognize the complexity of the issue or does not approach it with humility. That individual or group might firmly disagree with the generally accepted position while still experiencing considerable tension over the issue. To imply that a person who has a different position does not acknowledge the complexity of the decision is not helpful. This issue requires much more space than can be devoted to it here. May we hold on to well defined and articulated theological convictions, embrace individuals and families who are struggling with the choices before them, and do so with humility and grace.

> **Listening**
> When I listen to a person and understand the person's position, it does not mean that I will agree. Therefore, when I am told, "You do not understand the matter," this might actually mean that I do not agree.

i. Embracing Individuals with Compassion

How will we best represent Christ as we walk with individuals, their families, and their close friends as they contemplate, consider, and even request MAiD? I find an answer in the two words "position" and "posture." I believe we will not likely all come to a place where we will agree on our theology and biblical understanding in the matter of MAiD. That is, we are unlikely to convince everyone else of the merits of our "position." The ministry PostureShift illustrates how to have and accept a position but to also have the right posture towards other people. These words from Bill Henson, creator of PostureShift, apply to any situation where our goal is to express compassion and care in difficult and sensitive circumstances: "We encourage you to maintain your biblical *position* to honor God and adjust your *posture* to love like God has loved you" (Bill Henson, *Guiding Families of LGBT+ Loved Ones: For Every Pastor and Parent and All who Care*, Acton, Massachusetts: PostureShift Books, 2020).

The Confession of Faith of my own denomination, the Mennonite Brethren, is clear on this issue, and I am committed to affirm it. Further, I do not think the metaphor of a balance is helpful where we place our "position" (our beliefs) on one end of the scale and our "posture" (our practice) on the other end of the scale and then choose which has more weight or significance. Rather, I suggest that we focus on our "posture" towards everyone, including the individuals and families dealing with MAiD, as well as one another, even though we might hold varying theological positions. May our posture be one of embracing, listening, and caring for all people concerned in this difficult journey. May our words and our actions affirm that every person is created in the image of God. May we never exclude any person from our care on the basis of their beliefs or even their actions.

11. Youth-oriented versus Intergenerational Churches

Throughout the Bible, elders are honored and respected for their wisdom and experience. Two examples are in the book of Proverbs. Proverbs opens with a description of the person who fears the Lord (Proverbs 1:1-7) and concludes with an acrostic poem describing the wife of noble character who also fears the Lord (Proverbs 31:10-31). In between, the whole book of Proverbs is an appeal to younger people, frequently identified as "my son," or "my sons (1:8,10,15; 2:1, 3:1, 4:1, 5:1,7, 6:1), to follow the example of wise and godly people and to avoid people who are ungodly.

In contrast, has our contemporary Christian church exchanged respect and honor of elders for a youth-orientated culture that is focused primarily on activities and success? Are we expecting and demanding that church elders, with all their wisdom, submit to the youth?

> **How the Western church and Western Society Honor Youth at the Expense of the Elderly**
> • A disproportionate number of medical doctors have specialized in treating children in comparison to seniors. According to the Canadian Medical Association, in 2019 there were 304 doctors in all of Canada specializing in geriatric medicine (0.8 per 100,000 seniors). However, there were 2,973 pediatricians in Canada, (8.0 per 100,000 children).
> • Music in most evangelical churches is geared to youth even though seniors have difficulty participating because of hearing aids and the inability to stand for long periods.

James M. Houston writes, "But today, novices are too readily assumed to be fully equipped because of their rapid seminary training, their musical skills or their management training." Citing the example of what happened in one church, Houston continues, "Now, instead of a church community that was ruled by godly elders, it was ruled by youth. This was a reversal of both Chinese and Christian values" (James M. Houston and Michael Parker, *A Vision for the Aging Church*, 92).

A personal example illustrates how the Western contemporary church has largely abandoned the biblical teaching about the wisdom of the elderly. At the age of 53, I was in a chaplain residency program at a health center in Winnipeg, preparing for further ministry, either as a chaplain or as a pastor. At that time, I was told that one of our provincial denominational ministers would not recommend any person over the age of 45 to a pastoral position. However, my understanding is that the chaplaincy training I was in normally would not consider individuals unless they were at least 40 years old. The University of Winnipeg, which supervised and credentialed the chaplaincy program, recognized the value of experience and wisdom and required that individuals have these attributes to be suitable for their program, even though my denomination seemed to see these as a deterrent or at least of lesser importance for a pastor. The chaplaincy program that was training individuals to be care providers required a certain level of maturity and experience, whereas it seemed these were not a priority for the pastorate.

> **A Good Death**
> "As children of a culture radically, even religiously, devoted to youth and health, many find it incomprehensible, indeed offensive, that the word 'good' should in any way be associated with death." Richard John Neuhaus, *The Eternal Pity*, 1, quoted by W. Ross Hastings, *Where Do Broken Hearts Go?*, 16.

> **"Old School" versus "Hearing our Elders"**
> How might we dismiss the wisdom and experience of our parents and denigrate them with labels such as "old school" or "not with the times"? How might our seniors have accepted the belief that old people are of little value, and how might this contribute to their thoughts about their own funeral? What feelings are evoked by expressions such as "going downhill," "a senior's moment," and "slipping fast"?

In Moses' song at the end of his life, he described the Lord God and all the miraculous deeds God that had done. In case individuals had questions about the Lord, Moses said, "Ask your father and he will tell you, your elders, and they will explain to you" (Deuteronomy 32:7). In our churches, are we telling our congregations to ask the youth to explain things, instead of asking the elders with their wisdom?

As you read about this feature of our Western society, you might question how this relates to the focus of this book, which is about walking with individuals in their last years and then helping their loved ones as they prepare a funeral service. May I suggest that when a society focuses on youth and looks to youth for wisdom and direction, this will have a bearing on the priority this society gives to elderly people and therefore also to their funeral services. In a funeral service and in the sharing of memories, families and friends will in effect follow Moses' instruction. The stories told about a godly father and mother concern their lives but also give them an opportunity to pass on the core lessons of life to the next generations. This will not happen if we focus on youth and set aside the wisdom and experience of older people.

> **The Tried and True Way**
> "This is what the LORD says: 'Stand at the crossroads and look; ask for the ancient paths, ask where the good way is, and walk in it, and you will find rest for your souls.' But you said, 'We will not walk in it'" (Jeremiah 6:16). The Lord confronted his people about not following the tried and true ways of their ancestors.

12. Consumerism

How we perceive people in their declining and final years and months will determine how we make decisions about the care that will be provided for them. This includes decisions about the time and money spent on their care in their final years, as well as the cost of their funerals. I begin with two presuppositions:

1. Care for our elderly people costs.
2. There are only limited resources available for their care.

Human care is often spoken of in terms of supply and demand. The elderly person, with failing health and in need of extensive care, becomes the consumer. Then the care professional becomes the merchant of care. With such a perspective, humans are nothing more than a commodity in the competitive world of high finance where care is paid for by an insurance company, a government subsidy, or wise estate planning (although sometimes there is minimal or even no estate planning). Elderly people are more, much more, than a buyer or user of care. They are precious people, needing care and deserving care, not because they or their loved ones can afford it and have set aside money for their care, but because they are created in the image of God.

These two presuppositions apply from the moment a person is born and last throughout a person's lifetime. Every parent has a limited amount of resources to provide the necessary care for a child through all the stages of infancy, childhood, and youth. But these premises seem to become more critical in the final years of a person's life. This is especially the case when a society is ageist, that is, when it has a bias against older people. In fact, the manner in which some funeral establishments promote themselves indicates that they operate with these two presuppositions in mind. They perceive the deceased person as a consumer and the funeral home as a business that will supply the cheapest product for the least money.

A story will illustrate how consumerism impacts not only end-of-life care of elderly people, but even how we think about the cost of the final expression of care—the expenses associated with a funeral. Several years ago, the director of a funeral business requested to see me. He knew I was the pastor responsible for planning funerals in our church, and he was aware that in the previous few months very few church families had selected his funeral business. After listening to his business presentation for a considerable time, in which he attempted to convince me that his business was a better alternative to another funeral home, I interrupted him. I said, "I have not heard anything about care and compassion. The way you present yourself, a funeral is simply a business deal." Until I stopped him, he seemed to have had little awareness that he was merely selling a product and not caring for grieving families.

> **Quality Counts**
> "Take care of the service, and the sales will take care of themselves." (Edward Lynch to his son Thomas Lynch, both funeral directors, in Thomas G. Long and Thomas Lynch, *The Good Funeral*, 24.)

As a pastor who partners with various funeral establishments, I recognize how consumerism has permeated funerals. The focus seems to be on selling a product and not providing compassionate care. I realize that a funeral home needs to ensure a profit for the services that it provides. Yet funeral homes should be remembered for the care they provide and not for the deal they give a family.

Imagine with me that I am a spouse whose marriage partner of sixty years has passed away. Together with my family, I meet with the funeral director. He emphasizes the good offer he has for us and how little his products cost. Examples are the cost of a coffin versus the cost of an urn, cremation versus embalming, honorariums, a notice in the newspaper, flowers, and food for a reception. After a while, two things become evident:

1. The funeral director will not state this in these words, but, based on his offer, my spouse is worth very little. In fact, she is worth as little expense as I can get away with.

2. My spouse is not even worth being emotionally cared for. This funeral director has yet to express any compassion to me and my family.

I wish such a scenario would never take place. But on several occasions when a family has requested my presence as they met with a funeral director, I have perceived that what was happening was more like a business offer, like negotiating the price of a car, rather than an act of compassion.

Consider this comparison. Imagine a bride visiting several bridal stores with her mother, looking for the most beautiful wedding dress. Would a bridal store present itself as the discount bargain alternative to the other bridal stores? Would a bride want people to know how little she paid for her wedding dress? Have we accepted the notion that one funeral home is better than another funeral home because it provides fewer services at a discount price?

Life and death are more than an occasion to get a "good deal" and save money. We must take funerals out of the realm of consumerism and the marketplace and place them where they belong—within a caring faith community.

> "We are rapidly becoming the first society in the history of the world for whom the dead are no longer required—or desired—at their own funerals." (Thomas G. Long and Thomas Lynch, *The Good Funeral*, 93.) Is this motivated by an avoidance of death or by a desire to minimize expenses, or both? Or are other reasons involved?

Thomas Lynch, a funeral director, attended the convention of the National Funeral Directors Association, where over 1,200 funeral directors were discussing the serious business of what a funeral was. Whereas the exhibits across the street from this convention "proclaimed that the chief product of the mortuary were the cars and caskets and vaults and urns, piped in music and embalming, this think tank viewed such things as accessories only to the fundamental obligation to assist with the funeral. A death in the family was not a sales op, rather it was an opportunity to serve" (Thomas G. Long and Thomas Lynch, *The Good Funeral*, 24).

13. Restricting Care to Only Those in the Church Family

On two occasions in my first pastorate, a funeral director requested that I provide funeral services for people who were not part of our church. I sensed an openness on the part of our church to provide compassionate care that included a luncheon for people whom we did not know but who needed care. I trust that this caring spirit will be evident and demonstrated in every church. I realize that people might relocate in their retirement or later years. They might hesitate to become involved in a church in their new location for various reasons. They might not be comfortable affiliating with a church that is not part of the denomination they were previously committed to. They might sense that they have little that they can contribute. Or they might have heard rumors such as, "You only want to join our church so that we will help with your funeral service." May grieving families never have a sense that their grief and loss would be an unwelcome burden. In the crisis of loss and grief, may we as Christian churches never refuse to provide compassionate care or refuse to offer a memorial service to any family.

When we as pastors are prepared to serve individuals outside our church family, this introduces a challenge that is also an opportunity. This relates to caring for people we don't know. I realize that we are more comfortable with providing care for people we know. This is only natural. In response, I will offer several questions and a challenge: Is providing care and compassion a matter of doing only what we are familiar and comfortable with? Does it really matter whether we know the person or not? Does anyone really know the person's heart but God? Here is the challenge: to refuse to offer a memorial service to any family in the midst of their grief is unthinkable! (Read further on this in W. Ross Hastings, *Where Do Grieving Hearts Go?*, 127-132.)

Reflection #1: Summary Comments

In this chapter, I have attempted to describe the context, both cultural and spiritual, in which we, as pastors, are called to provide care at the moment when a person dies. In some cases, we are serving in a local context where the pattern or tradition of a funeral service will be very clear and understood by the family members who are grieving. But, for many of us who serve in an urban setting, the expectations might not be clear, familiar, or agreed upon. Furthermore, some of us pastors may be unfamiliar with planning what is possibly one of the most important services—a funeral. We have little or no experience and very little specialized training. Also, we might encounter some people attending the funeral who have unrealistic and unhelpful expectations, which we will not be able to meet and should not even attempt to fulfill.

> Respond in this culture with joy and grace. Process issues and concerns in a gracious spirit.

We will never know all who are present at the funeral services we lead. However, may we be faithful and open to God's Spirit as we give hope in the process of planning and carrying out the various aspects of a funeral service.

We have heard the simple challenge: "Bloom where you are planted." This was explained in a profound way by Larry Osborne as he described Daniel. Daniel lived in what was the most God-rejecting and wicked society in all history. Daniel knew his pagan culture. Yet he was faithful to God in this sinful culture because he knew and trusted the Lord, knowing that it was God who was in control, not the king who claimed to be (Larry Osborne, *Thriving in Babylon: Why Hope, Humility and Wisdom Matter in a Godless Culture*, Colorado Springs: David C. Cook, 2015). As we seek to fulfill our calling to God, we do so in a culture that might be more similar to the culture in which Daniel fulfilled his calling than we realize. May we be aware of our culture and true to our calling, serving with compassion and gentleness. The Apostle Peter's directive is helpful: May we do our pastoral ministry "with gentleness and respect" (1 Peter 3:15).

In this book, I will touch on the many elements that are part of a funeral service. First, though, I will provide an image that demonstrates how I seek to approach funerals—and, in fact, all of life. Imagine with me the strongest, tallest apple tree. The roots are deep in fertile soil. The branches produce the largest leaves and the most delicious fruit. This tree is planted beside a constant source of fresh water. My goal is that my life be like that tree, rooted in my almighty God. My hope is in God, in his love, in his grace, in his forgiveness, as well as in his compassion. My commitment is to follow his teachings. My desire is that all of us who provide care for grieving families will be like this strong tree. (This metaphor is explained in Psalm 1, John 15, and Galatians 5:22-26.)

I trust that this image will challenge us, inspire us, and give us hope and compassion. As ministers of the gospel, we have something to offer that the funeral director normally will not provide. (Having noted this, I will add that funeral directors often express deep compassion and sensitivity even as they provide a necessary service.) Unless we have a deep-rooted faith in God, we will not be able to give the hope and confidence that come from God. I trust my thoughts will help all of us who walk with families in the "valley of the shadow of death," pointing them across the finish line to the promises God has for them and for their loved ones. May we also proclaim the hope we have in the time before we cross the finish line, knowing that a caring God is with us now.

Besides this, I have a far deeper aspiration: that our faith will become strong in a loving God. It is one thing to make wise choices about a funeral service. It is altogether different and far more important that we renew our own faith in God, who will help in this time of loss and in every challenge we will ever face. As those whom God has called to lead in all areas of life, including funeral services, my prayer is that we will do so as the person described in Psalm 1 did—placing our trust in God and meditating on God's Word. The ultimate reason is that we will only be able to help people find comfort and hope in their time of loss as we are rooted in God and in his Word.

I have concluded this chapter with these words because we are called to bloom in a cultural and spiritual context that might not be what we desire. Yet we are called to express God's compassion in the context where we are planted. May we be faithful.

Reflection #2: Which of these Aspects of Our Culture Have You Recognized in Your Ministry?

1. The minimal training about death and funerals in theological institutions
2. The minimal value placed on funerals by some pastors
3. Ageism
4. Professionalism
5. Individualism in a spiritual community
6. Selfishness
7. An avoidance of intense pain and suffering and therefore an avoidance of the ultimate pain—death
8. An avoidance of embracing the declining years
9. An avoidance of death itself
10. MAiD (Medical Assistance in Dying)
11. A youth-oriented rather than an inter-generational church community
12. Consumerism
13. Restricting care to only those in the church family

Reflect on the issues above, and consider what positive steps you will want to take in response.

Reflection #3

Consider the following questions:

1. Training: As a pastor, there are always areas in which I will realize that I need further insight, training, and reading. How have I sensed this need when helping individuals prepare for end-of-life issues?

2. Priorities: When I hear that someone in my church has passed away, what are my emotions?

3. Myths on ageism: How might I be inadvertently demonstrating that I believe the myths of ageism? How have my attitudes to the elderly changed over the years?

4. Individualism: As a pastor, I am fully aware of the biblical teaching on the body of Christ and the reality that believers are connected to one another. But how might I be unconsciously demonstrating that I believe

Christianity essentially involves an individual's personal relationship with God and does not involve anyone else?

5. *"No service by request":* A notice such as this in the newspaper will impact how people perceive the value of a funeral service. How do I feel when I hear that someone I love will not have a funeral service—do I respond with compassion, sadness, anger, or some other emotion?

6. *Consumerism:* How might I be demonstrating that I believe the funeral home of choice should be the one that provides minimal services and the lowest cost?

7. *Avoidance of pain:* How familiar am I with the various issues related to the topics of euthanasia and MAiD? Have I taken the time to do a biblical study in these areas? How familiar am I with my denomination's position on these areas? How knowledgeable am I about medical and government guidelines and rulings?

8. *Providing care for those not in our churches:* How do I exhibit openness to walk with a family in their grief when I know very little or nothing about the loved one who has died?

> Daniel not only survived but thrived in successive pagan cultures. Through courage and compassion, wisdom and humility, Daniel stood firm so that those who disagreed with his values and rejected his God still listened to God's Word through him. May we be bold, even in our contemporary society.

Prayer

Heavenly Father, we come to you, realizing that we are called to walk with people in their loss and grief in a specific cultural and spiritual context. We do not have all the answers to the concerns, questions, and challenges people have. Yes, we are committed to being aware of the issues facing us as we provide care, but may we know our limitations. Our greater commitment is to see the world as you see it and then respond as you desire us to. Even as Jesus was Immanuel in a specific context and to a particular people, may we also be Immanuel in the context you have placed us. Give us grace to discern how best to respond with your words and actions. In the name of Jesus, who is Immanuel, we pray, Amen.

Chapter Three
Changes in Funeral Practices

I recognize that there are shifts in contemporary funeral practices from those in earlier centuries. Families will be aware of some of these changes and might expect that we, who are pastors, will suggest which the best practices are (often those most recently adopted). However, at times I have sensed families demanding these new practices and not being open to consider any other options. At times, it even seems that the families who are insisting on a specific practice are reluctant to admit that it is a very recent practice. Said differently, numerous aspects of funerals have only been practiced recently. I will note six examples.

> **Recent Changes in Funeral Practices:**
> - Funeral → memorial service
> - Fewer people at the cemetery
> - An emphasis on joy rather than sadness
> - No viewing of the body
> - A service → no public service
> - Traditional burial → cremation

1. A Funeral or a Memorial Service?

Possibly the most obvious shift is from having a funeral service to having a memorial service. In a funeral service, the body will be present, and the burial will follow. But in a memorial service, the committal service takes place before the memorial service and therefore the body will not be present. Even when the burial service is after the funeral service, the body will not be present in the memorial service. This also applies to ashes, which might or might not be present.

2. The People Present at the Cemetery

In the past, the community or the whole church family gathered at the cemetery. Presently, usually only the immediate family will gather. At times, invited friends and extended family will also be at the committal service. However, even now in some ethnic circles and in smaller, rural settings, many people will accompany the immediate family at the burial service.

3. An Emphasis on Joy rather than Sadness

In a funeral service, there will be a recognition of the somber reality of death. But, in a "celebration of life," there might be a deliberate avoidance of loss and grief, and the emphasis will be on celebrating the life of the deceased.

4. Viewing of the Body

The standard practice in many cultures is that the body will be placed in a prominent place in the home of the deceased, in a church, in a building dedicated for a religious purpose, or in a funeral home. Then, family and friends will gather to pay their final respects and comfort each other as they remember their loved one. Canadian First Nations often hold a "wake" in which family and friends will gather at the home of the deceased and stay awake all night as memories are shared and as people comfort one another. Yet, today in our Western society, it is becoming more common that families will decide not to view the body. When there is a viewing of the body, this might happen in several ways. Usually, the viewing will be the evening before the memorial service. Occasionally, there will be two time periods for viewing, one for the immediate family and then a public viewing for the larger family and friends. Also, there might be a final viewing just before the body is taken to the cemetery for the burial service or is taken into the sanctuary where the funeral service will be held.

5. No Public Service

Several years ago, I received a request to conduct a burial service for one of our elderly female church members. As I talked to her son and the funeral home personnel, I soon realized that the son did not want a memorial service in the church for his mother, even though she was a committed member in our church and had many friends who would want to be at her service. This elderly mother had no other children. The son had scheduled a winter vacation. He did the least possible for his mother—which included a brief burial service—so that he would not need to adjust his winter vacation plans. The issue was not finances but, sadly, an unwillingness to change his wants so that he could care for his mother.

As I read obituaries in the newspaper, I find it disappointing that an increasing number of people do not want a public service. What I see as even more regrettable is that, after individuals have desired a public service and have even written down their wishes, their children will decide to go against their parents' requests and not provide a public service for their parents.

6. Burial or Cremation

When a family is planning a funeral service, they will need to choose to have either a traditional burial or a cremation. I will briefly reflect on the choice between the two. Here, as in all components of helping a family in their time of loss and grief, it is critical that we, as pastors, walk with people with sensitivity and compassion.

I recall several individuals in our church coming to me, expressing anger and disappointment that their family members had chosen cremation for a loved one. In one situation, the nieces and nephews had chosen cremation for a person's sister, and in another situation, a son-in-law had selected cremation for the church member's daughter. In both cases, the grieving person declared, "The Bible is clear—cremation is written against in the Bible."

The opposite alternative might also be an occasion for family conflict—some family members, who prefer cremation, will be upset if the more costly traditional burial is chosen.

How was I to respond to these people who were confident that their interpretation of the Bible was the right one, as well as angry toward other family members who had chosen to have a loved one cremated? What would be the compassionate and wise response?

What I said and did might not be the only response, but I trust it was a compassionate response. My first priority was to respond to the immediate need, this being to comfort the grieving people, who were also angry and feeling let down by loved ones. My desire was to express God's compassion in a time of loss. I believe that when a person is grieving and angry, that is not the time to do a Bible study on the topic of cremation. At that moment, did it really matter what I believed the Bible taught on this topic or what my beliefs were? My answer then and now is the same—my interpretation of the Bible regarding cremation was not the key issue before me then, nor is it now.

Recognizing that the topic of burial versus cremation can be controversial, I wish to emphasize three points.

1. As pastors, we need to be sensitive in processing the topic of traditional burial versus cremation. May we never be judgmental, but empathetic and compassionate, and may we take time to listen to families.

2. Recognizing that opinions on the matter of traditional burial versus cremation are often strong and cause divisions within families and between friends, our goal should be to provide an atmosphere of listening and openness. When we sense divisions on this matter, may we encourage

a spirit of understanding one another and accepting one another, even when people disagree with each other.

3. May I encourage us, as pastors, to become familiar with this topic. Recognizing that much more has been written on this, I will briefly note reasons cremation is chosen, and then reasons for a traditional burial. My desire is to present these two sections with an attitude of compassion and understanding.

a. Reasons Cremation Is Chosen

1. Cost. Comparison is made between the total cost of burial (that will include embalming the body, a casket, and a large cemetery plot) to the total cost of cremation (that will include the cremation, a small urn, and possibly a small plot of land in the cemetery). However, at

> **Reasons Cremation Is Chosen:**
> • Cost
> • Scarcity of land
> • Ecological considerations
> • Family mobility
> • Disgust with the Western way of death

times, a family will have a viewing, possibly even a traditional service with the body, and then proceed with cremation. In these situations, the body will be embalmed and a coffin will be rented before cremation takes place.

2. Scarcity of Land. Only a small area of land is required for cremation if the ashes are buried in a cemetery. No land is needed if the ashes are scattered in various ways such as in a stream or from an airplane or in a garden.

3. Ecological Considerations. There are ecological reasons for choosing cremation. First, since land is limited, cremation is a better use of land when compared with what is needed for large burial plots. Second, very little material is used to construct an urn, compared to the cost of constructing a casket. Third, with cremation, the few pounds of ashes that remain can be scattered in a garden. Fourth, the toxic chemicals that are needed for embalming are not necessary.

> The cremation industry does not promote itself as green. Considerations are the tremendous energy required to burn a body (1600 to 2000 degrees Fahrenheit), the release of pollutants from the metals in tooth fillings, the release of materials from surgical implants into the atmosphere, and the embalming of bodies for viewing before cremation. (Lauren Markoe, "Cremation is popular, but is it eco-friendly?" *The Christian Century*, Vol. 131, No. 4, February 19, 2014, 18).

4. Family Mobility. Recognizing the extensive mobility in Western society, there might be little loyalty to the place of origin and therefore no need to be buried where a person's ancestors were buried. With cremation, the argument of family mobility takes on another dimension. On a fairly regular basis, families are choosing to bury the "cremains" (cremated remains) of a loved one at a family plot. This will normally be done at a date when the whole family can gather, which could be a considerable time after a memorial service.

5. Disgust with the Western Way of Death. This includes the argument that embalming has little value since it merely slows the decomposition of the body. This line of reasoning might also include a rejection of the belief that the person is "just sleeping" because, with a rejection of the Christian hope of resurrection, then the person is not sleeping but is no more. Therefore, why not just be cremated and "get it over with" as quickly as possible (William Phipps, "The Consuming Fire for Corpses," *The Christian Century*, Vol. 98, no. 7, March 4, 1981: 221-222

When we recognize that cremation is an accepted method of disposing of bodies, not only in Eastern societies, but also in our Western society and even among many Christians, we need to remain true to our calling and provide pastoral care, no matter which is chosen, cremation or traditional burial. I repeat that our mission as pastors is to care for families and not debate the method of disposing of a body. However, I believe it is good for us, as pastors, to be familiar with reasons for burial as well as reasons for cremation. Therefore, I will now note the reasons that Christians, throughout history, have chosen burial.

Some Christians will respond that there is no theological basis for burial over against cremation. They will state, "The real person is not here anymore. The body is just a shell of the person that used to be here. Therefore, it does not matter whether the person is cremated or buried." If that was the case, then the early Christians would have adopted the practice of the Romans and cremated their loved ones. But the Christians opposed and rejected Rome's longstanding pagan practice of cremating the dead, which brought Christians derision, ridicule, and persecution. The accepted reason why the early Christians chose burial—even though no church council or synod issued a canon regarding cremation—is that none was needed because the Christians never had any questions about cremation. Nikolaus Müller, a church historian, stated that there was "an unwritten law" that told Christians they were not to incinerate their dead. The early Christians saw cremation as biblically and theologically wrong and sinful. (Nikolaus Müller, "Koimeterein," *Realencyclopädie für Protestantische Theologie und Kirche*, Leipzig, Germany: J.C. Hinrichs'she

Buchhandlung, 1901, 10:815, cited in Alvin J. Schmidt, *Cremation, Embalmment, or Neither?*, Bloomington, Indiana: WestBow Press, 2015, 85.)

As you read these reasons Christians chose burial, may these be received with the spirit they are given—a pastoral concern for grieving families and a commitment that God be honored in whatever method the bodies of people are taken care of.

b. Reasons Christians, Beginning with the Early Church, Have Chosen Burial

Following are the main reasons Christians have chosen burial.

1. They are committed to follow Jesus—not only in life, but also in death. Therefore, they want to be buried or entombed as Jesus was. As Jesus was buried and raised bodily from the dead, so Christians believe that their burial is a witness to the coming resurrection.

2. They follow the biblical precedents of earth burial throughout the Old Testament and the New Testament.

3. They believe in the sanctity of the human body and that this sanctity does not come to an end when a person has died. The human body is the crown of creation and the temple of God's Holy Spirit (Genesis 1:27, Psalm 8:5, 1 Corinthians 3:16). The dignity of the human body is evident in Christians washing their dead, which was a radical act since the early Christians were Jews and any contact with a dead body would have made them ceremonially unclean (Acts 9:37). The body of every human is created by God, bears his image, and therefore deserves to be treated with respect.

4. Believers hold to the centrality of the Incarnation. When the Word, God's Son, became flesh, God uniquely hallowed life and bodily existence forever.

5. Believers hold to a doctrine of death as sleep. This was not an empty metaphor for early Christians but an expression of hope in death, even in persecution, that they would awaken to new, eternal life. Believers also had hope that when they laid their deceased loved ones to "rest" in the grave, they could look forward to the moment when their loved ones would hear the Lord's trumpet call and awaken. Several people in the Bible, including Daniel, Jesus, and the Apostle Paul, describe death as sleep (Daniel 12:2, Mark 5:39, John 11:11, 1 Corinthians 15:20, 1 Thessalonians 4:14). The metaphor of sleep for the Christian's hope is enhanced by the burial of the loved one. The assurance of a bodily resurrection can be envisioned equally with cremation, but a grieving family might easier understand this with a burial than with cremation. As an aside, the English word "cemetery" is derived from the Latin *coemeterium*, "a sleeping place" (Alvin J. Schmidt, *Cremation, Embalmment, or Neither?*, 93).

6. Believers want to return the deceased body to where it came from, in keeping with the Lord's words: "By the sweat of your brow you will eat your food until you return to the ground, since from it you were taken; for dust you are and to dust you will return" (Genesis 3:19).

7. Our liturgy and rites embody our biblical teaching in favor of burial. This becomes evident when we analyze our liturgy, hymns, and other words we use in burial and funeral services. Two key elements of concern are the absence of the body (which our liturgies assume is present) and the saying, "ashes to ashes." For Roman Catholics, a question is whether there is a funeral liturgy that is appropriate for the disposition of ashes. (Answers are considered in two articles: H. Richard Rutherford, "Forum: Cremation American Style: A Cultural Revolution for Catholics," *Worship*, 66, No. 6, November 1992, 544-549; and H. Richard Rutherford, "Honoring the Dead: Catholics and Cremation," *Worship*, 64, No. 6, Nov. 1990, 482-494.) Recognizing that many Christians practice cremation and that in some countries cremation is required by law and burial is prohibited, I cannot agree with Alvin J. Schmidt, who insists on burial and rejects cremation with the words: "Belief in the resurrection of the body assumes burial and graves, whereas cremation does not" (Alvin J. Schmidt, *Cremation, Embalmment, or Neither?*, 107). My answer to this is that the Christian faith is built on what the rituals and practices symbolize and not on the rituals and practices themselves. Certainly, we need to find and use the best symbols possible to express the reality behind them. I believe that Jesus' death, burial, and resurrection, as well as our death, burial, and resurrection, can better be understood with the symbol of burial than that of cremation. But it is not helpful, correct, nor pastoral to state that "cremation does not assume belief in the resurrection of the body." The primary issue is always the spiritual reality—Jesus' resurrection and our resurrection, which is based on his resurrection. Biblical teaching explains the core Christian faith. Rituals and practices are always secondary and never primary. They are helpful only as they point to and help us envision the reality.

8. Burial can provide for a more complete grieving, whereas cremation might minimize grieving. The following instruction by a dying man demonstrates our tendency to avoid pain and grieving: "When I'm gone, just cremate me." This person just wanted it all to be over. (Thomas Lynch, "The Holy Fire, Cremation: A Practice in Need of Ritual," *The Christian Century*, 127, No. 7, April 2010, 22-29.) This urgency that our life should be terminated quickly when the quality of life is no longer present and the assumption that our loved ones will forget us certainly do not represent the desires of many people who request cremation. As a pastor who has walked with families when both cremation and burial were practiced, I sense that it is more natural to feel the deep loss and grief as we view a body, carry the coffin, and then watch it being lowered into a grave. Having said this, I can recall many burial services of cremains that were equally moving and very meaningful to the family members.

9. Burial more naturally provides a specific place that loved ones can return to and remember the faith and life of a loved one. When there has been a burial of cremains, the family will usually install a marker so that the family members can come and remember their loved ones. However, when a loved one's ashes are scattered in a river or on a golf course or from an airplane, there is nothing physical to remind the survivors of their departed loved one and of their hope.

A funeral director gave this insightful observation about what should be done with the cremains. He suggested that "a good test of what is done with cremated remains is to ask if there is any parallel with what we would sense as proper to do with a body" (Richard Peterson, referred to by Thomas G. Long, *Accompany Them with Singing*, 176). This simply means that we will want to treat the cremains no differently than a body. There are two concerns I want to note about cremation and specifically cremated ashes. First, most funeral homes say they have unclaimed urns. Second, some families who choose not to have a committal service of the ashes immediately when the person dies will not have planned how to deal with the ashes. There might be a feeling of shame and guilt, even helplessness, as time lingers after the memorial service and the family remains unsure of what to do with the cremains.

Following is an example of the second point. A family had chosen cremation but did not bury the cremains at the time of the memorial service. Six years later, the surviving spouse requested that I read several Bible verses as the family placed the cremains in a "crematorium." I sensed God's gentle, compassionate Spirit touch the hearts of the family members as they shared memories and heard God's Word and a committal prayer. Would it not have been better to have had the service of committal at the same time as the memorial service was held and not wait six years? I chose not to ask the spouse this sensitive question. Here, as always, we walk with families where they are in the journey of grief.

Having given the above reasons for both cremation and traditional burial, I emphasize that we need to be sensitive when expressing our views on this topic, recognizing that our primary purpose is to provide compassion in a time of grief and loss and not to be engaged in a debate on viewpoints.

7. The New Way of Death

In the previous six sections, I noted six specific changes in funeral practices. These are neither minor nor insignificant. But I am making a distinction between those practices and the ones in this section. Someone might argue the difference between the changes in the previous sections and the changes in this section are only a matter of degree. However, as I review some of the literature describing contemporary memorial services, I perceive a new approach altogether. Here are several books that describe the "new way of death": Betty Breuhaus, *When the Sun Goes Down: A Serendipitous Guide to Planning Your Own Funeral* (New York: iUniverse, 2007). Lisa Takeuchi Cullen, *Remember Me: A Lively Tour of the New American Way of Death* (New York: HarperCollins, 2006). Elizabeth Fournier, *The Green Burial Guidebook* (Novato, California: New World Library, 2018). Jeltje Gordon-Lennox, *Crafting Meaningful Funeral Rituals: A Practical Guide* (London: Jessica Kingsley Publishers, 2020). Lucinda Herring, *Reimagining Death: Stories and Practical Wisdom for Home Funerals and Green Burials* (Berkeley: North Atlantic Books, 2019). Doug Manning, *Don't Take My Grief Away from Me: How to Walk through Grief and Learn to Live Again* (Oklahoma City: In-Sight Books, 2005).

I will begin this section with an illustration. The concert maestro will ensure that all the musical instruments are perfectly in tune before the curtain opens for a symphony. How does this illustration apply to the topic of funerals and end-of-life concerns? I begin my answer by noting that how we treat our bodies when they are dead is an indication of how we treat our bodies when they are alive. Further, our funeral rituals expose core personal and cultural values and beliefs. Imagine a symphony in which all the musical instruments were out of tune—we would walk out because the sound would be a chaotic clatter, unpleasant to any musical ear. I believe many

> "Who among you fears the LORD and obeys the word of his servant? Let him who walks in the dark, who has no light, trust in the name of the LORD and rely on his God. But now, all you who light fires and provide yourselves with flaming torches, go, walk in the light of your fires and of the torches you have set ablaze. This is what you shall receive from my hand: You will lie down in torment" (Isaiah 50:10-11).

contemporary memorial services are a glaring sign of a society that is not aware of how out of tune it is with deeper, genuine God beliefs and values. As I review the literature on the "new American and Canadian way of death" and the stories and guidance on "reimagining death" there, I have three initial observations. First, this "new way of death" is simply one ritual replacing another, that is, the historic traditional funeral is replaced with an untried "contemporary model." Second, this new model seems to have little basis or foundation in a Judeo-Christian belief structure. There is little reference to the core meaning of life that based on an almighty and compassionate God. And there is minimal reference to any hope beyond this life, specifically not to the hope that is rooted in a gracious God and his resurrected Son, Jesus Christ. Third, these new expressions of dealing with the dead and the topic of death expose how void of a moral framework our society is now. I am not negating all new aspects and styles of funerals, but I invite us to examine our own beliefs as I list some aspects of contemporary funerals:

- Green cemeteries: an unembalmed body is placed in the earth in a biodegradable box or shroud. A green burial is environmentally friendly, perceived as a vehicle to save the planet. No monument or marker will help locate the body, only a global positioning system.
- In planning the service, people are "free to personally define exactly the type and style of life celebration" they prefer (Betty Breuhaus, *When the Sun Goes Down*, xxv).

> **Looking Back**
> Do Isaiah's sobering, shocking, and even sarcastic words about those who follow pagan gods apply to some of the new ways of doing funerals? "You were wearied by all your ways, but you would not say, 'It is hopeless'" (Isaiah 57:10). Do the depressing features in some of the funeral practices convict us of our mission to bring a message of hope and purpose that is only found in Jesus Christ?

- People are told that the funeral service should accomplish two things and only two things: memorialize the loved one and comfort the person planning the service. It should be governed solely by the survivors (Doug Manning, *Don't Take My Grief Away from Me*, 8).
- Speedy, personalized, affordable options are recommended over the supposedly "unaffordable" options offered by the commercial funeral industry, which is said to "prey on the emotions of grief."
- New processes to preserve a body include alkaline hydrolysis (known also as water resomation, bio-cremation, and flameless cremation), mummification, cryonic freezing, plastination (infusing the human corpse

with a mix of plastics, thereby preserving it), and compressing ashes to produce diamonds and jewelry.

After describing "the changing landscape of funerals," Thomas Long gives this sobering analysis: "The stakes are high here. I am persuaded that in this, our moment in history, we are going through one of those periodic upheavals in the ways we care (or don't) for the dead that are inevitable signs of an upheaval in the ways we care (or don't) for the living. To put it bluntly, a society that has forgotten how to honor the bodies of those who have departed is more inclined to neglect, even torture, the bodies of those still living. A society that has no firm hope for where the dead are going is also unsure how to take the hands of its children and lead them toward a hopeful future." Thomas Long continues with this conviction: "that there is a broad but identifiable Christianly way to honor the dead, to walk with them in hope, and to mark well the meaning of death and life" (Thomas G. Long, *Accompany Them with Singing*, 4-8).

> Funerals expose the answer to the question, "Who is at the center of the universe—me or an almighty God?"

> **New Expressions in Dealing with Loss**
> When Jeremiah saw the depravity and wickedness of God's people, as well as God's judgment, he responded, "Since my people are crushed, I am crushed; I mourn, and horror grips me. Is there no balm in Gilead? Is there no physician there? Why then is there no healing for the wound of my people?" (Jeremiah 8:21-22). What is our emotional response to these new expressions at the loss of loved ones? I trust it is grief and compassion.

My critique of the "new way of death" is that, while there are elements to be commended, such as the emphasis on the need to honor a loved one in a personal manner, I sense that many of the elements demonstrate a sense of hopelessness. Is our society attempting to find direction without a moral compass or attempting to tune its values without an absolute tuning fork—to continue the comparison I made at the beginning of this section. We will only be able to walk in the dark challenges of life, function in times of crisis, and face up to our frailty, disability, and imminent death, when we believe we are sustained by a caring and compassionate God. We will only be able to stand with hope at the grave of a loved one when we believe in an eternal God who resurrects the dead. In contrast, I believe that many of the new expressions of dealing with death and then with the dead are a vain attempt to make sense out of a confusing situation when the core belief in a Creator God, a sustaining God, and an eternal God is rejected.

Reflections

1. Which of these changes in funeral practices have you noticed and have had to deal with:
- a memorial service rather than a funeral
- few people present at the cemetery
- an emphasis on joy rather than sadness
- no or limited viewing of the body
- no public service
- cremation rather than traditional burial

How have you dealt with these changes? What is your attitude toward them?

2. Have you encountered a change in the philosophy underlying funeral practices? How have you dealt with these situations? What is your attitude toward them?

Prayer

Our heavenly Father, we come to you in the name of your only Son, who declared, "I am the Way, and the Truth, and the Life." As we perceive the hopelessness evident in many new expressions of dealing with loss, we know this is a direct result of a society that has rejected you and has therefore lost the guiding compass in all phases of life. With David, we have assurance that you walk with us in the valley of the shadow of death. This gives us comfort and hope in our grief. Therefore, give us a sensitive heart as we walk with and hear about families who have rejected you, the Good Shepherd, and therefore grieve without your compassion and comfort and without hope. Give us a gentle heart of Jesus, who responded with compassion when he observed the crowds, harassed, helpless, and like sheep without a shepherd. May we walk with grieving people strengthened by your loving embrace, giving sympathy and hope. In the name of Jesus, who is compassionate and full of forgiveness, Amen.

Chapter Four
Planning the Funeral Service

When families come to share their loss and to plan the funeral service, I stress the importance of them planning as a family. Most families will want to consider the desires of all the family members in making funeral plans. However, on a few occasions, we pastors will become aware that there is not full agreement within a family on the decisions made. We might discover that some family members are making all the decisions without consulting the other family members. These family members might justify their actions based on the fact that they are the executors who will carry out the will of the deceased and do not need to consult other family members. In these circumstances, we will sense friction between family members in the midst of grief. How we walk with the family members in this sensitive time is crucial.

Deciding on the date of the funeral will usually take considerable discussion. Often the date will not suit everyone involved. I encourage the family to postpone making the decision on the date of the funeral until all immediate members of the family have been consulted, and if possible, an agreement has been reached.

I realize that each pastor will have her or his own approach to planning the funeral service. Also, how we do things may change over time. This has happened with me. But there are several key principles I follow:

1. Plan Ahead

There is an awareness in our church that I encourage individuals to plan ahead, well before a death occurs. People will come to see me, and I will go over funeral planning forms with them.

2. Have Clear Guidelines

Our church has developed a handout which includes the basic forms that can be used to help with the planning.

3. Plan with Compassion

When a family comes to process the funeral details, the members might be in extreme grief. Therefore, I will listen to discern where a family is in their grief and, if appropriate, process only the basic items in the first visit. I will ensure that all the details will be attended to, but these do not need to be finalized in the first planning meeting.

4. Proceed with Gentleness

Usually in the initial visit, the family will not know many of the details they need to decide on. However, the family members will have the forms and know what decisions still need to be made. Then I will state that the family and I will communicate numerous times as we arrive at the decisions regarding items such as the pictures for the bulletin, the life story, and the selected hymns. I do not know all the discussions the family members will be having in order to reach agreement among themselves. But I know that time is of the essence, and therefore I will request that the necessary items be decided on and communicated to me in a timely manner—but I will do so with gentleness.

5. Lead and Listen

As a pastor, I have led many funerals and I recognize that the family might not be familiar with planning a funeral service. Therefore, I want to give the family a sense of assurance that all the details will come together, even if they are in grief and are unsure of what is next. This means I will lead with a component of gentle authority. At the same time, I will always listen to the family, ensuring their questions and uncertainties will be answered.

6. Plan with an Awareness of Our Own Limitations as well as Our Own Issues

As pastors, our commitment is to walk with families in their grief. However, there might be instances, such as a sudden tragic death, in which some family members will be in severe grief and shock and will need to be referred to professional help, be it medical (prescription drugs) or counseling of some kind. Are we aware of such support services to which we might make appropriate referrals? (This will be addressed in Chapter Nine, "A Word to Fellow Pastors," specifically the section on "Acknowledging Our Own Brokenness and Limitations.")

Reflections

When we meet with the family to plan a funeral, we need to hold two values or goals in balance. One is to express compassion and care, and the other is to ensure the service is being planned in a timely manner. When we have finished the initial meeting with a family, how will the family members sense that we were present with them? On the other hand, what might we be doing that might lead them to feel we are rushed and attempting to shorten the meeting in any way possible? How are we showing the family that we are committed to walk with them and that we feel their loss? How are we assuring them of our support?

Prayer

Heavenly Father, as a family comes to me in their grief, may I have a compassionate heart, listening to their heart and sensing their grief. May I never perceive a meeting with a family as another item to check off my list in a busy schedule. May I instead be present, expressing the compassion that you have for me. In the name of Jesus, who is Immanuel in all of life's circumstances, Amen.

Chapter Five
Partnering with a Funeral Home

When a family plans a funeral service, there are three groups that are involved: the family, the funeral home, and the church. All three of these need to work together.

As the pastor, you might be consulted as to whether you have a preference or recommendation for a funeral home. Families will even ask, "Are all funeral homes the same? Which is the best funeral home?" Sometimes I am asked these questions even though the family has already selected the funeral home. When a family does insist on an answer on which funeral home I would recommend, I will assure the family of these three things:

1. It is up to the family to make this decision, and I will respect their choice.

2. I will work with whatever funeral home the family chooses and will ensure the best possible service will be provided.

3. There is a third thing I will say, but only when I sense the family has concerns about the differences between funeral homes. The family knows that funeral homes provide different levels of service and therefore the costs will reflect this. When a family selects a funeral home that has fewer services, I will assure the family that I will do my best so that the family will have all their needs and wishes met even though the funeral home will not or cannot provide some services.

Here are two examples of providing a service that a funeral home cannot meet:

1. A funeral establishment might have very limited room for viewing, and therefore I will offer that the viewing can be in our church.

2. A funeral home might be further away or in an industrial section of town. Then I will make the offer that the family can meet at our church and proceed from our church to the cemetery together.

There is great variation among funeral homes. But when we are consulted on this matter, we as pastors need to keep our purpose and calling clear. We are called to help a family plan a very critical service in their time of grief. At that time, the difference between funeral homes is of minor consequence. The important thing is that we do all we can to walk with the family, representing a caring God and giving hope and comfort.

Therefore, instead of making comparisons and offering our personal preferences in regard to funeral homes, an alternative approach is to have materials (advertising, etc.) from all funeral homes and crematorium services available. We thereby simply make people aware of their choices without promoting one funeral home over the others.

In the book, *Accompany Them with Singing: The Christian Funeral*, Thomas G. Long makes helpful observations in the section, "The Funeral Director" (pp. 178-180). He is not optimistic that it will happen, but he would like to recover the older designation—*undertaker*. A funeral *director* does not, or at least should not, *direct* the funeral service. He or she is responsible to *undertake* the responsibilities that the rest of society will not or cannot do. The directing, planning, and leading of the funeral service, if it is to be a Christian funeral, must remain the responsibility of those who direct the sacred funeral rituals.

Reflections

Our goal as pastors is to ensure that the family's needs are met, and it does not essentially matter which funeral home is selected. Therefore, we need to be cautious about making any negative or critical comments about any funeral home. How are we demonstrating to the family that we affirm their selection of a funeral home, even if we, as their pastor, might wish they had chosen another funeral home?

Prayer

Heavenly Father, as I partner with a funeral director, may I do so with respect, honoring the role and ministry that the funeral director provides. May I keep my purpose uppermost: leading a family through their valley of loss and grief. In Jesus' name, Amen.

Chapter Six
Components of a Funeral Service

1. Naming of the Service

Traditionally, the service has been called a "funeral service." However, when the burial precedes the ceremony, then the service is usually called a "memorial service." Frequently, this ceremony is also called "a celebration of life." This last designation denotes that the family is thanking God for the life and faith of their loved one and thus celebrating the person's life. The title "memorial service" denotes that the family is thanking God for the memories of a person. (In effect, they will also be celebrating the life and legacy of the loved one.) The choice of what to call the service is a significant matter and might also be a sensitive issue. As pastors, we will want to encourage the family to think how they wish to label their service. If at all possible, we should ensure that all the family members agree on how the service is designated.

Having said this, I believe that we, as pastors, need to give consideration to how a service is named. When we reflect on the name of the service, or if a family asks for our suggestion, there are some questions we will want to consider and even suggest that the family take into account:

• If a life was worth anything and the relationships were deep, then its end must represent a painful and permanent void for those left behind.

• If we genuinely loved a person and that person is no longer with us, this will result in deep grief and loss. Can this loss and separation be celebrated with any honesty?

• When a family is grieving the loss of a dear spouse, mother, or grandmother, do we not need to acknowledge the intense grief?

The answer to these questions is that we certainly want to thank God for his faithfulness in the life of the person whose service we are planning and for the eternal inheritance he is preparing for us. But I invite us to review our easy acceptance of a title that I suggest is confusing. I believe the label "celebration of life" might be a futile attempt to numb the pain of grief and ignore or minimize what is obvious—the family and friends are in their greatest moment of loss.

I mention this to encourage us to both be sensitive regarding whatever name the family will select for the service but also be prepared to reflect with the family on what is the most appropriate designation for them. However, I suggest that we will want to withhold a conversation on the name of the service if the family is agreed on a name, even if we might believe another name is more appropriate.

My own journey and thinking in this matter has evolved. There was a time when I encouraged using the label "celebration of life." However, after planning funerals with many families, I became more aware of the pain and challenges within families and more cognizant of the core essence of the service. Therefore, I am now suggesting the service be given the title "memorial service" or "funeral service."

However, this reflection on the various possible names for the service might not be helpful in a situation where the family's faith tradition provides only one option on the name of the service.

2. Viewing

As I was planning the various aspects of the funeral service with a family, an adult daughter commented, "My children can't stomach viewing Grandma's body. Why would we have a viewing anyway?"

Some pious Christians will say, "The person—our mother or grandmother—is not here anymore. So why do we gather around the shell of a person? The spirit of our mother is with Jesus. That is her real self. She is gone. This body is not her."

> **Personhood**
>
> A funeral service is not an ideal time to process the dualistic way of understanding human personhood that is widespread in Western society and is influenced by Platonic Greek philosophy. W. Ross Hastings explains that people, even though they are dead, "*are* an animated body, a body animated by the life or soul God has given them (not 'a body housing a soul'). After they die, when Christ returns...they will be resurrected and once again be living, integrated body-soul, whole persons" (W. Ross Hastings, *Where Do Grieving Hearts Go?*, 103).

As we plan a funeral with the family, it might not be an appropriate time to go into an explanation of the biblical understanding of the body. However, I believe that we, as pastors who lead a funeral service, should reflect on both the practice of viewing the body of a deceased person and the theology/biblical understanding of personhood. Here, as in all areas of life, values, ideology, and theology determine attitudes and actions.

An excellent place to begin to build a biblical understanding of care for the body of a deceased person is with the Gospel accounts of how people treated Jesus' body after he died. The Gospel writers describe in detail the tender care given to the body of Jesus by Joseph of Arimathea and Nicodemus. Then the Gospel writers mention the love shown by the women who purchased and prepared spices to care for Jesus' body. The Gospel writers stress the importance of these acts by naming the men and also the women: Mary Magdalene, Mary the mother of Jesus, Mary the mother of James, Salome (Matthew 27:57-61, 28:1, Mark 15:40-16:3, Luke 23:50-24:3, John 19:38-20:1).

The following words point to the respect and care we need to give to a body: "Caring attentiveness to the 'mortal remains' is a token of care and respect both for the one who has died and for those who grieve. The person is dead, the body will decay; relationships are broken; communities are dismembered. But the body was once—and still is—identified with the person who has died. The body was once—and still is—the medium by which we display the affection, loyalty, and honor due the person" (Allen Verhey, *The Christian Art of Dying*, 254).

Some people hesitate or refuse to come to a viewing for another reason. Their rationale is, "I want to remember her (our mother or my friend) when she was strong, healthy, and beautiful. I want to keep those memories as my final memories." Will these people hesitate to visit their friend, even their mother, after she has had a stroke and cannot speak? We expect they will, but we don't know. Yet, we need to be sensitive to those who are reluctant to see people in their weakness. When a friend has suffered a stroke or another debilitating disease, this is precisely the time we must come alongside to express our love, our presence, and our compassion. We cannot desert a person when he or she is suffering physically and is unable to respond. Further, will these people wish that their family members and friends will visit them when they are weak and frail? I believe that in most cases they would desire that their loved ones visit and care for them particularly when they are not well.

> **Honoring a Person whose Mortal Remains Are not as Desired**
>
> These reflections on viewing might give the impression that a body, at least the face, will offer a positive representation of the person. Yet, what about a situation where the body is severely damaged by an accident or fire? What about a situation where a person died but was not found for several days? We will want to have a sensitive and compassionate word in such situations—and then respond with grace.

a. Reasons for Viewing

Why then do we gather at a funeral home, or even in a home, to view a dead person? I will offer several reasons for doing so, recognizing that in our Western culture the practice is becoming less common. A related practice that is also less observed is for the community to gather at a graveside service. The following reasons are not given in any order of importance. When a family requests counsel or guidance regarding viewing, we can begin with these reasons.

> **Reasons for Viewing**
> 1. To express honor and gratitude
> 2. To remember special moments
> 3. To support one another in our grief and loss
> 4. To hold high the torch or baton of our loved one
> 5. To shut one door
> 6. To proclaim our Christian hope

a. To Express Honor and Gratitude

We gather to express our honor and our gratitude to the person who has meant so much to us. We pause, reflecting on the impact this person has made in our lives.

At the funeral home, the coffin is placed in the front of the chapel, allowing people to come quietly to the coffin and reflect. If the funeral home does not have a chapel, I recommend that the coffin be placed in the front of a church sanctuary. Individuals can visit in the foyer or further back in the sanctuary while other people pray and quietly reflect about the loved one in the coffin.

We are familiar with the fifth commandment: "Honor your father and your mother, so that you may live long in the land the LORD your God is giving you" (Exodus 20:12). When I observe families gathering at the coffin of a loved one, I must come to the deep conviction that here is a family that honors their father and their mother. God will bless this family in return. The command "Honor your father and your mother" is placed in a significant spot within God's Ten Words (Decalogue) that form his basic covenant between himself, the Lord God, and his redeemed people. God prefixed his Ten Words by noting his identity, "I am the LORD your God," and his act of redemption, "who brought you out of Egypt, out of the land of slavery" (Exodus 20:2). Then he declared how his people must live in relationship with him and with each other (Exodus 20:3-17). Applying this to ourselves, as those who follow the Lord God and are his redeemed people, we need to carefully consider the fifth word, commonly known as the fifth commandment, "Honor your father and your mother." I will briefly examine and apply this word as it applies to a funeral service.

We begin by noting that the entire command is, "Honor your father and your mother, so that you may live long in the land the LORD your God is giving you." Some people refer to the promise connected to this command and make this argument: "When children honor their parents, then they should live long and prosperous lives." But what if their days are neither long nor prosperous? The reverse argument is that when children abuse, disrespect, and neglect their parents, they should not live long and prosperous lives. But what if the children who do not honor their parents happen to live long and enjoyable lives? This interpretation is based on the Western attitude of individualism and what is best for each person. A better interpretation of the fifth command is based on the understanding that the overall good of the community must be the focus. Parents are the ones who will pass on the teaching and values of the community. When parents are not respected and revered in the community, then the assimilation of God's truth will suffer. The ultimate result is that the community will cease to exist and prosper under God's hand. The above thoughts are drawn from Rod J. K. Wilson, who explains that conversion is not simply an individual experience but a commitment to discipleship within a faith community. This means that the core issue throughout the Bible is relationships—our relationship with God, which is in the context of the Christian community. When children honor their parents and follow their parents' teaching from God, which will include the other nine words or commands from God, this will result in a healthy community where the life expectancy will be longer than in a community where these commands are violated (Rod J. K. Wilson, *Counseling and Community*, 60-66).

In summary, viewing a body in a coffin is certainly a fitting way in which children, family members, and friends honor a loved one. This is an expression of who we are—not merely separate and isolated individuals in a relationship with God, but people in relationship to God and people in loving and caring relationship with one another.

b. To Remember Special Moments

We gather to remember special moments, some painful but many pleasant and joyful. We gather to share these memories with an intimate circle of family and close friends. I will never forget the viewing of my mother, with our daughter holding her grandpa's hand. With family members solemnly standing around the coffin, individuals recalled moments about Grandma. Nothing can replace the impact of gathering around a grandmother or around a husband and sharing memories with family and friends.

We live in a time of mostly shallow communication. We text and communicate with many people, many of whom we hardly know—and we quickly forget almost everything we text or see on Facebook. But we will never forget an emotional sharing by an uncle or a brother as we gather around a dear mother. Also, we will never forget our own words, spoken out of a heart of love and gratitude. Yes, Grandmother will not hear us. But our cousins and all our family will know how much we loved our grandmother or mother.

c. To Support One Another in Our Grief and Loss

When we gather around the body of a loved one, we accept the harsh reality: "We have many memories with our dear mother or grandmother, but we will not make any more memories. We will never again hold her hand. We will never hear her words of love nor feel her warm embrace. This loss cannot be put into words. We are left speechless, numb. Nothing can replace what we are losing. We feel our loss and grieve deeply." Therefore, as we gather at a viewing, we support one another in our grief and loss. We live in a culture that attempts to minimize pain and grief. The Apostle Paul, who wrote, "Rejoice with those who rejoice," also wrote the next line: "Mourn with those who mourn" (Romans 12:15). In the Psalms, there are many more laments than psalms of praise. This is important to note because it reminds us that we are created to bring our griefs and losses to God and to do so in the company of other people.

At a viewing, a deliberate decision has been made to gather and support one another in our grief. I realize that some believers argue that, since we are anticipating the eternal home Jesus has prepared for us and we will be with him for all eternity, then there should be no sadness nor grieving in a funeral service. Further, these people maintain that Christians should not gather to grieve their loss. I will speak to this argument by drawing on two incidents in Jesus' life to demonstrate that he grieved deeply when he felt a major loss.

The first incident is when Jesus was with his friends, Martha and Mary, who were grieving the death of their brother Lazarus. As I read the graveside story about Jesus' friend Lazarus in John 11:1-44, I notice eight references to Jesus' deep emotions, particularly his grief and compassion. Certainly, we must affirm Jesus' words of assurance, "I am the resurrection and the life. He who believes in me will live, even though he dies, and whoever lives and believes in me will never die" (John 11:25-26). But even in the story when Jesus declared these reassuring words about himself, he expressed deep grief. As pastors, we make a serious oversight when we ignore Jesus' deep emotions, particularly Jesus' grief, as he wept with two sisters at the grave of their brother and his intimate friend. As we carefully read this graveside story, we will clearly perceive Jesus' emotions, as well as Jesus' focus on Martha and Mary's deep grief:

1. Jesus responded to Martha's statement of faith with the assurance, "Your brother will rise again" (verse 23).

2. When Martha answered, "I know he will rise again in the resurrection at the last day," Jesus assured Martha that she did not need to wait to receive the benefit of the power of God's resurrection because

standing in front of her in her time of grief was Jesus, "the resurrection and the life" (verses 24-26).

3. When Jesus saw Mary and the Jews who had come along with her weeping, we read, "He was deeply moved in spirit and troubled" (verse 33).

4. Jesus' question "Where have you laid him?" indicates that Jesus was interested in the loss of his friend Lazarus. Jesus did not minimize the grief but instead asked where the grave of his friend Lazarus was (verse 34).

5. The words "Come and see, Lord" were addressed to Jesus because these Jews knew that Jesus was caring and compassionate. They knew he would come with them and the two grieving sisters, Martha and Mary, to the tomb of Lazarus (verse 34).

6. The short sentence, "Jesus wept," points to Jesus' compassion and emotions (verse 35).

7. The Jews recognized Jesus' compassion and said, "See how he loved him!" (verse 36).

8. "Jesus, once more deeply moved, came to the tomb" (verse 38).

These eight expressions of Jesus' grief and compassion apply to the context of our deep grief. Even when our trust is secure and firm in Jesus, the Resurrection and the Life, we must and we will weep deeply for the loss we are feeling at that moment—a dear brother, mother, father, or child who is no more with us. When we follow Jesus' example, then deep grief and absolute trust will go together.

The second incident from Jesus' life that instructs us to grieve when we feel a deep loss is when Jesus was in the Garden of Gethsemane with his disciples. This story has three lessons we can draw from Jesus' example in regard to feeling and sharing grief:

1. As Jesus felt the intense pain in Gethsemane, he knew that he would be alive three days later. The hope of the resurrection did not keep Jesus from feeling the grief of the moment. This means that even though we believe that we and our loved ones will be with Jesus for all eternity, we still need to recognize the grief we are feeling in the time of a funeral and burial service.

2. We usually consider grief a response to something that has happened to us or to a loss we have experienced in the past. But the story of Jesus in Gethsemane tells us that we will grieve over an event or a loss that will happen in the future. In Jesus' case, he was anticipating all the abuse and suffering, rejection, and humiliation he would endure in the next hours.

3. When Jesus instructed his disciples to pray with him, he demonstrated that he needed them. The lesson is that we need one another in a time of loss and grief.

Genuine Christianity does not shrink back from death. It does not force a smile to mask our grieving. When we are sad because of the loss of a dear loved one, it will be obvious in our sorrow. We cannot cover up grief, nor should we attempt to do so. We must come alongside one another, even as Jesus did with his friends Martha and Mary. A Honduran proverb is: "Grief shared is half grief; joy shared is double joy." But even grief shared that becomes half grief is still grief. We should not try to hold back our grief. Nor should we forsake one another in our grief.

This is a lengthy argument for a viewing. Taking the time for viewing provides an opportunity for us to carry each other's burdens. We must come to a viewing to "weep with those who weep."

d. To Hold High the Torch or Baton of Our Loved One
Here I think of the metaphor of a relay race where one runner passes the torch or baton on to the next runner. When a family gathers around the coffin of a dear mother, there is a sense that the family members and friends are saying, "Mother, we thank God for your legacy, and we are committed to lift high the godly legacy you have given us." I believe that when a son or daughter walks into a quiet sanctuary with the coffin of a loved one, he or she is recommitting himself or herself to God and saying, "I thank God for you, Mother. I want to become like you. I want to follow God as you, my mother, did."

e. To Shut One Door
The fifth reason includes all the above reasons—to express honor, to remember special moments, to hold high the baton of a loved one, and to support one another in our grief. In the past, I have used the phrase "bringing closure." I am becoming convinced that this is neither a helpful nor an accurate phrase. I agree with these words, "The deepest rituals of death make it clear that 'closure' is neither achievable nor desirable" (Thomas G. Long and Thomas Lynch, *The Good Funeral*, 176).

As I stood in front of the coffin of my mother with my father, my wife, my children, and my siblings, I was saying a final "Goodbye." Yes, I thanked God for all that she meant to me. Yes, I was taking up the torch she had handed me throughout my life. Yes, I was supported by a loving family. But I was in deep grief because I knew this was the final time I would see her. From that moment on, I could recall memories but I could not make any more memories.

Viewing is necessary so that we can be released to move through our grief and on to the next phase, a difficult phase which will not include our loved one. Viewing is one aspect of closing a door so that we can open another door, stepping out of the room where our loved one remains behind and stepping into a room without the loved one.

Such a transition is necessary to make a partial closure when a loved one has left us. Having said this, the reality is that we can never achieve full closure. We simply move from a room where a loved one is left behind, shut the door, and move on—holding the memories and the loss in our hearts.

f. To Proclaim Our Christian Hope

This is the ultimate reason for viewing. How I wish that over every coffin were the words, "We preach Christ crucified and risen" (1 Corinthians 15), the church motto on the wall at the front of our church sanctuary. How I wish that over every coffin there was displayed a cross and an open grave. We gather to bow before the cross of Jesus, whose blood secured our salvation and the salvation of our loved one. We gather in grief, knowing that we will not see our loved one again here on earth. We gather in hope, knowing that we will see our loved one with Jesus in heaven. We gather in hope, knowing that Christ was crucified and rose from the dead. We gather in hope knowing that when we believe in Jesus crucified and risen, our sins are forgiven, we are daughters and sons of God, we have peace with God, and we will live eternally with Jesus. We gather to celebrate that our loved one is alive because Jesus rose from the dead.

> **Proclaiming Christian Hope**
> Even as we proclaim our Christian hope, a solemn question is, "How do we do this when we, as well as those in attendance, are fairly certain that the deceased was not a believer?" This difficult concern will be addressed in Chapter Ten: The Life Story: A Personal and Faith Legacy.

b. Three Concluding Thoughts on Viewing

1. Should a viewing include a brief meditation and prayer? A family might request that a pastor share some Bible verses and lead in a prayer. Or the family might select one of their own members to bring their hearts together under God. This might be a very short but compassionate and personal word, indicating that a family is stating, "Mother's life revolved around God, and when we gather for the last time with her, we will focus on God, as she did."

2. As family and close friends gather for a viewing, there might be a spontaneous time of sharing or even singing. Singing was very much a part of one family's life together. Therefore, they were considering whether they should sing one of their mother's favorite songs after the fellowship meal that followed the memorial service. What was planned to be one song expanded into an hour of singing their mother's many favorite songs. A viewing can be an opportunity to do something special as a family and

as close friends. May we be open to one another, hearing each other's hearts and walking together with sensitivity in this special moment.

3. Even as I have emphasized the value of viewing the body, I don't want to say that similar meaningful acts cannot be done without the body. Families might well have meaningful and personal times of sharing memories at other times and in other ways. But reflecting on photos of a loved one is not the same as reflecting on the actual face of the loved one.

3. Flowers

Flowers are a visual expression of our love—both for the deceased and for the family that remains behind.

Some people might respond, "Why provide flowers that will perish in several days?" This argument has as little validity as a husband excusing his refusal to give flowers to his wife, even on their anniversary or her birthday, with the argument, "Why should I give her flowers that will perish and wilt in several days? I want to give her something that she can keep and that has some practical value."

Other people might ask, "Why spend money for flowers for a person who is not able to appreciate them?" Flowers are for both the dead and for the living. Flowers are an expression of our love and of our support, and they will be seen by the living. But these flowers also express our love for the dead. The flowers show how much the loved one meant to us.

In some European cultures, the giving of flowers is a daily and regular practice, far more prevalent than in our Western culture. A husband will pick up a bouquet on his way home to express his love for his wife. He will not wait until her birthday or their anniversary. I believe we need to express our love in regular, tangible ways. Then, the giving of flowers at a funeral will be another natural expression of our love. May our expressions of love be extravagant and generous.

4. Donations in Memory of a Loved One

As noted above, I believe flowers should be bounteous and plentiful at a funeral service. I encourage the giving of flowers as something distinct from donations. They should not be made "in lieu of flowers."

When a family is choosing to encourage people to give donations in memory of their loved one, I suggest these words be used: "Donations in memory of (the name of the loved one) may be given to the (the name of a specific ministry or agency)."

I am aware that some families do not want to highlight any specific ministry. Their loved one might have given frequent and consistent contributions to a particular ministry or to many ministries. The family might choose not to direct people to give to a specific ministry but will instead say, "Please give a donation to the agency or ministry of your choice."

I propose another approach. I believe that a funeral service is an appropriate and natural venue in which to highlight a ministry, mission, agency, or foundation that a beloved mother believed in and supported. Can we, as pastors, be so bold as to go one step further? I suggest we ask the family whether they know if their mother or loved one supported a specific ministry. If so, they could select that ministry as the designated mission people can give donations towards—and then follow their mother's example and give to that ministry as well. I encourage the children to set an example that other people will follow. Having said all this, I never pressure any person in the matter of recommending donations but simply explain that this can be a loving way to follow the example set by their loved one, as well as to honor that person.

I will add two practical notes regarding donations:

First, if donations are designated for a specific ministry or agency and individuals expect to receive donation receipts, it is important that this ministry or agency is legally registered with the government.

Second, when some ministries or agencies become aware that donations will be given at a memorial service, these ministries might want to send a representative and set up a display. As the pastor responsible for the memorial service, I need to assure the family that there will not be any large display nor promotion of any ministry. Some ministries will want to use the occasion to promote themselves. However, the setting is a memorial service and not a promotional opportunity for any group, however worthy the ministry is.

5. Obituary, Eulogy, Life Story, Words of Tribute

It is necessary to be clear on the differences between the various written or spoken words about the loved one.

> **Obituary:** a short account of a person, comprised of key items
> **Eulogy or Life Story:** a spoken or written composition that honors a person and expresses good things about this person
> **Tribute:** words that express love for and honor of a person

a. An Obituary

An obituary is a short account of a person, relating highlights of the person's life. This is the account that will be forwarded to a local newspaper. This might also serve as a notification to people in the community that a person has passed away. A family might choose to place two notices in the paper, first a brief account that their loved one has passed away and then a longer announcement giving the details of the service time and place when these have been finalized.

b. A Life Story or Eulogy

The word "eulogy" is a compound word consisting of "*eu*," meaning "well" or "good," and "*logos*," meaning "word"; that is, a eulogy is "a good word" about a loved family member or friend. I use "eulogy" and "life story" interchangeably. In a life story, a person will begin with the basic facts that comprise an obituary and then expand on several parts of the person's story, including personal reflections or memories.

We all have a story. A funeral service provides an opportunity to write and then share our story. But our story is much more than "a string of biographical facts."

There are several questions regarding the eulogy. Who will write our story? What is the purpose of our story, either written or spoken? What will be included in our story?

I strongly encourage each of us to write our own story. We have the opportunity then to write out how we want to be remembered. What do we want included in a written or spoken legacy?

If we do not write our own story when we can choose what to include and when we have clarity of mind, then our children will need to compose a story when they are in grief. Also, if we have several children, would we prefer one of our children to write our life story?

Some families will maintain that there is no purpose in having a written life story if this will be read in the service. Even though a spoken life story and tributes will be given at a funeral, I encourage families to take the following perspective. A funeral is an ideal occasion for a family to provide a written legacy of their loved one, one that will be read and reread and cherished, not only by family but also by friends.

I compare a life story to a will. A will defines the legal distribution of a person's material possessions. However, through a life story, a person has the opportunity to leave a spiritual and personal legacy. In a life and faith account, a mother can record how she met God, list specific landmarks on her faith journey, recite favorite Bible verses, and explain what God meant to her. We will never fully know how our lives impact our children and grandchildren and friends, but in our faith journey we can share, "This is how Jesus impacted me. This is why I love Jesus."

What if the person has not written her eulogy/faith journey before she passed away? This provides the family with an opportunity to honor their loved one. As family members recall and write down memories of their mother, they have a wonderful opportunity to express their love. They will be able to let the other family members and their friends know who their mother was in a deeper and more genuine way than by merely giving a list of facts and minor events.

I remember one family who wanted to express their love for their mother in the best possible eulogy they could provide in the available time before the memorial service. Their intention was to have this available as a print-out with pictures at the memorial service. But the family member responsible for writing the life story kept on revising it and adding new items until shortly before the service. There were so many things she wanted to include. As a result, this family was unable to provide a printed life story at the time of the funeral, but they made a printed copy available to anyone who requested one afterward. They took the time to write a treasured story of their mother, a keepsake of her faith in God, and a reminder of her love for her family and of their love for her.

As pastors, we have an opportunity to encourage the children to take the time to show their love for their mother or father. We can encourage them to discover things they never knew about their grandmother. We can suggest that they include pictures that show how much their mother loved her family and they loved their mother. In our church, we help families print longer stories of their loved ones. Children will never be sorry for taking the extra time to write, not only a short obituary of core facts, but also a eulogy packed with memories and highlights of their parent's relationships, both with God and with people.

c. A Tribute

In a tribute, a person will share specific memories and express how the loved one made a positive impact on her/his life. Here I wish to offer two suggestions:

1. Every child and every grandchild might want to give a personal and even a lengthy tribute. We will want to affirm their intention to express their love for the one who has died. Therefore, when there are many children, many more grandchildren, and sometimes even great-grandchildren, my suggestion is to have one child speak for all her/his siblings and then have one grandchild speak for all the grandchildren. This suggestion also applies to the great-grandchildren. If this approach is not taken, the service can become very lengthy. If the service does run longer than usual, I assure the family that this is all good as well. It is the only time that family will provide this service for their loved one. Time should not be the final factor in selecting what to include in a service.

2. It is also a good idea to encourage more informal sharing during a luncheon. At that time, the children and other family members who might have hesitated to speak in the memorial service or did not have the opportunity to do so will be able to share more freely.

Having said all of the above, I never want to make anyone feel guilty or ashamed for not developing and presenting a life story. Some families and some specific members within a family find this relatively easy, but other families are not as comfortable with writing and public speaking. I want to emphasize that the thing that matters the most is what is in the heart, not how a life story will sound.

6. Grieving during a Public Service

In this section, I want to repeat the biblical injunction to "weep with those who weep" (Romans 12:5).

After a memorial service, a friend of the family approached me and said, "What is wrong with all of us? No one cried. No one showed any emotions. Did no one love our dear friend? Did none of the family love her?"

In many Western churches, we will likely never be accused of wailing loudly and tearing our clothes as expressions of grief. But have we gone too far in suppressing and restraining our emotions? If we genuinely love our mother (or whomever we are conducting the funeral service for), and if we believe we will never see her again here on earth, then this should be obvious in the expression of our deep sorrow.

I recall hearing the testimony of a widow whose husband was murdered while they were serving as missionaries. At that time, I was just beginning my pastoral ministry and had conducted only one or two funerals. But I sensed something was not right as I listened to her testimony. There seemed to be no expression of deep grief, but only a constant, glowing testimony of how God was with her. Certainly, I rejoiced that God was with her and that she felt God's presence. But why did she, a Christian leader, not hint at the grief of losing not only her husband but also the vision of being a missionary with him? Why did she need to be silent about her pain? Why did it appear as though only I sensed something was amiss as she told the story of the murder of her husband?

The words of the Teacher, son of David, king in Jerusalem, in Ecclesiastes 3:1-8 are regularly cited at funeral services. These words begin, "There is a time for everything, and a season for every activity under heaven." Then the Teacher lists fourteen opposites, such as a time to be born and a time to die, a time to plant and a time to uproot, and a time to embrace and a time to refrain from embracing. The two sets of opposites that apply to a funeral service are "weeping and laughing" and "mourning and dancing." I cannot go into detail on the subject of grief, loss, and mourning. That will require more space that I can give here. But I have heard how this passage has been misinterpreted and misused so that grieving people were pressured not to express their grief and loss.

I recall the close friend of a grieving widow who phoned and implored me to visit this widow. Her husband had passed away several years earlier. The reason this close friend wanted me to visit the still grieving widow was to counsel her that "She had grieved long enough and she needed to get over it and get on with life." This friend thought that I, as the pastor, could coerce the grieving widow out of her grief. Possibly some other pastor might have read Ecclesiastes 3:1-8 to her and then admonished her, "Sister, there was a time to weep and a time to mourn. But that time is long past. Now is a time to laugh and to dance. God gave you many good years with your husband. Remember those years and thank God for them. Now you need to move on." I trust that we, as pastors who are committed to diligently and accurately study the Bible, will see such counsel as a misinterpretation of Scripture as well as a lack of understanding of human nature. May we never cause people to feel guilty for grieving even if they believe in Jesus.

> **Ecclesiastes 3:1-8**
> When the Preacher listed fourteen opposites that begin with the words, "There is a time for everything," he did not:
> - promote a type of fatalism.
> - declare that everything that happens is good and is meant to happen when it does.
> - declare that since these things happen, we are to accept them with thankfulness and not with grief.

Jesus' words apply: "Blessed are those who mourn, for they will be comforted" (Matthew 5:4). Jesus did not promise, "Blessed are those who refrain from mourning." A stiff upper lip in a time of sorrow and not breaking down when we share a tribute to a dear mother might be good stoicism, but it is certainly not good Christianity.

Fellow pastors, I believe we have a lot to learn about grief and expressing it. We need to allow people to grieve and even to lament openly. We need to invite grieving and never tell people to stop grieving. Nor should we give Bible promises in an attempt to hold back grief-laden emotions. Why do we need to come to people's rescue with "cheer up" words and superficial and shallow promises? May we never shut down someone's weeping by quoting a Bible promise and offering a prayer—simply because of our own discomfort with displays of emotion. Often silence is the best expression of love when a person is in grief. Our body language, an embrace, and a listening ear will bring more comfort than words.

When we do not permit people to grieve in our midst, are we telling these people, "You cannot grieve. I don't know what to do with your loss"? When we stop people from grieving, they will submerge their grief and hurt, pushing it deeper inside. And they will conclude that God can't carry them in their grief and is not walking with them in the "valley of the shadow of death." They might also conclude that we, God's spokespeople, do not fully believe that we can trust God with our loss and our disappointments.

At a graveside or in a funeral service, we confidently (and rightly) declare the words of the Apostle Paul: "Brothers, we do not want you to be ignorant about those who fall asleep, or to grieve like the rest of men, who have no hope. We believe that Jesus died and rose again and so we believe that God will bring with Jesus those who have fallen asleep in him" (1 Thessalonians 4:13-14). Paul had no doubt that we would grieve when a loved one dies. When we experience loss, we must grieve. But we will not grieve "like the rest of men who have no hope." Our grieving includes hope—the hope that Jesus will return and receive each of us who believe in him. We must grieve, knowing that even though we can expect a glorious reunion in heaven, we will never see our loved one again here on earth.

> **Suffering**
> "Suffering is not a problem to be solved or a riddle to be explained, but rather it is a reality to be confronted in cooperation with God's own expressed intentions in the world." – the premise of *The Roots of Sorrow* by Phil C. Zylla

We must proclaim that Christ, as the last Adam, came into the fallen creation and fallen humanity in order to reconcile both to God. Jesus dealt the death blow to suffering and death in his own death. But, despite death having been dealt a death blow—the crucial victory in the war—the war is not yet over. There will come a day when Christ will return, and then he will "wipe every tear from their eyes" (Revelation 21:4). In this "in between" time, tears are the order of the day, along with mysteries, losses, sadness, and tragedy (W. Ross Hastings, *Where Do Broken Hearts Go?*, 99).

Sometimes I wish I was more courageous and had challenged more often the platitudes that some preachers and some other people have used. There is a powerful promise that was proclaimed many times by the famous preacher, Tony Campolo: "It's Friday, but Sunday's coming." As believers, we hold high the reality of Jesus' death and his triumphant victory over death on Easter resurrection morning. But, by popularizing these two key days in Jesus' life that are the foundation of our faith (crucifixion Friday and resurrection Sunday), do we ignore that we are living in Saturday time, with our weaknesses, our diseases, our grief, and our losses? Yes, praise God, Sunday's coming, but today is still Saturday. With the Apostle Paul, and with all believers, we have a solid and certain hope. We do not grieve like the rest of men. But we grieve. We must.

A painful story comes to mind. Several years ago, our church provided our facilities for a memorial service. During the luncheon, the pastor from another church went to various family members and friends and in a boisterous voice spoke so everyone could hear, "We are not here to grieve. We are here to celebrate. Let's all be happy." What if there was a little granddaughter present who deeply missed her grandmother? Any natural emotions of sadness in her would have been shut down by this unwise pastor who did not accurately represent a loving and compassionate God.

Jesus wept with the two sisters Mary and Martha at the death of their brother Lazarus. Jesus wept even though he knew that within minutes he would call Lazarus back to life. Paul described God as "the Father of compassion and the God of all comfort, who comforts us in all our troubles, so that we can comfort those in any trouble with the comfort we ourselves have received from God" (2 Corinthians 1:3). I have a sense that the pastor who told people not to grieve did not know what it felt like to mourn. Or, at least, he was unable to accept the full range of human emotions, including those of grief and loss.

In our Western society, we want formulas, answers, and solutions. How has our theology of suffering become compromised as we seek to fit into our modern world? Is this not what happens when we present a view of suffering that is neither true to life nor true to the Bible? How can we, as those who are committed to speak God's truth and apply it faithfully, attempt to explain away suffering, to avoid suffering, or even to try to explain what God is doing?

7. Children

As pastors, we have the opportunity to lead on the question of how children will be included in the funerals of their grandparents, parents, and dear elderly friends. We do so both by our caring example and with our words. Do we unnecessarily keep children from experiencing the loss of a grandparent or another loved one? Children might have watched as a family pet, a cat or a bird, has died. We take little children and show them newborn babies and want them to appreciate the joy we experience. Yet, we hesitate to have children see the still body of a grandmother and sense our deep sorrow. However, as children observe the death of a grandmother and know their grandmother will never be there for them again, they must be conscious of our love and support. They must know that we will walk with them through their valley of the shadow of death because little children can best experience God's love and care through us, their parents, uncles, and aunts.

8. Bulletins

A memorial bulletin is an opportunity for the family to express their love to the one who has died. A bulletin is also a short, clear legacy that family and friends can take home. One item to be included is the eulogy or life story. I encourage families to take as much space as they wish to express affection for their loved one. Friends appreciate a printed family tree that includes the children and grandchildren. If the deceased had a special poem or a favorite Bible verse, this could be included as well. There should also be a list of the pallbearers. Pallbearers should understand it is a privilege to serve and an honor to be recognized. The bulletin should also include a note of thanks for the love and support expressed, an invitation to a luncheon after the service, and an explanation regarding donations in memory of the loved one.

I realize a funeral home might provide a small card that includes the most basic items, such as the name of the person, the person's date of birth and date of death, a photo, the time of the funeral service, and possibly a poem or familiar Bible passage such as Psalm 23. Pastors must never minimize the value of the card the funeral home provides. But we have a distinct opportunity and, I believe, a responsibility to encourage and to help families to provide a larger bulletin that will be a valued memory of a loved one.

When a family asks how many bulletins should be printed, my answer includes the following: First, unlike other church bulletins that will not be kept, family members and friends will want their own bulletin and will want to take copies for people who cannot attend the service. Second, if more people come to the service than expected, we will want to do our best to have more copies available. As soon as I realize that more are needed, I ask the church office staff to print extra copies and make them available during the service if possible.

9. Hymns and Special Music

As a pastor, I encourage people to plan their own funerals. By this I do not just mean that they meet with a funeral director. I also urge them to think through what they wish to have included in their funeral service. As people plan their funeral service, I encourage them to write down the titles of the songs they would like sung. Sometimes they will write down the names of the musicians they would like to be asked to perform. The family will usually appreciate it when detailed instructions are left by the loved one.

When a parent has not written down clear instructions that include favorite hymns, the family might turn to the pastor and ask, "What were some songs our mother loved?" or "What songs do you recommend we sing?" Usually, as pastors, we will not have a specific answer to the first question. In that case, we will want to be clear about the purpose of songs in a funeral service and suggest that this give direction to the songs that are selected.

Our faith is rooted in a powerful, loving God who is with us now and who desires a relationship with us, his creation and redeemed people, forever. Our faith has a future. It is going somewhere—to a glorious union with our Creator and Savior. Hymns and songs which express confidence, trust, and hope in our faithful God are an excellent way to remind the grieving family of these truths. When they feel deep-seated grief and might even feel deserted and forgotten by God, hearing the old familiar hymns can be comforting. If one of the mourners has turned away from God, these hymns will remind this person that God does care. The songs assure the people in a funeral service that their faith is based not only on a sovereign, almighty God, but also on a compassionate God. He is Lord of today, when they feel grief, but also of tomorrow, when they will be with Jesus, their Savior and their Creator. Today they can sing "What a Friend we have in Jesus." But the grieving family members can also joyfully sing, "There is coming a day when my Jesus I shall see." As pastors, we want to encourage families to sing songs of their faith.

Reflections

1. What title do you prefer to use for a service you lead—funeral service, memorial service, celebration of life, or maybe something else? What are the reasons for your selection?

2. As pastors, we want to be aware of our own opinions on sensitive matters such as having a viewing. Here again, our goal should be to express compassion and walk with the grieving family. May we never consciously or even flippantly dismiss the family members' suggestions.

3. When we, as pastors, talk about the purpose and contents of a eulogy, it is best that we can do so as those who have carefully thought through and written our own life story. In other words, we should want to set an example which will be an encouragement to others regarding the value of writing a life story.

Prayer

Heavenly Father, as I lead a family in this special service, may I do so with a spirit of compassion. Certainly, I wish that all the parts of the service will come together smoothly. But when I realize all the details that are involved in a funeral service, may I not get stuck on things that are not central or over which I have no control. May my focus be on what is core—on your faithfulness and mercy in the lives of all of us. Above all, may you, God, be glorified, and may people feel your compassion in the funeral service. In Jesus' name, Amen.

Chapter Seven
The Burial, Interment, or Committal Service

On one level, the name "committal service" implies that the body or the ashes are committed to the ground. However, we want to perceive this service on a deeper level—it represents our final act of committing or entrusting our loved one to our God.

The same service is appropriate for the burial of a body or for burying cremated ashes or for placing the ashes in a columbarium.

The word "interment" refers to the act of interring or burying. It comes from the Latin *"in"* (in) and *"terra"* (earth) and therefore means placing "in the earth."

This chapter is divided into two major parts. The first concerns the words spoken in a burial service, and the second offers guidelines for the specific parts of a burial service. Regarding the words spoken, I will first make suggestions from a free church tradition and then from a more liturgical tradition.

1. Burial Words from a Free Church Tradition

When I prepare for a burial service, I realize this is often the most significant event for the grieving family. My goal is to hear God's heart and mind. I ask myself what might be the words that God wants this family to hear. Then I want to speak from my heart so that the family and friends will be comforted with God's love. I can also draw upon a rich church heritage of words that godly men and women in the past have written for a burial service. I will include some of these words in the section on committal words and the committal prayers.

A normal burial service will last about eight to ten minutes. There will be several parts to the service: personal words to the family, words of comfort, words of hope, committal words, and a committal prayer.

a. Personal Words to the Family

In three or four sentences, I seek to make a personal connection with the family, noting the finality of this moment and the reality that it is the last time they will be with the deceased loved one. I will also usually mention a positive experience I have had with the loved one. The reason I include this is to give the grieving family an assurance that I have a relationship with the one who has died. Often, I do not know many of the family members, but I believe they will sense my compassion—and, I trust, God's care for them—when I relate a personal incident. Having stated that I will often begin with a personal remembrance, I must add that there will be times when I believe this is neither necessary nor appropriate. Here, as in the other parts of the burial service, I seek to be sensitive to God's leading.

b. Words of Comfort

Next, I offer words of comfort and hope. This is the main part of a burial service. At times, I will introduce these words with a question such as, "Can I invite us to ask: if your mother or grandmother could address you one final time, what might she say this morning as we gather around her casket?" Then I will speak words of comfort and words of hope, all based on God's promises. Here are some selected themes with Bible readings.

i. You are not alone.

I reassure the people who are gathering at the grave of a loved one that they are not alone. They have one another, and their family and friends are with them. I also state that other people are supporting them with their prayers and love.

ii. God will comfort.

We are comforted by God, whom the Apostle Paul worshiped with these words: "Praise be to the God and Father of our Lord Jesus Christ, the Father of all compassion and the God of all comfort, who comforts us in all our troubles, so that we can comfort those in any trouble with the comfort we ourselves have received from God" (2 Corinthians 1:3, 4).

Jesus assures us, "Blessed are those who mourn, for they will be comforted" (Matthew 5:4).

God's Holy Spirit is present. The familiar words from Psalm 23 assure us of God's compassion: "Even though I walk through the valley of the shadow of death, I will fear no evil, for you are with me" (Psalm 23:4).

We are assured that God is attentive to our prayers. When we are unsure of what to pray, or our grief is too deep for us to pray, we know that the Holy Spirit is "interceding for us with groans that words cannot express" (1 Peter 3:12, Romans 8:26).

The Apostle John described how Jesus comforted Martha and Mary at the graveside of their brother Lazarus. John recorded that when Jesus saw Mary weeping, He was deeply moved and wept as well (John 11:33-35). I reassure the grieving family that Jesus feels their grief as they are standing at the graveside of their loved one just as Jesus felt the grief of his friends Martha and Mary at that graveside near Bethany nearly two thousand years earlier.

As those who lead a family in a burial service, we pastors will select which Bible passages and words from God are most appropriate. This principle applies in this part of the service as in the other parts—we must be fully convinced that we believe what we are saying. This will be evident in how we convey these truths. If, however, we are not fully convinced that our God is a God of comfort, then we need to search our own hearts. We are not only sharing truths from the Bible. We also need to speak out of a personal, deep relationship with a loving and compassionate God. May God give us grace to speak his word and share his love through us.

iii. God is gracious and compassionate.

Lamentations 3:21-26 say, "Yet this I call to mind and therefore I have hope: Because of the LORD's great love we are not consumed, for his compassions never fail. They are new every morning; great is your faithfulness. I say to myself, 'The LORD is my portion; therefore, I will wait for him.' The LORD is good to those whose hope is in him, to the one who seeks him; it is good to wait quietly for the salvation of the LORD."

At any graveside service, there will likely be regrets on several levels. Possibly the family members know that the loved one whom they are laying to rest expressed concerns and raised issues that were not resolved. Also, the people at the graveside might have their own regrets. There might even be unresolved difficulties or conflicts. When people are gathered at the graveside, they need to be reassured that God is forgiving and compassionate.

iv. God is faithful in keeping his word.

As individuals gather at the graveside of a loved one, they might have doubts or questions. Therefore, I believe it is appropriate to include Bible passages that speak of God's commitment to his promises. The following verses express God's commitment to his covenant, words that speak of assurance at the time of death:.

• "Yet to all who received him, to those who believed in his name, he gave the right to become children of God—children born not of natural descent, nor of human decision or a husband's will, but born of God" (John 1:12-13).

• "For it is by grace you have been saved, through faith—and this not from yourselves, it is the gift of God—not by works, so that no one can boast" (Ephesians 2:8-9).

• "That if you confess with your mouth, 'Jesus is Lord,' and believe in your heart that God raised him from the dead, you will be saved. For it is with your heart that you believe and are justified, and it is with your mouth that you confess and are saved. As the Scripture says, 'Anyone who trusts in him will never be put to shame.' For there is no difference between Jew and Gentile—the same Lord is Lord of all and richly blesses all who call on him, for, 'Everyone who calls on the name of the Lord will be saved'" (Romans 10:9-13).

Often, the pastor who presides at a graveside service will say something such as this: "The person who passed away (use the name) will have heard words such as Jesus gave to the faithful servant: 'Well done, good and faithful servant! You have been faithful with a few things; I will put you in charge of many things. Come and share your master's happiness!'" (Matthew 25:21). Having said this myself, I am reflecting on whether I can be so bold as to declare that the person will hear this from Jesus. Will I myself hear the words, "Well done, good and faithful servant"? I trust I will. But is this not up to Jesus to declare and not myself or any other pastor? Only he knows our hearts.

Similarly, is it appropriate for us to say that these words by the Apostle Paul can be claimed by the deceased: "I have fought the good fight, I have finished the race, I have kept the faith. Now there is in store for me the crown of righteousness, which the Lord, the righteous Judge, will award to me on that day—and not only to me, but also to all who have longed for his appearing" (2 Timothy 4:7-8)?

c. Words of Hope

Next, I will offer words of hope such as the following:

i. Jesus is the resurrection and the life.

Our faith is placed in Jesus, who declared, "I am the resurrection and the life. He who believes in me will live, even though he dies; and whoever lives and believes in me will never die. Do you believe this?" (John 11:25-26). These words reassure us that Jesus is the basis of our hope. I might read these words and then conclude, "(Give the name) answered 'Yes' to Jesus' question. Therefore, we can be assured that she is alive today."

ii. Jesus' resurrection is the basis of our resurrection.

Paul's words in his first letter to the Christians in Corinth assure believers that Jesus' resurrection is the foundation of our resurrection. I often use selected verses from 1 Corinthians 15: "For what I received I passed on to you as of first importance: that Christ died for our sins according to the Scriptures, that he was buried, that he was raised on the third day according to the Scriptures....But Christ has indeed been raised from the dead, the firstfruits of those who have fallen asleep....Listen, I tell you a mystery: We will not all sleep, but we will all be changed—in a flash, in the twinkling of an eye, at the last trumpet. For the trumpet will sound, the dead will be raised imperishable, and we will be changed. For the perishable must clothe itself with the imperishable, and the mortal with immortality. When the perishable has been clothed with the imperishable, and the mortal with immortality, then the saying that is written will come true: 'Death has been swallowed up in victory.' 'Where, O death, is your victory? Where, O death, is your sting?' The sting of death is sin, and the power of sin is the law. But thanks be to God! He gives us the victory through our Lord Jesus Christ" (1 Corinthians 15:3, 4, 20, 51-57).

iii. Jesus is preparing a home for us.

Jesus assures us of an eternal home with him. Jesus' familiar promise in John 14 is taken from the cultural setting of his day. When the groom and bride were engaged, the groom would return to his father's house and prepare a home specifically designed for his bride and himself. When the room was ready, the groom would return to get the bride, and then she would live with him. Jesus, the Groom, has paid the necessary price for us, the church, his bride, with his death on the cross. After his ascension, he returned to God, his Father, to build a home for us. At times, I will explain the Jewish cultural custom out of which Jesus developed his promise to first build a home for us and then return and take us, the bride, to be with him forever.

The Bible is rich with numerous metaphors that describe Jesus' relationship with us. At a funeral service, we frequently read Psalm 23 and note the Shepherd-sheep relationship. This is certainly a comforting metaphor to emphasize that Jesus is with us during life and especially during difficult times of loss and grief. But the Shepherd-sheep relationship clearly will not have the comforting and intimate expression that the Groom-bride relationship presents: "Do not let your hearts be troubled. Trust in God; trust also in me. In my Father's house are many rooms; if it were not so, I would have told you. I am going there to prepare a place for you. And if I go and prepare a place for you, I will come back and take you to be with me that you also may be where I am. You know the way to the place where I am going....I am the way and the truth and the life. No one comes to the Father except through me" (John 14:1-4, 6).

iv. We have been promised an eternal glory.
　　The Apostle Paul assured us: "Therefore, we do not lose heart. Though outwardly we are wasting away, yet inwardly we are being renewed day by day. For our light and momentary troubles are achieving for us an eternal glory that far outweighs them all. So we fix our eyes not on what is seen, but on what is unseen. For what is seen is temporary, but what is unseen is eternal. Now we know that if the earthly tent we live in is destroyed, we have a building from God, an eternal house in heaven, not built by human hands" (2 Corinthians 4:16-5:1).

v. We are assured that Jesus will return to take us home to be with himself.
　　The Apostle Paul also wrote: "Brothers, we do not want you to be ignorant about those who fall asleep, or to grieve like the rest of men, who have no hope. We believe that Jesus died and rose again and so we believe that God will bring with Jesus those who have fallen asleep in him. According to the Lord's own word, we tell you that we who are still alive, who are left till the coming of the Lord, will certainly not precede those who have fallen asleep. For the Lord himself will come down from heaven, with a loud command, with the voice of the archangel and the trumpet call of God, and the dead in Christ will rise first. After that, we who are still alive and are left will be caught up together with them in the clouds to meet the Lord in the air. And so, we will be with the Lord forever. Therefore encourage each other with these words" (1 Thessalonians 4:14-18).

vi. We have the promise of heaven.
　　In Revelation, the Apostle John gave us this description: "Then I saw a new heaven and a new earth, for the first heaven and the first earth had passed away, and there was no longer any sea. I saw the Holy City, the new Jerusalem, coming down out of heaven from God, prepared as a bride beautifully dressed for her husband. And I heard a loud voice from the throne saying, 'Now the dwelling of God is with men, and he will live with them. They will be his people, and God himself will be with them and be their God. He will wipe every tear from their eyes. There will be no more death or mourning or crying or pain, for the old order of things has passed away'" (Revelation 21:1-4). The vision continued in the next chapter: "Then the angel showed me the river of the water of life, as clear as crystal, flowing from the throne of God and of the Lamb down the middle of the great street of the city. On each side of the river stood the tree of life, bearing twelve crops of fruit, yielding its fruit every month. And the leaves

of the tree are for the healing of the nations. No longer will there be any curse. The throne of God and of the Lamb will be in the city, and his servants will serve him. They will see his face, and his name will be on their foreheads. There will be no more night. They will not need the light of a lamp or the light of the sun, for the Lord God will give them light. And they will reign for ever and ever" (Revelation 22:1-5).

d. Committal Words

On the basis of God's Word, knowing that a loved one trusted in Jesus, and knowing God is true to his character and to his promises, I conclude with words such as:

- Today we take comfort that ____ was faithful to the very end.
- We are assured of the better life that she has.
- Now she is with God. This is a precious thought!
- God, in his love and wisdom, has taken ____ out of this world. As a kind Shepherd, God has taken her to be with himself.
- We therefore commit her body (or ashes) to the ground, earth to earth, ashes to ashes (if the body has been cremated), dust to dust.
- We look forward to Jesus' second coming when her body will be transformed to be like Jesus' body.

A Model of a Committal Prayer

Our Heavenly Father, you are the Giver and Sustainer of life, but you also take away life through death.

We thank you for the memories we have of ____.

We thank you for her/his love to____ and to the family.

Above all, we thank you that she believed in you and then shared your love, your Word, and your compassion with so many people.

We have peace today, knowing that her sins are forgiven, she received you as her Savior, and she is now with you in heaven.

As we lay her body/ashes to rest, we pray that you watch over this hallowed place in holy remembrance until the trumpet shall sound and the dead shall be raised in glory.

Father, bless the family that wait here on earth until that triumphant day when those who know you as Savior shall be joined together in heaven.

To him who is able to keep you from falling and to present you before his glorious presence without fault and with great joy—to the only God our Savior be glory, majesty, power, and authority, through Jesus Christ our Lord, before all ages, now and forever more. And now, may the peace of God, which transcends all understanding, guard your hearts and your minds in Christ Jesus.

In the name of our gracious and loving Lord Jesus Christ, we pray, Amen.

e. Committal Prayer

The committal prayer should contain these elements:
- thanksgiving for the person's life
- an expression of hope in God
- committal of the body
- committal of the loved ones to God's care
- a benediction

2. Burial Words from Other Christian Traditions

The burial words from a free church tradition in the previous section are the words I use at a graveside service. I will never use all the Bible passages listed there. I will adapt, add, or change as I sense appropriate for each situation.

However, I firmly believe there is also much benefit in studying the manuals, handbooks, and prayer books from various denominations. Thomas Long notes, "The free-church pastor can gain much from tracing the maps of the prayer-book traditions" (Thomas G. Long, *Accompany Them with Singing*, 151). When we have the awesome responsibility to lead a family in a funeral service and then a burial service, I trust we do not just put together these services with minimal thought or preparation and without recognizing the significance of the event. I trust that we have carefully planned the journey we are leading the family and the congregation on. May our words be chosen carefully to point all of those present to our faithful and compassionate God. A comprehensive resource that draws from eleven denominations is *The Baker Funeral Handbook*. In the appendix is a list of other books and resources.

At a burial service, the community of faith carries the deceased to the grave and bids farewell, entrusting her or him to God. My strong desire is that the larger community of faith, not only the immediate family, would be present at a graveside service. As a church family, we have worshiped and served with this member. Now, in her or his final moments, we want to entrust this person to God as we then will continue the service God has for us, grieving the loss of this person but serving with the hope we have.

a. Commendation and Committal

The burial service consists of two main parts: the commendation to God of the one who has died and the committal of the body of the deceased to the planned burial. The following words of commendation and committal are drawn from several sources, particularly from Perry H. Biddle, *A Funeral Manual;* Paul E. Engle, ed., *The Baker Funeral Handbook*; and John Rempel, ed. *Minister's Manual.*

i. The Commendation of the One who Has Died to God
Into your hands, eternal God, we commend [your servant] ____. [Receive unto yourself, we humbly ask, a sheep of your fold, a lamb of your flock, a sinner of your redeeming.] Receive ____ into the arms of your mercy, [into the company of your saints, into everlasting peace]. Amen.

Let us commend __ to the mercy of God, our Maker and Redeemer.

ii. The Committal of the Body of the Deceased to the Plan of Burial
"Seeing that the earthly life of [our brother/sister] ____ has come to an end, we commit his/her body to be buried, earth to earth, ashes to ashes, dust to dust, [confident of the resurrection to eternal life through our Lord Jesus Christ].
(The body is lowered into the grave, where applicable.)
____, may God bless you and keep you. May the very face of God shine upon you and be gracious to you. May God's presence embrace you and give you peace. Amen.

b. An alternate Commendation and Committal
Leader: Give rest, O God, to your servant with your saints, where sorrow and pain are no more, neither sighing, but life everlasting. Creator and Maker of humankind, you only are immortal, and we are mortal, formed of the earth, and to the earth we shall return: for so you did ordain when you created us, saying, Dust thou art and unto dust thou shalt return.
People: All we go down to the dust, and, weeping, over the grave, we make our song: Alleluia, alleluia, alleluia. Give rest, O Christ, to your servant with your saints, where sorrows and pain are no more, neither sighing, but life everlasting. Amen (from *Minister's Manual*, edited by John Rempel, 194-197).

c. Lutheran Commendation and Committal
The Commendation
Pastor: Into your hands, O merciful Savior, we commend your servant (name). Acknowledge, we humbly beseech you, a sheep of your own fold, a lamb of your own flock, a sinner of your own redeeming. Receive him/her into the arms of your mercy, into the blessed rest of everlasting peace, and into the glorious company of the saints in light. Amen.

The Committal
Pastor: One or more of these scriptures may be sung or said.
- "In my anguish I cried to the LORD, and he answered by setting me free....It is better to take refuge in the LORD than to trust in men. It is better to take refuge in the LORD than to trust in princes....I was pushed back and about to fall, but the LORD helped me....Shouts of joy and victory

resound in the tents of the righteous; the LORD's right hand has done mighty things! The LORD's right hand is lifted high; the LORD's right hand has done mighty things!...Open for me the gates of righteousness; I will enter and give thanks to the LORD. This is the gate of the LORD through which the righteous may enter (Psalm 118:5, 8-9, 13, 15-16, 19-20)."• "I know that my Redeemer lives, and that in the end he will stand upon the earth. And after my skin has been destroyed, yet in my flesh I will see God" (Job 19:25-26).

• "For none of us lives to himself alone and none of us dies to himself alone. If we live, we live to the Lord; and if we die, we die to the Lord. So, whether we live or die, we belong to the Lord" (Romans 14:7-8).

• "I am the resurrection and the life. He who believes in me will live, even though he dies; and whoever lives and believes in me will never die" (John 11:25-26).

Prayer
Almighty God, by the death and burial of Jesus, your anointed, you have destroyed death and sanctified the graves of all your saints. Keep our brother/sister whose body we now lay to rest, in the company of all your saints, and at the last, raise him/her up to share with all your faithful people the endless joy and peace won through the glorious resurrection of Christ our Lord, who lives and reigns with you and the Holy Spirit, one God now and forever. Amen.

Lessons
One of the following lessons may be read:
• "Jesus replied, 'The hour has come for the Son of Man to be glorified. I tell you the truth, unless a kernel of wheat falls to the ground and dies, it remains only a single seed. But if it dies, it produces many seeds. The man who loves his life will lose it, while the man who hates his life in this world will keep it for eternal life. Whoever serves me must follow me; and where I am, my servant also will be. My Father will honor the one who serves me'" (John 12:23-26).
• "Listen, I tell you a mystery: We will not all sleep, but we will all be changed—in a flash, in the twinkling of an eye, at the last trumpet. For the trumpet will sound, the dead will be raised imperishable, and we will be changed. For the perishable must clothe itself with the imperishable, and the mortal with immortality. When the perishable has been clothed with the imperishable, and the mortal with immortality, then the saying that is written will come true: 'Death has been swallowed up in victory.' 'Where, O death, is your victory? Where O death, is your sting?' The sting of death is sin, and the power of sin is the law. But thanks be to God! He gives us the victory through our Lord Jesus Christ" (1 Corinthians 15:51-57).

- "But our citizenship is in heaven. And we eagerly await a Savior from there, the Lord Jesus Christ, who, by the power that enables him to bring everything under his control, will transform our lowly bodies so that they will be like his glorious body" (Philippians 3:20-21).

Prayer
The coffin is lowered into the grave or placed in its resting place. Earth may be cast on the coffin as the minister says:
In sure and certain hope of the resurrection to eternal life through our Lord Jesus Christ, we commend to almighty God our brother/sister (name), and we commit his/her body to the ground/the deep/the elements/resting place; earth to earth, ashes to ashes, dust to dust. The Lord bless him/her and keep him/her. The Lord make his face to shine on him/her and be gracious to him/her. The Lord look upon him/her with favor and give him/her peace. Amen.
Lord, remember us in your kingdom, and teach us to pray: Our Father in heaven, hallowed be your name, your kingdom come, your will be done on earth as it is in heaven. Give us today our daily bread. Forgive us our debts, as we also have forgiven our debtors. And lead us not into temptation but deliver us from the evil one. For yours is the kingdom and the power and the glory forever. Amen.
Lord Jesus, by your death you took away the sting of death. Grant to us, your servants, so to follow in faith where you have led the way, that we may at length fall asleep peacefully in you and wake in your likeness; to you, the author and giver of life, be all honor and glory, now and forever. Amen.

The Blessing
The minister blesses the people:
The God of peace—who brought again from the dead our Lord Jesus Christ, the great shepherd of the sheep, through the blood of the everlasting covenant—make you perfect in every good work to do his will, working in you that which is well-pleasing in his sight; through Jesus Christ, to whom be glory forever and ever. Amen.
Let us go in peace.

3. Parts of a Burial Service

a. Practical Guidelines for a Burial Service

As pastors, we have the God-given responsibility to speak his words in a burial service. But we will also have the opportunity to provide guidelines and suggestions on practical items involved in a burial service.

Before I address these, I want to make the following comment. A burial service is, in my perception, the most critical and solemn ceremony in our society. Therefore, it is very important not only that all things will be done with excellence but also that the family receives the assurance that all will be done correctly and as they requested. This is critical when the family has given specific instructions. In this regard, it is very important that a pastor connect with the funeral director in all phases of what takes place at the cemetery. Funeral directors will each have their way of carrying out their responsibilities, even as they all strive to do what is best. It is up to us, as pastors, to be alert to know how each director is leading the service and to work together with her/him. For instance, the funeral director will instruct the pastor on the specific path to take from the hearse to the gravesite. Then, it is our responsibility to lead the way.

The following are several specific items that I, as the pastor, ensure are taken care of:

• When the family has arrived at the cemetery and before the casket is taken from the hearse, I will ask a family leader whether everyone who is expected to be present is at the cemetery. If a family member is still on the way, I will insist that the burial ceremony be delayed until everyone is present.

• Before I begin the ceremony, I, along with the funeral director, will invite those in attendance to come as close as possible. I will then speak slowly, clearly, and loudly.

• I will ask whether there are any specific items to be used in the ceremony and ensure that these are arranged where they need to be.

• At the end of the burial service, I will ensure that instructions are clear on where the family will gather before the funeral service.

b. Cremation

Are there any specific concerns if the burial is a cremation?

My words will be similar, except that in the committal, I will add "ashes to ashes." However, a common practice with cremation is that a funeral director will not be present at the cemetery. Then I, as the pastor, must be clear on all the details and lead with confidence. I need to be certain about who will lower

---

Preparing for a Funeral

In a how-to manual on preparing your own funeral was an expression something like this: "Whenever something is made, someone can make it cheaper." The intent seemed to be to give guidelines on how to spend as little as possible on a person's funeral. However, in some cultures it is a sign of honor to provide the best for a person's memorial service, and it is considered a shameful act to be perceived to be trying to save money.

the urn into the specific hole. Will I do this or will a designated family member?

c. Caskets and Coffins

A question that is implied, if not asked, is, "Why spend money on an elaborate coffin?" Coffins, like many other aspects of a funeral, can be approached in several ways. (The issue of whether to have a coffin, which is related to the question of whether to have a traditional burial or a cremation, was addressed in the "Consumerism" section of Chapter Two.) Once the choice for burial has been made, the next question is the type and cost of a coffin. Certainly, cost is a factor, and the funeral director will provide specific options, including the costs. I will be so bold as to

> **Casket or Coffin?**
> Is a casket the same as a coffin? In common usage, these will often be interchanged. The term "casket" denotes a chest or container intended for treasured items. When this word is used in the funeral context, it certainly implies that the body is treasured. The term "coffin" comes originally from the Greek word "*koffinos*," meaning "a basket."

comment briefly on the matter of caskets or coffins. It seems that the general public has come to the conclusion that funeral directors' primary purpose is "the sale of boxes" (coffins) and that they will take advantage of people's grief to pressure them to purchase a product they don't want and cannot afford. I have not found this to be the case with the funeral directors I have been involved with. But there are other aspects that cannot be measured by dollars, as will be evident in the following scenarios:

> This might seem to be a strange comparison but perhaps a useful one. We won't mistake a large diamond for a good marriage, nor will we conclude that a walnut, elaborate casket is a sign of a good funeral. An expensive casket might be either a sign of honor by the family or a recognition of the selection made by the deceased. We don't know. However, when a family is wealthy and selects the cheapest coffin, this might raise questions. In all situations, may we never be judgmental. We will not know the reasons a certain casket was selected. And even if we do, may we still be gracious.

- Will a grandson ever forget the time he stood between two cousins, carrying the coffin of his dear grandmother?
- Will a widow ever forget the moment she placed her hand on the coffin of her deceased husband, saying, "I love you. We'll meet again"?
- Will a family ever forget the time each family member

carefully and lovingly placed a flower on the coffin of their dear mother?
• When a granddaughter has lost her way but is standing with a loving family, will not her heart be softened as she watches a coffin holding her grandmother being lowered into the ground?

My intent in providing these few words comparing a traditional burial and a cremation is not to place a higher value on one over the other. I simply wish to help us recognize that there will be adjustments in the burial service. When these are acknowledged, our ministry as pastors is to lead in the best possible manner.

d. Pallbearers

There is something that happens in the heart of a son or a daughter, a grandson or a granddaughter, as this person helps carry the casket of a mother or grandmother. This person will sense a special bond to the person she is carrying, as well as to the other people who are carrying the coffin with her.

It is important to include the names of all the pallbearers in the bulletin. If there are more than six people whom the family desires to be involved as pallbearers, I suggest that the other people be designated as "honorary pallbearers." In the event that the family has seven or eight people and only six can carry the coffin, I recommend that the other one or two individuals walk immediately behind the coffin.

When the family requests direction in the selection of pallbearers, I urge the family to ensure that all groups within the family are represented. At times, a young granddaughter or grandson is invited to walk with me, the pastor, as we lead the pallbearers. This may seem a small gesture towards the young member of the family, but I believe this person will be deeply touched to be given this special honor.

Also, when a family has a very small group of people who can serve as pallbearers, we, as pastors, along with the funeral director, need to ensure that enough other people will be available to help. It is our responsibility, along with the funeral director, to ensure that the family's wishes are met.

Here, as in all the planning of a funeral, this reality applies: the family will usually be unfamiliar with the necessary details, but we, as pastors, will normally have considerable experience and therefore should be aware of the details. This means we need to think ahead to ensure the details are in place. Then the family can best do what is their responsibility and privilege—carry their loved one to the final resting place.

4. Special Features in a Burial Service

One of my goals is to make each funeral service, as well as each burial service, special for the person involved. I will ask the family if they are planning to have a specific feature included in the burial service. Then, just before the burial service begins, I will make certain that all the details are clear. Special expressions of love might include the following:

a. Placing Flowers on a Coffin

These flowers represent a distinctive but final expression of the relationship between the family members and their loved one in the coffin. The funeral director or the oldest family member will give the flowers to the family members, beginning with the immediate family members. When family members place flowers on a coffin and then observe the coffin with their flowers being lowered into the ground, there is a final, but loving sense of farewell. What better way to say, "Good-bye, until we meet again in heaven," than with roses, symbols of love, that have been placed there by each family member.

b. Distributing Flowers from the Casket Spray

Taking flowers from the coffin spray and giving one to every family member and close friend at the burial service is a wonderful way to have each person take something home as a remembrance of their loved one.

c. Releasing Balloons

As these balloons fly into the sky, the family reflects on how the spirit of their loved one has gone up to God. Even more, the family members are looking forward to the time when they "who are still alive and are left will be caught up together with them in the clouds to meet the Lord in the air. And so we will be with the Lord forever" (1 Thessalonians 4:17).

Having noted the symbolic meaning of releasing balloons, I will mention a concern about balloons. They might fly for a long time and land in the water and then be ingested by sea animals.

However, I will also offer a rationale for releasing balloons at Christian funerals. Consider the millions of helium balloons that are released into the air at birthday parties, sports events, and other celebrations and the few balloons that are released at cemeteries where Christians celebrate the hope we have. If we are concerned about our environment, then should we not restrict all balloons? If balloons are going to be released, when should this be done if not when we gather to celebrate the greatest hope we have? Should it not be at the burial services of those who believe in the resurrection of Jesus and therefore the resurrection of the bodies of their loved ones?

d. Releasing Homing Pigeons

As the pigeons are released and begin their flight "home," the family is given a distinct and pleasant illustration that the spirit of their loved one has flown "home" to be with Jesus.

e. Singing a Hymn

The family might choose to sing a song that was a favorite of a dear mother or grandmother. In the event that the family will sing a hymn or song, I suggest that the words of the hymn be printed and that everyone has a copy. On several occasions that I can recall, a son or daughter suggested that a song be sung, and then he or she began singing. After the first couple of lines, it became evident that only a few people knew the words. Children and grandchildren especially might not be familiar with the favorite hymn of an older person. These family members might feel left out if they cannot sing along with the rest of the family.

Another comment about singing at the graveside is that the important issue is what's in our hearts, not how we sound.

f. Playing a Trumpet

At either the beginning or the conclusion of a burial service, sometimes a person will play a familiar song on the trumpet. Family members will likely never forget hearing the trumpet play the song, "When the trumpet of the Lord shall sound and time shall be no more," as the coffin is lowered into the grave. Those words give the assurance that, even though Mother's body will remain in the grave as the family leaves the cemetery, one day Jesus will call her home to be with him. The notes of the trumpet will keep ringing in the hearts of the children, assuring them of their mother's home-going and their eventual home-going as well. If the cemetery has a small hill, a suggestion is to have the trumpet player stand on top of the hill, even if it is a considerable distance from the gravesite.

g. Pouring Sand on the Coffin

When it comes to the act of pouring sand, I want to be sensitive to the individuals concerned. As sand is poured and the words said, "Dust to dust, earth to earth," the family members have a visual sense of the finality of life—that they are committing a loved one's body to the earth and it will return to dust.

At times, between the words of committal and the committal prayer, I will add these words: "At a burial service, we often pour sand (or dirt) to visually express the reality that we are committing to God one member of his creation, our loved one. Today, I wish to use this same sand to form two symbols, a heart and a cross. Together they illustrate the strongest comfort and hope. Even as we see this sand that symbolizes that our bodies will return to the earth, may this same sand have two additional meanings. First is the heart, which speaks of God's love, forgiving, caring, embracing, and comforting. Because of God's love, we have hope. This heart also reminds us of the love you have received from a dear (mother, father, sister), the love you have for her, and the love you have for each other. Second is the cross, which is the ultimate expression of God's love. It symbolizes that God sent his only Son to die for us, taking upon himself what we deserve. The cross gives us hope. It reminds us that all is well between (name) and God. The reason is that (name) confessed she/he was a sinner and believed that what Jesus did on the cross was for her/him."

It is possible that those two images will be remembered far longer than all my words. A heart represents the love of the person in the casket, and the cross represents the love of God, who is present to bring comfort. These two symbols give hope and comfort in the midst of grief.

h. Including a Special Symbol or Item

Families often create a display of items that illustrate the life of their loved one. This display will be on a table for people to see as they come to the . However, there might be an item that represents the loved one in a very profound way that the family wishes to have at a burial service. One family made the effort to drive to the original family home and gather some stalks of wheat. The family members placed these on the coffin, and on top of these stalks they placed roses. I give this as an example of how we can honor our loved ones and make the most of previous memories, even as we lay them to rest for a final time.

i. Placing Items in the Casket

A common practice is to place the person's favorite Bible in the casket. However, the issue of placing items in the casket is a conversation that family members will want to have among themselves. Some children might wish to have a keepsake, but other family members might insist that this keepsake should be placed in the casket. As pastors, we will want to take notice of these items and might choose to make reference to them in our words of committal.

j. Writing Care Notes on the Coffin

I remember one particular time as the family gathered in the cemetery. The pallbearers carried the coffin a few feet from the funeral coach and placed it on a stand. Then all the children, grandchildren, and great-grandchildren were given marking pens. The surface of the coffin was such that writing would be easily visible on the light-colored wood. As the family members wrote their final words of love to their mother and grandmother, there was a spirit of joy mingled with sadness. Numerous photos were taken of the people writing the care notes, as well as of the notes themselves.

k. A Civil Ceremony Element

The deceased person might have been part of a group, such as the military or the police force, and the family or this group might request that an additional ceremony be included. I speak from personal experience as both a prison chaplain and as a pastor. I have provided funeral services for officers, both those still working as officers and those retired, and I have provided funeral services for former inmates. At times, there would be a request for the institution to participate in the funeral or burial service. This might be perceived as a "civil ceremony" element. I mention this matter for two reasons. First, we want to be respectful to the family and the group of which their loved one was a part. In this regard, I suggest that we provide the opportunity to have a suitable word from this group included. The second reason is to say that the core issue for me was that I was leading a Christian funeral or burial service and this added part would not change the purpose of the funeral or burial service.

Reflections

I realize that there are many possible components in a graveside service. As pastors, we need to ensure that the family hears God's words of comfort, assurance, and hope, as well as words of commendation and commitment. The concern then becomes how best to include these vital parts and also make the service specific for each person. This will mean that we will want to ask the family whether they have any special requests. Reflect on how you, as a pastor, can invite the family to consider adding special components that will express their love and care for their loved one.

Prayer

Heavenly Father, in all aspects of the funeral service, beginning with the first planning meeting, may I walk compassionately with the grieving family, knowing that you care deeply for the family members. As I gather them around the casket of their loved one, there is the deepest sense of finality. Therefore, may I be fully assured that you—and you alone—are the Father of compassion and the God of all comfort, who comforts us in all our troubles, so that I can comfort those in any trouble with the comfort I have received from you. May my words be filled with comfort but also hope and trust. May my words provide assurance of the resurrection of Jesus and therefore of the resurrection of the person whose body will be laid to rest. In Jesus' name, Amen.

Chapter Eight
Words of Caution

1. Recognizing Family Brokenness

When a family gathers to plan a funeral service, this special event is an opportunity for caring, remembering, and even reconciling, if necessary. There might be hurts and unresolved problems in a family. If so, a funeral might be an occasion that will expose family brokenness and pain. Family members hope that the other members will be compassionate, pleasant, considerate, sensitive, and understanding, but this may not be the case. Instead, unresolved bitterness and offences, simmering under the surface, might explode or at least dampen the compassion and the ability to work for the common goal of preparing the funeral service.

As pastors, we might also know that the person for whose funeral the family is gathering has caused pain, even abuse, to the people who are still here and are planning the service. Or the person whose funeral is being planned might have caused division within the church or the community. There might be people in the church or the community who have been offended or hurt by the person whose funeral we are conducting. A father who was a church leader might not have represented God as a loving, caring father at home. He might have had a critical and controlling spirit within the church. Wishing this had not happened will not make it disappear, and it won't erase hurtful memories at the time of the funeral service. Unkind, judgmental words always hurt. Harsh criticisms and putdowns always destroy. A daughter might have conflicted feelings as she stands by the casket holding her father's body, as she remembers a father who controlled, shamed, and even abused her, and who demeaned his wife, her mother, who is standing beside her. This daughter is aware that her mother knew about the abuse and rejection yet did not protect her, the daughter who is planning the funeral service. The daughter might acknowledge that the mother was threatened or powerless in dealing with her husband. Therefore, the mother, the daughter, and other family members will have feelings of grief and loss but also conflicting emotions about unresolved issues.

As a pastor, I am sometimes aware that a parent has caused pain. What should I say to these children as they plan their father's or their mother's funeral service? They might or might not know that I am aware of their family's problems. I do not believe I should open a hurtful and sensitive wound at this difficult and complex time. However, if the family opens the matter of their father's abuse and unresolved issues, I believe I need to listen and acknowledge their hurt. I cannot undo what has happened. The last thing these children need to hear in their grief, compounded by anger, guilt, and shame, are admonitions that they need to forgive and forget, let the past be forgotten, and just work together. They will have heard this already. They believe this is what the church wants or even demands. But is this the best word for hurting and grieving children? My passionate and fervent answer is "No." Instead of judging them and commanding them to forgive, I need to assure them that I, as a pastor, will accept them where they are. Then they will be in a better position to accept and to receive the other things I will say, both in planning the service and then at the funeral itself.

> **Reconciliation**
> We have heard of miraculous moments of reconciliation within a family around a bed in the final days or even hours of a person's life. Yet, I know of hurting and rejected children going for a final time to the bed of a father, wishing desperately that he would confess and admit his wrong and the hurt he inflicted—and being disappointed that this hoped-for reconciliation did not happen. We rejoice and celebrate when reconciliation happens, and we acknowledge the truth, grieve, and walk with individuals when grief is mingled with hurt and abuse.

2. Extending Grace to Those who Are Hurting

There will be opportunities when we, as pastors, will be asked to provide a funeral service for someone who has left a trail of profoundly broken relationships and bitter feelings—towards God, towards the church, towards the family, and towards those in the community. This provides an opportunity for us to lead by demonstrating grace and forgiveness. Here, as always, our facial expressions and body language will convey whether or not we are gracious. Our words must be supported by our attitudes and actions.

Some people become more mellow, compassionate, and understanding as they get older. The opposite is true of other people, who become more irascible, judgmental, and hardened in their stubbornness and divisiveness. Regrettably, some of these people have been church leaders. Their families, the church congregation, and many friends are aware of the damage these people have caused. At times, they have caused deep pain, even on their death bed. There will be times these people will suffer from dementia in their last months and therefore be unable to confess their wrongful behavior and attitudes even if they wanted to. Therefore, the family is left to care for a parent who has dementia layered over unresolved issues. The family might feel compelled to express compassion for their ailing parent. Then, when this parent dies, the family will have conflicting emotions and even bitter and angry memories of this parent.

How do we, as pastors, respond to a request to provide a service for a person who has caused major conflict, division, hurt, and even abuse? Again, we need to be clear on our calling. There was an occasion when I was advised not to offer a funeral service for an abusive parent who was also a destructive church leader. How should I have responded if this person's child requested that I help plan the father's service? This is not a theoretical question. It has actually happened.

> **Guidelines for Making Difficult Decisions**
> - Don't be surprised when they come.
> - Pray for love, grace, and wisdom.
> - Apply the Lord's Prayer, asking, "What will bring God's kingdom to this family, this group of friends, or this church?
> - Consult trusted, wise, and mature leaders.
> - Don't decide without consulting others.
> - Don't share information or concerns that will shame or disgrace a family.
> - Protect the church staff, who often do not need to know what we know.
> - Be guided by our calling.
> - Remember that our purpose is not to be popular, but rather to be caring, even when the decision is unpleasant and unpopular.
> - Give difficult answers in person, welcoming a response and a conversation, never in writing and certainly not in a public email. Emails are not for sensitive matters.
> - Remember that grief coupled with sensitive decisions demands utmost care.

As pastors, we will need to make difficult decisions and some decisions that will not be appreciated nor welcomed. We will need to act in ways that might not be understood, even by church members and other pastors. May our decisions honor God and extend Jesus' grace and compassion. Children of difficult and stubborn parents need our grace and assistance when they are in grief. Members of churches that were splintered and divided by carnal and arrogant leaders need a demonstration of compassion. Those outside the church are also watching. What will the church do when one of its leaders passes away, a leader who has left a negative impression in the community? May we be faithful!

I offer the following perspectives as "words of caution" because they are a necessary reminder to myself. Satan will stop at nothing. His goal is to kill and destroy. Satan does not care whether a family is in intense grief. He does not care how great the loss is. Satan's goal is to destroy families while they are at the most vulnerable time in their lives. Satan will do all he can to drive a wedge between family members and then widen the gulf that separates these family members.

May I take this concern to another level? Satan's goal is not only to destroy families who have experienced pain from the actions of a parent. Satan's goal is also to destroy the church or at least drive wedges between church members. And what better occasion than the funeral of a former church leader who has caused pain and divisions? May God give us wisdom, courage, grace, and unity, especially in the vulnerable times of grief.

Also, Satan knows everyone present will be listening carefully at a funeral service or burial service for a person who has caused pain and division. Will the pastor leading these services use the occasion to demonstrate unity and compassion? Will the pastor speak untruthful words, maintaining that the person was not as bad as many people experienced him to be? Will we, as pastors, speak hurtful words, adding to the harm already caused?

> **Abuse**
> The sensitive matter of abuse cannot be ignored. But we need to recognize that the reverse side of abuse is withholding honor and blessing, shaming, and not affirming. The seriousness of abuse, in all its forms, was addressed in Chapter Ten of the Guide for Families and Individuals.

We are called to follow the Apostle Paul's words: "Love keeps no record of wrongs. Love does not delight in evil but rejoices with the truth" (1 Corinthians 13:5-6). How do we apply this to a person who was abusive and even cruel whose funeral we must lead? Part of my answer involves being clear about our purpose. I believe it is not up to us to list any wrongs. However, we will also not speak any falsehood. In such a situation, we need to be fully convinced of our role as a pastor. Here, as always, we want to draw individuals to a compassionate God, who is also a just and holy God.

At the same time, a funeral service, with all that goes with it, can be an opportunity for great spiritual victories and personal repentance and growth. I have observed as children and grandchildren recommitted their lives to God. I have been humbled and inspired as a son challenged his siblings, nieces, and nephews that it was now up to them to take up the baton of faith handed to them by their parents. Jesus' story of the lost son "coming to his senses" and returning home to his father and his family (Luke 15:11-32) illustrates how people return home to their heavenly Father in the context of the death of a loved one. Satan knows that when a loved one dies, believers might recommit themselves to God and wayward children and grandchildren might come home to the faith of their parents. Satan will do all he can, by any means, to thwart the convicting moving of God's Spirit. Therefore, we must be on our knees as we lead in these services and walk with grieving families.

At times, we might sense God calling us to walk with family members, seeking their personal resolution to a life of estrangement from the person whose funeral is being conducted. This is an area I am convinced needs to be addressed, and resources must be provided for it. How I wish I had a clear answer to the hurt and pain I feel in the children who have been abused by a parent.

Reflections on Extending Grace to Those who Are Hurting

Here are some reflections for the times when we speak to the pain and hurt of the people whom we have the opportunity to lead in a memorial service:

• We can only touch a person's heart when we speak from our heart. Speaking from our heart requires that we listen quietly to God's heart—this demands silence and waiting.

• Each of us has been hurt and abused, and each of us has hurt and abused other people. This is a reality of living in a fallen world. These are two related, yet distinct issues. May we never excuse destructive behavior with the cliché, "Hurt people hurt people"; in other words, we should never use the excuse that since we have been hurt, we can therefore excuse our own hurtful behavior.

• Therefore, we are called to ask ourselves: "How have we responded to hurt? How do we respond to hurt?"

• We can never say, "We have fully dealt with hurt in our lives." Forgiving and responding to hurt are a daily, ongoing choice we need to make continually.

• Never, ever give simplistic answers. When I hear words such as, "The children just need to get over their father's abuse or control and forgive and forget," I become upset and angry. These words have been given as explanations, admonitions, or even as minimizations of the wrong done. They are not wise and certainly not helpful.

Concluding Reflections

Here, more so than in any other area of the funeral, we will need God's grace and compassion and will need to recognize our dependence on God. How we respond to brokenness in people's lives will be evident at the time of a funeral. Family members will perceive any element of judgment or criticism on our part.

Prayer

Heavenly Father, may the topic in this chapter, that of brokenness and hurt, touch me deeply as I acknowledge my own bent to sin and to hurt other people. As I hear stories of abuse and see how individuals were devastated by those who were responsible for them, I pray that I may respond with wisdom and compassion. May I also respond with boldness and courage, seeking wisdom on when to speak the truth in love. May I claim the reality that you have given me a spirit, not of timidity and cowardliness, but of power, of love, and of self-control. Therefore, may I speak the truth with love and grace. In Jesus' name, Amen.

Chapter Nine
A Word to Fellow Pastors

Up to this point, I have addressed many components of funeral and burial services. My goal has been to write about these matters from a pastor's point of view. Earlier, in Chapter Four, I raised the issue of our limitations, of recognizing that we do not know everything. This in itself might be hard to hear. An even more important matter is that we, as pastors, need to be aware of our own issues. Therefore, in this chapter, I will become more personal, speaking pastor to pastor. I will note some items that I have found important. Although I have given them separate headings, these comments flow from one to the next and are related.

1. Recognizing Our Pastoral Priorities

When a family comes to our church office and requests that we provide a funeral service, we have an opportunity and a responsibility that will come only once in the lifetime of this family. It is critical that we are absolutely certain of our God-given responsibility. A family is coming at a time of their deepest pain and loss. Each family member will have her/his own relationship with the loved one, as well as with God. Therefore, we must be sensitive to their feelings.

However, even as we want to be sensitive to the grieving family, we need to be aware of the balance between listening to their desires and providing an appropriate sacred church service. At times, I have said to a family, "I want to assist you to fulfill your wishes as we plan this service for your mother." But I could only say this because I was absolutely certain that this mother and her family would want a service that glorified God and encouraged and inspired those in attendance. I can never say, "Whatever you'd like at the funeral, whatever would be meaningful to you, will be fine." Our responsibility as pastors is not merely to give people the things they want or believe they need. We have a responsibility to lead them to a gracious God—to encompass them with God's presence and help them receive what God desires to give and only God is able to give. (This is further explained by Thomas G. Long, *Accompany Them with Singing*, 145-149.)

2. Walking with God

Who we are is more important than our skills as we seek to help a family in their time of loss. We need to "walk with God" if we expect to walk with a grieving family with integrity in their valley of death. These words by James Houston emphasize the need to pay attention to our inner life at all times, especially in expressing compassion and care: "We cannot pray for others when we are inconsistent, shallow, unkind and unsympathetic in relationships. Nor can we transmit the values we say we believe in without the truth dwelling richly in us and expressed outwardly in empathy and mutuality" (James M. Houston, *Joyful Exiles*, 162).

> **Walking with God**
> *Walking with God* is necessary if we wish to be *speaking for God*. "Enoch walked with God; then he was no more, because God took him away" (Genesis 5:24). "Noah was a righteous man, blameless among the people of his time, and he walked with God" (Genesis 6:9).

3. Listening and Reconciling

The family members might not be in agreement among themselves on how things should happen. In some situations, we will be aware of disagreements within the family. At times, some family members will tell us that they are not in agreement with the decisions being made by other family members. Again, our role is to listen and to be patient, nonjudgmental, and gracious.

Also, the family sitting in our church office might never have planned a funeral before. One thing is certain—they have never planned a funeral for the loved one they are now missing. Therefore, we must do all we can to assist this family, ensuring them of our support. During our initial visit with a family, we need to give them the assurance that we will help them in this difficult time. I provide as much contact information as possible so that the family can contact me whenever they need to. When I meet with a family, I will provide several forms, note items they will need to address, and then assure them I will be available for any questions, concerns, or needs they might have.

4. Leading as a Shepherd

The biblical metaphor of a pastor as a shepherd is very applicable in a family's time of loss and grief. We will want to gently care for the hurts of the grieving people as a shepherd cares for an injured and hurting lamb. We will want to both care for them and lead them through the planning of a funeral service.

Another factor plays into planning most funerals today. The person who passed away and whose funeral is being planned is almost always part of our congregation. But the individuals planning the service are normally not part of our church family. They will be children who participate in other churches, maybe in other cities, provinces, or even countries. Or they might have no Christian faith, might have rejected the faith of their parents, and might not wish to follow the church's directives and practices. They might not even be familiar with our practices. They might assume that we will adjust to their wishes. Therefore, we will need great wisdom and compassion.

I have made a shift in how I plan funerals with families. In the past, I attempted to make as many decisions as possible in the initial meeting with the family. Now, I take a different approach. My primary goal in the initial meeting is to extend care and invite the family to express their grief and pain. Only after I sense the family has expressed their grief and I have assured them of my compassion and support will I note the items that the family will need to decide on. Then, I will assure the family that I will be available as often as they wish until the funeral service. I say that my initial meeting with the family is only the beginning in the planning for the funeral. In planning for a particular funeral, there will be many emails, phone calls, and personal visits with family members.

I have made this shift for several reasons. First, it is impossible to process all the issues on an initial visit. Second, I believe it is not caring or sensitive to expect the family to make major decisions when they are feeling intense loss and grief and might still be in shock. Third, this shift sends a message to the family that their input and suggestions are valued and wanted. Finally, I see myself not merely as a professional who does a service for the grieving family, but instead I as a fellow pilgrim and shepherd who walks with them in the valley of the shadow of death, sharing their grief.

5. Respecting Clergy Confidentiality

Recently, I have come to a deep conviction that we, as ministers, need to recognize our unique role. This applies especially to the area of the eulogy and the message we provide. We might know a lot about the person we are remembering. But we cannot and must never share publicly what has been shared with us in confidence. In this regard, I have felt exasperated and annoyed when pastors have shared stories about the weakness of a person whose funeral they were conducting.

We might know things about the individual that are embarrassing. On one occasion, I cringed as a pastor (that he was from another congregation did not minimize what he said) described in vivid detail, and with not a little humor, how the person whose memorial service was being "celebrated" had slipped into dementia. Did the pastor's elaboration of the person's dementia add to the family's celebration or express his compassion? The answer is an emphatic "No."

I chose not to approach and confront this pastor because I did not believe he would recognize how insensitive and inappropriate his comments were. I also sensed he was showing signs of dementia himself and therefore might not have been able to fully comprehend what he was saying. I felt pain as he was engaging in behavior that regrettably is normalized even among church leaders. Why do we feel the need to share stories about a member in our church, especially stories that put this person in a negative light? Yes, we will want to recognize her or his faith and express the church's gratitude for the person's legacy. But I believe we need to let the family and friends give the eulogies and the tributes. Certainly, we should never share embarrassing life stories.

6. Representing God Faithfully and Compassionately

We have a distinct responsibility to speak God's words. We must pray and ask God for discernment, so that the people in attendance will hear a particular word of God that offers them hope and grace.

Family members might have feelings of regret and wish they could have another chance to speak with the loved one. They might desperately want to seek reconciliation and to have another opportunity to express love and appreciation. Will they feel God's grace in our words?

Family members might have a negative view of God and might blame God, not only for the death of their loved one but also for the wrong done by the loved one. They might be angry at God. Will they hear that God is able to receive words and feelings of anger towards himself? Will they hear God's tenderness and compassion in words spoken from our heart?

Family members might not have spoken with each other for many months, even years, at least not in a caring and gracious manner. Then they come together in our church office to plan a memorial service. We might know that some family members will not be present because of conflict within the family or because some members have personal mental health issues or maybe emotional difficulties. A critical question is: "How do we speak to those present, knowing that we are aware of the family conflict?" An even harder question is: "How do we speak with courage and faithfulness when the family knows we are aware of their struggles and difficulties?"

I have been in this situation several times. Again, I refer back to the metaphor that I noted earlier, that of being a shepherd who walks with and is committed to carrying wounded lambs. A specific example was when I was requested to help plan a funeral service for a parent in whose family there was significant conflict, even abuse. The adult child who made the request had been forbidden to be present at the funeral service of the first parent. This child said that there had been some reconciliation within the family but not to a full extent. Therefore, some of the family members were still estranged from the family and would choose not to be present. At the funeral, as another family member was giving the life story, it became very evident in this child's tone that there was still major conflict within the family.

In another funeral service, the family was gathering at the funeral home, ready to drive to the cemetery. Two of the sons came to the funeral home but did not come to the cemetery nor to the church service. The division and conflict within a family might be so intense that we will be warned that some family members are not welcome and that we, along with the funeral directors and church ushers, will need to be on the alert for disruptive behavior. We need to take these warnings seriously and respond wisely and also compassionately as we lead a family who will be feeling grief and in which some members will also be fearing an ugly incident.

7. Accepting Brokenness as Stories Are Shared Publicly

The sensitive matter of family brokenness has a bearing on the matter of having an "open mic" time where memories are shared. Before I discuss positive and negative aspects of having an open mic, I wish to mention two things.

First, no family is perfect with only open, caring, and loving relationships. Every family has elements of brokenness.

Second, there will be sharing of memories. By providing an open mic, we hope that positive memories will be shared and remembered and condolences will be given publicly.

a. Positives of an Open Mic
- It provides an opportunity for children to publicly honor their parents as they express words of appreciation.
- It provides an opportunity for individuals to publicly express their commitment to God and also to challenge other people to do the same. In a public setting, family members and friends will commit to "take up the baton or torch" and carry on the faith of their loved one.
- It provides an opportunity for family members and friends to learn positive aspects about the person who is being remembered.
- It is a forum where appropriate humor is welcome.

b. Negatives of an Open Mic
- On rare occasions, some people have spoken unkind words. Therefore, I will introduce the open mic with clear instructions so that people will

understand that negative words are not welcome and are out of place. I might even clearly state, "This is not a roast."
- There is also the problem of minimal participation. What if there is silence and no one is prepared to share or has the courage to speak? I will be prepared with appropriate comments. I might say, "Thank you for coming to express your support and love for the family. I recognize it is difficult to share publicly. I know we have memories we wish to share with the family. Therefore, please take the time to do so personally."

On two occasions, knowing that negative and hurtful words might be said, I was prepared not to have an open mic. On neither occasion was this necessary in the end, but the family knew that I was prepared, and this gave them a sense of peace. We never know all that has transpired in a family, all the hurt, the bitterness, and the absence of forgiveness. Our goal is that the family members will be at peace and have confidence in us as we lead them through a difficult time, a time that might have disruptions. Will they be assured that all will be well, knowing that both we, as pastors, and the family members who have confided in us are trusting God for wisdom and courage? One step towards minimizing unnecessary or hurtful comments is to request that anyone who wishes to speak approach me or a family member to alert us to their intention before the open mic time.

c. Further Reflections

I wish to offer some further reflections on the practice of giving mourners at a funeral an opportunity to share memories. An open mic illustrates the challenge of being a pastoral guide amidst the frailty of life. Families might respond with hesitation when we raise the issue of whether there will be a structured open mic time. There might be concerns that unpleasant memories will be recounted. As a pastor, I cannot guarantee what will be said. But I can say that from my experience almost everything that has been shared at such opportunities has been encouraging. Also, when I am responsible, I will introduce this time with guidelines such as, "When you come to the mic, please introduce yourself and give your relationship with the person whose funeral we are celebrating. As well, please remember that this time is not about you but about your memories of the person whose life we are remembering, specifically memories that will be an encouragement to the family. Humorous stories are always welcome. And please keep your stories short so we all will have time to share."

Humor might seem out of place at a funeral, but it is not. An elderly friend shared her deep love for the deceased after a memorial luncheon. To express how much she loved her friend, she said, "I loved her to death." We all had a good laugh, realizing how this sounded, but that it was appropriate in the context. We can hold both together—clean humor and deep grief and compassion.

Again, we cannot undo the past, nor can we say a lot in a short time. It is important that we consider how what we say might be perceived. How might our faces express more than we think they do? Also, references to God might have the desired, positive response. But these might also produce an unintended, negative reaction. We must depend on God to guide our responses and how we share God's love. Offering Bible promises, however well-meant, might have an unexpected negative impact.

8. Acknowledging Our Own Brokenness and Limitations

As we lead a family in planning a funeral service, we will become conscious that we, as pastors, are wounded shepherds who are carrying wounded sheep. The people whom God has placed over them, their parents, might have wounded and abused them. There might be conflict and disagreements among the family members. But, as pastors, we also need to recognize and admit our own brokenness and limitations.

> **Resting in the Lord**
> Pastors, perhaps more than anyone, need to remember that resting in God is as necessary as working for God. After God worked six days, he rested. How are we, as pastors, resting in God and aligning ourselves with God?

The Bible reminds us that we are merely frail earthen vessels: "But we have this treasure in jars of clay to show that this all-surpassing power is from God and not from us" (2 Corinthians 4:7). As pastors, God has entrusted us with a "treasure." A few lines earlier, the Apostle Paul acknowledged that "we do not preach ourselves, but Jesus Christ as Lord, and ourselves as your servants for Jesus' sake" (2 Corinthians 4:5). This means that we are entrusted with the best message every grieving family will need—Jesus Christ identified with humanity, took its sin upon himself, and gave new life through his resurrection. This is the hope we share with families in their loss. Paul reminded the Corinthians that he, and all of us, are merely clay jars that, in comparison to the treasure inside us, have little value and should not attract attention to ourselves. A study of the life of Paul and of the biblical people that God called and commissioned reveals that they were not merely frail and fully dependent on God, but also that they were flawed and broken.

The relevant point for us is that we, as pastors, need to be aware of our humanity and limitations. When family members come to us with intense grief and loss and sometimes also with raging anger, unsettled feelings, and deep divisions, we cannot ignore these issues and assume we can plan a service as if all is good. We do not have all the answers for all situations. We certainly want to sit down with families and listen. We want to hear their concerns and feel their pain. But we need to accept what we can do and what we cannot do, what our responsibility is and what the responsibility is of the people who have come to us to plan a funeral.

Here are several specific issues that demonstrate we have our limitations and areas of brokenness as pastors:

a. Stewardship of Time

We have a limited amount of time. In this limited time, we need to plan the funeral service with all the details that involves. Therefore, we cannot take the valuable time to deal with critical issues, as much as we might want to.

b. The Need to Refer

We should be prepared to refer the family to other people for answers that we cannot provide or for situations that we are not competent to deal with. Such openness is very necessary as we plan a funeral with a family. It is often necessary for us to consult with experts and ask for direction and also to refer the family to those who have more answers or expertise than we do. Here are some examples of issues where we need help and people we can refer the family to:

- Medical concerns: direct the family to consult their family doctor.
- Pensions and wills: direct the family to the funeral director and to the family lawyer.
- Family conflict: certainly listen to their concerns and then direct the family to a professional counselor.
- Legal concerns: direct the family to consult a lawyer.

In this matter, it will be helpful if we are prepared ahead of time with names of professional people such as lawyers and counselors.

c. Sharing Care with Other People

We have the privilege and responsibility to validate people who have a deeper relationship with and more intimate knowledge of the person who has died than we do. Therefore, we should never perceive ourselves as being indispensable and as the only people who can speak God's truth and comfort in a funeral. We will want to ask, "Is there someone who knows the person more deeply than we do and therefore can offer hope and God's word as well as we can?" If so, we will want to invite this person to have a part in the funeral service as we walk with the grieving family.

I realize that in some Christian traditions, a member of the clergy is recognized as the only person who is authorized or ordained to be God's spokesperson. If, however, you are in a tradition where there is a shared leadership in the church—multiple pastors, elders, or ministers or a leadership team—it is wise to provide the opportunity for several people to provide care to the grieving family. Recognizing that numerous people have poured God's healing oil on wounds with their words and care, it would be consistent to invite these people to bring healing and comfort when it is most needed, at a time of loss and grief.

d. Personal Brokenness

When a family comes to us in their loss and grief, their pain and unresolved issues might trigger unresolved problems in our own hearts. How they have been hurt might remind us of how we also have been hurt. When this happens, we have a choice and several options. Even though we can identify with the grieving family, this is not, in any shape or form, the time to express this. So, the first choice we need to make is to not focus on ourselves. The only right option is to recognize our responsibility—to walk with this family and care for them. Yet, if their sharing triggers an issue or issues in our own lives, then we cannot ignore this. We need to deal with our own stuff—and we all have enough of that!

e. Specialized Areas

We might wish to be knowledgeable in a variety of areas. But we need to choose which area or areas we believe are most important for us and focus on the ministry God has called us to. This choice will mean that we cannot be well-informed in other areas. A good exercise is to know which areas we are unfamiliar with and recognize what our limitations are.

f. Being with Jesus

Our awareness of our humanness must be placed over against the realization that we are not speaking in our own power. We must "be with Jesus," who gives us a word from God. Jesus called the apostles that "they might be with him," and only after they had been with Jesus were they able to do his work (Mark 3:14). Peter and John had the courage to boldly speak about Jesus and his death and resurrection because they "had been with Jesus" (Acts 4:2, 10, 13). The Apostle Paul reassured us with this promise: "For God did not give us a spirit of timidity, but a spirit of power, of love and of self-discipline" (2 Timothy 1:7). We have the greatest message to share in a time of greatest loss. May we be faithful. May we be with Jesus.

g. The Greatest Need

Paul's concluding line to his eloquent description of love is necessary in every situation of life, but possibly none is as critical as when we are in grief and when we walk with people in grief. Paul affirmed: "And now these three remain: faith, hope and love. But the greatest of these is love" (1 Corinthians 13:13).

Reflections

In this chapter, the focus has been on brokenness and frailty—brokenness in the people who are grieving and brokenness within our own selves as pastors. Therefore, it is right to ask:
• What necessary steps am I taking to own my brokenness and begin dealing with my issues?
• How am I taking the necessary time to "be with Jesus"?

Prayer

Heavenly Father, we come in our brokenness and frailty. We are wounded and fully dependent on you. With the Psalmist, we pray: search us, know our hearts, test us, know our anxious thoughts, and see if there is any offensive way in us. We confess any known sin. Yet, we do not know ourselves, but you know our hearts. We need your healing fire and light to cleanse us so that we can see with your eyes and hear with your ears. Lead us in your everlasting way to bring healing and hope. We pray this in Jesus' name. Amen.

Chapter Ten
The Life Story:
A Personal and Faith Legacy

As pastors, we have a unique opportunity to guide people in writing their life stories. When we do this, we can invite them to reflect on their lives. They will choose what they will focus on as they write their life story, or a family member will write the story of their loved one. This raises the question: "What will they want to be remembered by?" or "What will the person writing the life story want the other family members and friends to remember their loved one by?"

As I meet with families, I invite them to take a new look at the topic of the eulogy or life story. I encourage them to see it as more than a chronological chain of details. In discussing the life story, I will often receive one of these two responses: "There is not much to write about in my life. Very little happened" or "I'm only a sinner, saved by grace. So, what is there to write about?" Is this how we really want to be remembered—as an insignificant and worthless sinner?

Recognizing our need of God's grace, the Psalmist David openly admitted, "For I know my transgressions, and my sin is always before me. Against you, you only, have I sinned and done what is evil in your sight" (Psalm 51:3-4). The Apostle Paul confessed, "I was once a blasphemer and a persecutor and a violent man....Christ Jesus came into the world to save sinners—of whom I am the worst. But for that very reason I was shown mercy, so that in me, the worst of sinners, Christ Jesus might display his unlimited patience as an example for those who would believe on him and receive eternal life" (1 Timothy 1:13, 15-16). David and Paul unreservedly confessed who they had been and what they had done. David knew that because he had confessed his sin and then received cleansing and restoration from the Lord, he was able to say, "I will teach transgressors your ways, and sinners will turn back to you" (Psalm 51:13). Paul also knew that the transformation of his life, from persecutor to preacher, brought glory to God. This is why he concluded his brief testimony of being transformed from a blasphemer and persecutor to an example of

God's unlimited patience with, "Now to the King eternal, immortal, invisible, the only God, be honor and glory for ever and ever. Amen" (1 Timothy 1:17).

I mention David's and Paul's testimonies because they challenge us to review how we write our life stories and how children write or tell the life stories of their parents. As I read the life stories of people and the accounts children write about their parents, I have a growing misgiving. I ask myself and all of us who write these life stories: Why are we so intent on making ourselves appear as either worthless sinners or flawless heroes? Why do children need to make their parents appear more than they are? Why do people avoid talking about their brokenness, their pain, their failures, and their disabilities? A family member will note that the parent was not perfect and then add the comment, "But, neither is anyone perfect." However, seldom will a family member share how a parent acknowledged a weakness or even a sin and then asked for forgiveness. I believe I have yet to read that a parent felt he needed to confess to his family and then sought their forgiveness. Such humility and contrition will show how God brought healing within the family.

Yes, we want to honor our parents. The dilemma is balancing our desire to honor our parents and our recognition that they were not perfect. At times, a family will share openly in my office about their family. They will speak of the pain and heartache. Yet, they will be very guarded when they write their parent's life story and then read it in the service. I am not suggesting that they bring up unresolved and painful memories. But I am encouraging us to consider the example of the Psalmist who cried to God in his struggles, the example of Jeremiah who shared his questions and even his lamentations (Jeremiah 36-38), and the example of the Apostle Paul who prayed that God would remove his "thorn in the flesh" even while knowing that God did not answer his prayer. (2 Corinthians 11:16-12:10). These Bible passages point to the reality that the Christian faith covers all of life, including the difficult and challenging seasons. When we respond to Jesus' gracious call to follow him, the path will not be all pleasant and painless until we reach the finish line. This makes me question whether our life narratives and those of our loved ones would not bring more glory to God if we shared our struggles and doubts, along

> **Lessons from Ecclesiastes**
> Is there a lesson we need to learn from the author of Ecclesiastes? When he concluded his description of each human success and accomplishment with "vanity, vanity," what was he teaching us about major accomplishments? How might his words give us a new perspective on writing our life stories?

with God's faithfulness, than if we shared only our accomplishments, victories, our trophies. Would children not honor their parents even more if they shared how their parents were prone to fail and how they struggled yet kept on striving in their brokenness? Would this not be more believable than if the children only listed their parents' victories and successes? Will a eulogy that includes brokenness not be more honest and also offer more hope to those who listen to it? Many of the people at a funeral already know at least some of the painful stories about the loved one. Questions I ask are: "Why do we feel the need to present only the pleasant and positive experiences in our families? Have we portrayed a Christianity in which God cannot deal with our pain and brokenness? Do we honestly believe God is the strong and faithful Good Shepherd? Do we believe he will never leave us as we walk as broken people in broken families, as we travel through valleys of despair and discouragement, as we encounter death and hopelessness?"

David and Paul described how God transformed their lives, how God was there when they failed, and then how God turned them around. Malachi prophesied that a core marker of revival is that the Lord "will turn the hearts of the fathers to their children, and the hearts of the children to their fathers" (Malachi 4:6). I wish that our lives—and therefore our life stories—would contain many examples of such a revival in our families. May we who are fathers have the humility to admit our shortcomings, including our failures and neglect within our families, and then ask for forgiveness and reconciliation. May we have the humility and vulnerability to document how God restores and heals broken fathers, mothers, and whole families.

I invite us to hear the words of W. H. Auden: "To a Christian the godlike man is not the hero who does extraordinary things, but the holy man who does good deeds" (James M. Houston, *Joyful Exiles*, 34). My appeal is that we not make our parents into heroes but celebrate the times when they expressed their love of Jesus by their compassion and their good deeds.

I invite us to hear the words of God, our Creator, when he declared that we, his creation, are "very good." The Bible affirms that the essential worth and significance of each person is based in the reality that we are created in God's image. This is where the essence of our worth lies. We have incomparable value in God's eyes and have been called by him to fulfill what he desires (Genesis 1:26-31, Psalm 139). My appeal is that we never diminish our significance or the value of our loved ones but that we affirm our/their importance because it is given by God. Our worth is a given even before we have achieved great accomplishments or even when we believe we are failures. May none of us ever say, "I have nothing to write about my life because I did nothing extraordinary, exceptional, or outstanding."

I invite us to hear the words of Paul, that we are partners in the gospel with Paul (Philippians 1:4-6) and that we are ambassadors for God (2 Corinthians 5:20) in the work God is doing. This applies also to our parents who were committed to be faithful, obedient servants. They were not distinguished as heroes and exceptional people, at least not most of them. But that is not what will matter in the final analysis if they were faithful with what God had entrusted them with. My appeal is that we affirm them as faithful co-workers and partners with God. This is of far greater significance than any worldly achievement.

I invite us to hear the words of Micah: "He has showed you, O man, what is good. And what does the LORD require of you? To act justly and to love mercy and to walk humbly with your God" (Micah 6:8). My appeal is that we celebrate that our parents did what the Lord required and how they walked humbly before God. Even when they did not walk humbly before God—and who of us does so fully?—may we recognize that God's grace was there for them as well.

I invite us to hear the words of Jesus: "Blessed are the poor in spirit...those who mourn...the meek...those who hunger and thirst for righteousness...the merciful...the pure in heart...the peacemakers...those who are persecuted because of righteousness" (Matthew 5:3-12). My appeal is that we celebrate how our parents demonstrated these godly qualities.

In the above thoughts about writing our life story and the life story of our loved ones, I see our lives as a unit, in that everything that happens is under the watchful eye of a caring God. I don't see a separation between the normal area of life and the spiritual. However, it might be useful and easier to perceive our lives as having two parts—our personal life story and our faith life story. In the personal life story, we include information on our family, our parents and ancestors as well as our children and descendants. We will want to include important events in our life, such as education, work experiences, and special achievements. In the spiritual life story, we include our faith background, our conversion experience, how we became Christians, our growth in Christ, any special events in our faith journey, and our service for Christ. Did we have a life mission statement? What values motivated us? What do we wish to be remembered for? What faith legacy do we wish to leave or do we believe we have left? Similarly, when we write our parents' life stories, how will we answer these questions?

As I reflect on people in the Bible, I note two things. First, the biblical accounts are transparent and honest recordings of real people. Second, the

accounts often include a brief legacy or phrase of some people who can be considered models for us. Here are some of them:
- Enoch "walked with God" (Genesis 5:24).
- Noah "was a righteous man, blameless among the people of his time, and he walked with God" (Genesis 6:9).
- Abraham "believed the LORD, and he credited it to him as righteousness" (Genesis 15:6).
- Samuel is remembered for his words, "Speak, for your servant is listening" (1 Samuel 3:10).
- Mary affirmed, "I am the Lord's servant" (Luke 1:38).
- John was "the disciple whom Jesus loved" (John 13:23, 19:26).

May we emulate godly people, either people in the Bible or people we know personally. We become like the people we follow. If we do this, we will leave a godly legacy for our children and descendants.

In Summary

My desire is that we, who are pastors and are leading the funeral service, will encourage families to have a renewed look at the life stories that will be written and spoken. My desire is that our lives will focus on God. Then, may we lead individuals so that when their life stories are written and shared, they will focus on God. May they and their loved ones be revealed as examples of how God transforms human beings. May we invite people to share how God is gracious, is compassionate, and is continually transforming each of us, including the person whose life story will be shared. When this is our goal and passion, God will receive the glory, and people will receive hope in their journey of life.

Reflections

As pastors, we might know a lot about the person whose funeral we are conducting. How might our extensive knowledge of this person become the focus of our message?

What about our personal motives? Have we taken the opportunity to look at our motives, and what have we learned? How do we want to be remembered? How would we write our personal legacy?

Prayer

Heavenly Father, as I reflect on the topic of my life story, I am so grateful for the godly heritage you placed me in. Just as Paul spoke of Timothy's godly mother and grandmother, I can say the same for my parents. They lived and taught what it meant to be a follower of you. I sensed their blessings and their affirmation upon me. May I leave such a godly legacy, so that my children and grandchildren will feel your blessing through me. In Jesus' gracious name, Amen.

Chapter Eleven
The Funeral Service

When I first considered this chapter, I intended to focus on the funeral message. Upon further reflection, I realized I needed to broaden the topic and present a basic overview of the funeral service in which the funeral message will be preached.

There are several reasons for this. One reason is the phenomenon that was happening as I was working on this book—the COVID-19 pandemic with the accompanying restrictions. When these restrictions were in place, we not only could not have normal church services, but we could not have any funeral services. We had several burial services, but the restrictions against larger gatherings prevented us from having a funeral service as normal. Even at the burial service, only a limited number of people could attend. The extended family and close friends were completely excluded. There was no opportunity to share memories nor have a luncheon meal with a larger group of friends. I mention this to say that often it is only when something is taken away that we realize what we are missing. This also provides an opportunity to examine what we are missing. This leads to several critical questions and concerns:

• Can a funeral service have the same essence and serve the same function weeks or months after a person has passed away?

• What is the essence and purpose of a funeral service, specifically a Christian funeral?

The scope of this book does not permit a thorough answer to these questions. However, I will attempt to address them in this chapter.

1. A Brief History of the Christian Funeral

The early church was birthed within Judaism but also within the Roman Empire. I will address two core elements of early Christian customs that arose within this context.

a. Care for the Body

In Judaism, contact with a dead body rendered a person unclean. But, following Jesus' teaching on what defiles a person (Mark 7:14-15), the

Christians did not avoid contact with the deceased. Instead, they began perceiving the dead as holy saints worthy of being touched and caressed. This applied even to those people who had died in a plague. This meant that the early Christians cared for the dead, a practice very much at odds with the general customs within the larger Roman society.

b. Nature of Mourning

The nature of mourning for the first Christians was in sharp contrast to that of both Judaism and Roman society. A typical early first-century inscription on a Roman grave read, "*Non fui, fui, non sum, non curo*" ("I was not, I was, I am not, I don't care"). This demonstrates the hopelessness and sense of futility prevalent in Roman society.

Jewish mourning rituals were divided into three periods: a period of intense mourning by the family lasting seven days, a second period of less severe forms of grief lasting thirty days, and then a period of a year when the family members were commanded to carry out specific acts of devotion.

The early Christians were encouraged to replace the black and red mourning garments typically used by the Romans with white funeral clothing, the garments of baptism and eternal life. The Christians also replaced the loud and excessive Roman displays of grief with reverent quietness, the chanting of psalms, the singing of hymns, and confident expressions of resurrection hope. The early Christians practiced earth burial, "rejecting altogether the practice of cremation as a blasphemy against the body as a temple of the Spirit and a rejection of the bodily resurrection." Another element of the early Christian funeral was that the believers would, as an act of farewell, kiss the forehead or the cheek of the deceased. This was the "kiss of peace," the same sign of forgiveness and reconciliation that took place in Christian worship at the table before the Lord's Supper. (This brief summary of the history of the Christian funeral is taken from Thomas G. Long and Thomas Lynch, *The Christian Funeral*, 59-71.)

2. The Essence of the Christian Funeral

The preceding brief summary of the history of the Christian funeral points to the fact that the essence of the Christian funeral is rooted in the essence of the Christian faith. Said another way, we begin with the nature of our God. He is our creator who made us in his image. He is the giver of life and also the sustainer of life. Our lives are in his caring hands. He is also the compassionate God who sent his beloved Son for our redemption. Jesus, our Savior, rose from the dead, providing eternal life to all who believe in him. He has placed us, as his sons and daughters, in his spiritual family, where we find sisters and brothers who will care for us and walk with us in all phases of life, both the pleasant and the painful, both life and death. Even more, Jesus, our Savior, is our Bridegroom who has gone ahead to build an eternal home for us, his bride. This gives us hope, knowing we will be with Jesus and with one another for all eternity.

The essence of the Christian faith has many more components. The Apostle Paul presented the heart of the Christian message as the three acts of Christ: "that Christ died for our sins according to the Scriptures, that he was buried, that he was raised on the third day according to the Scriptures" (1 Corinthians 15:3-4). The Apostle John built his theology on his eyewitness account of the eternal Word of life who became a man so that his followers can be in fellowship with him and with one other (1 John 1:1-4).

The core issue for us in this book is to recognize that a Christian funeral must be rooted in and be an expression of our Christian faith. That is, it is essentially one part of a covenant relationship with our God and with his people, our brothers and sisters. This means that a funeral is Christian to the degree that it expresses the Christian faith. One reason I affirm the value of a minister's manual and specifically a funeral manual is that these manuals ensure that the core essence of the Christian faith will be proclaimed during a funeral. The next section speaks to the value of these manuals but also of the personal inner preparation of our hearts as we serve.

3. Funeral Manuals: Their Value and Some Reservations

I, along with many other pastors, have benefited from funeral manuals that contain core Bible passages, prayers, poems, hymns, and sermons. These guidelines might be for funeral services in general or might be geared to services for particular situations, such as the death of an elderly person, the death of an infant, a death caused by an accident, or a death caused by suicide. In the "Parts of a Burial Service" section of Chapter Seven, I drew from the manuals of other Christian traditions for the words of commendation and committal. I am developing a greater appreciation for the carefully worded readings and prayers from a rich Christian heritage. (Several manuals are listed in the Appendix.) At the same time, this has prompted me to be more careful with the words I speak during funeral services.

> **Coping with Dying**
> "There is no recipe for mixing the ingredients of Christology, Scripture, and theology into a guaranteed salve that will eliminate the utterly serious and often painful end-of-life struggle that is coping with dying" (Fred Craddock et al., *Speaking of Dying*, 140).

While I recognize the immense value of these funeral manuals, I wish to note that it is unfortunate that these manuals have saved some of us pastors from having to pray, struggle, and think deeply, so that each funeral will be appropriate for and unique to the deceased (Fred Craddock et al., *Speaking of Dying*, 129-130). One pastor told me that the funeral message and service should be identical for each funeral except that the names will be changed. Another pastor stated he has his favorite funeral message that he uses, with a little variation, for all funerals. Would we ever think of doing this with the weddings we plan? How might a bride and groom feel if they knew that their service was identical to all the other services we performed, except for the names?

a. Three Realities about Funeral Manuals
i. Manuals give detailed suggestions and even sermons to use for particular situations.

Manuals are helpful especially for pastors who are unfamiliar with preparing funeral messages. We can gather wisdom and guidance from the experience of other preachers. But a funeral manual or prayer book should never be used as a substitute for diligent prayer and Bible study to discern what God's word is for each funeral. I believe godly sermons will include the wisdom from both a funeral manual and personal reflection.

A biblical comparison is the book of Psalms. The Holy Spirit directed godly people to record these prayers and praises, which have been a resource for God's people throughout many centuries. We will not equate a pastor's manual to the Holy Spirit's inspiration of the Psalms, but I do believe godly women and men were guided by the Holy Spirit when they wrote these manuals. We can benefit from God's guidance and wisdom through these writers. We affirm God's active involvement in the writing of the Scriptures (2 Timothy 3:16-17, 2 Peter 3:15-16), making them useful for teaching, rebuking, correcting, and training. I believe the wisdom in pastor's manuals can be useful as well.

ii. Funerals are not given a high priority by many pastors.

This is evident in various ways, one being the above comment that a pastor should use the same message for all funerals with minor variations.

iii. The needed time for funeral preparations is limited.

The schedules and agendas of most pastors are full of numerous commitments. This means a pastor will need to remove other important items from her or his schedule in order to give the necessary attention to plan and lead a funeral. Therefore, when a funeral must be planned, a pastor must reschedule commitments and change priorities. The core issue then becomes: how important is the ministry of caring for a grieving family and providing a funeral service? How much time can or should a pastor take away from other important work to plan a funeral and a burial service? My answers to these questions are contained in the next section.

b. The Importance of Planning and Providing Funeral and Burial Services

My advice in this area has three parts.

i. Serve from your heart.

When it comes to a funeral service, my priority is not to have a fine-tuned message and polished music. A funeral service must come from the heart of a pastor. Only then will it reach the heart of the people. This must be the case with every service, but especially a funeral service. At the same time, as a busy pastor, I need to prioritize my schedule so that the service will not have elements that will distract from focusing on God and achieving the core goal of the service.

ii. Serve with integrity.

When we speak on the matter of death, loss, and grieving we do not have all the answers. But we must have done considerable serious personal biblical and theological study on what we believe. Before we speak, we must have taken the time to do diligent Bible study on what the Bible teaches on matters of death, loss, and grieving, as well as our Christian hope.

Even more, we must not only have thought through our theology on these critical issues. We must also have been with the dying and the grieving. I will take this one step further. We must be able to be present with, to sit with, the dying, to be fully there, listening to what God is saying to us. We will only be listening to God's Holy Spirit when we are not scrambling in our minds for a word for the person who is dying or for the family. Yes, the dying person and the family deserve a word from God. But it cannot come from our memory or from our heads. They deserve a word that we believe God is giving them from our hearts.

To be able to do this with integrity, we must have faced our own mortality before we speak to those who are dealing with death and loss. We need to do this on a regular basis. This is a major challenge since we are living in a death-denying society. Yet, has any society ever embraced death with hope? In the sixteenth century, Benedict of Nursia gave monastic Christians the imperative, "Keep death daily before one's eyes." Jonathan Edwards made it a regular practice to reflect on his mortality and wrote that he was resolved "to think much on all occasions of [his] own dying, and of the common circumstances which

> *Memento mori:*
> "Remember death"

attend death." J. Todd Billings, who references these two church leaders writes, "Only those who *know* they are dying can properly trust in God's promise of eternal life....The process of embracing my mortality is a God-given means for discipleship and witness in the world" (J. Todd Billings, *The End of the Christian Life*, 10-11).

iii. Use helps, and serve from your heart.

I encourage us to use all the excellent helps available. But what we say must come from deep within our hearts. This saying is true for all our services and ministry: "A mind will reach a mind, but a heart will reach a heart." We need to do both, but as we prepare a funeral in a time of grief and loss, our priority should be our heart.

We will want to think deeply on these core issues that people deal with at the time of the death of loved ones. Then we will be able to feel intensely on the matters before us. For some of us, therefore, the priority of funerals will need to be revisited. We will need to repent regarding our priorities.

4. The Christian Funeral Service

Based on what has been said on the essence of a Christian funeral and the valuable helps available, we will then conclude that a Christian funeral service will be rooted in the Christian faith. The essence will be the same, but the form may vary, following either a prayer book tradition or a free church format. From experience and training, I approach a funeral service from a free church tradition. Yet, even though I do not belong to a prayer book tradition, there is a clear and regular structure that free churches habitually use. I am not sure whether Thomas Long was writing in jest when he wrote, "Wearing dark suits and praying from the heart, rather than from a book, are vital ritual acts." His next comment points to a commonality that exists in funeral services, whether they belong to a free church tradition or follow a formal funeral liturgy: "Even though the emphasis appears in the free church to fall more heavily on the side of improvisation, most such funerals nevertheless are assembled on the same metaphorical chassis as their prayer-book cousins, namely, that the funeral is the enactment of the conviction that the deceased is a saint traveling on to be with God, surrounded by the songs and prayers of the church" (Thomas G. Long, *Accompany Them with Singing*, 150-151).

I will offer three outlines for the Christian funeral service: first, a general outline from a liturgical tradition; second, an expansion of the "service of prayer and word" section of the liturgical structure; and third, a common format from a free church tradition.

a. Structure of the Central Funeral Rite
The central funeral rite is composed of the following sequential movements:
- The Gathering
- The Procession to the Front of the Church
- Service of Prayer and Word
- Holy Communion
- Sending: Commendation and Committal

b. Service of Prayer and Word (often used in liturgical churches)
i. Invocation and Collect Prayer
- This opening prayer is like passing an offering plate, collecting thoughts, feelings, and hopes from those present and placing all of them before God.
- This prayer usually assumes the form of an expanded "collect," adding to the usual five elements of a collect (name of God, attribute of God, petition, reason, and closing).

ii. Prayer of Confession
- Recognizing that a death often stirs up feelings of anger and guilt, regret and remorse, a prayer of confession provides the means for these feelings and experiences to be offered to God.

iii. Scripture
- Generally, two or three passages of Scriptures are read, usually including one from the Gospels.
- It is fitting to read "favorite passages" of the deceased.
- The main purpose of these readings is for the whole congregation to be reminded, through Scripture, of the promises of God in the face of death and loss.

iv. Tributes and Eulogy
- The tributes should be a maximum of five minutes.

v. Sermon or Homily

vi. Naming and Witness
- This is very optional.
- The community explicitly relates the life story and memories of the deceased.
- The community's memories, sense of sorrow, and words of thanksgiving for the life of the person they have lost are now received and blessed.

vii. Creed
• Those present make a profession of the Christian faith using the Apostles' Creed.

viii. Prayers of Intercession
• The main theme of this prayer section is pleading with God, praying for the mourners that they will be consoled, praying for the church that it will continue along the path of discipleship, and praying for the deceased that she or he will be received into the mercy of God.

ix. The Benediction

x. Music
• Music is so important that it cannot be just in one place.
• There should be lots of music, and most should be congregational songs.
• The best funeral hymns are traveling music, pilgrim songs.
• Hymns that have been especially meaningful to the deceased and the deceased's family should be included.
• Solos and other special music offered by friends and family are important.
• Music by the church choir can also be included.

c. Funeral Order of Service from a Free Church Tradition
When we meet to plan a funeral, I provide a copy of this service order to the family, recognizing that many families will not be prepared to develop a service or are not familiar with planning a service. This order of a funeral service offers both structure and the opportunity for the family to give their own input.

i. Organ/Piano Prelude
• The songs might be requested by the family. Often the song when the family walks in will be a favorite song or a song that was meaningful to the deceased.

ii. Procession

iii. Opening Words and Prayer
• Core Bible verses will draw the congregation together under God.
• The prayer will begin with worship and thanksgiving, recognizing who our God is, a Father of comfort and our God of compassion. It will also include a petition that the people will be consoled in their grief and be open to receive consolation.

iv. Spiritual Song or Chorus
- This is either a favorite song of the deceased or a hymn recognizing God's faithfulness and compassion.

v. Special Music
- This might be provided by a group or a person whom the deceased valued.
- Often a family member will serve with music as an expression of love to the deceased.

vi. Family Component
- There are three options here: a life story, tributes, and a pictorial life story. All three may be used or only one or two.

vii. Message
- A Bible text might be requested by the family, or the message will draw on the deceased's favorite Bible passages to point the congregation to God.

viii. Spiritual Song or Hymn

ix. Concluding Words and Benediction

x. Recessional
- A favorite hymn may be played during the recessional.

5. Other Ministry Areas to Remember

a. Comfort in Grief
The church has not come together at a funeral to provide therapy, but to grieve with the family and to worship and focus on God. As they, the family and friends, mourn, they trust that God is faithful.

b. Hope in Loss
Christian hope is vital, but it is helpful to remember that that hope is not inconsistent with lamenting loss.

c. Hope in Our Medicalized Culture
Modern hope is often based on technology. Then, when a family had set their hope on a medical miracle and are now grieving their loss, we assure them that the ultimate hope is based on God's faithfulness, his

constant and enduring covenant. In keeping with his promise, his presence is with us now, and we will be with our God for all eternity.

6. Metaphor of a Baton or Torch

At a funeral, the family is called to pick up the torch of faith handed down by the loved one. There are 180 Bible passages that speak of passing the torch from one generation to another (Don Nori, *Breaking Generational Curses*, 17). The passing of the baton or torch has many aspects, including challenging the family to:
- Fix their eyes on Jesus.
- Eliminate sin.
- Repent of wrong.
- Examine their priorities and values.
- Eliminate weights and other hindrances to Christian living (Hebrews 12:1).
- Imitate and follow the godly example of their loved one (1 Corinthians 4:16, Hebrews 6:12, 13:7).
- Recommit to the mission to which God has called us (Matthew 28:19-20).

Reflections

A Christian funeral will be rooted in the Christian faith. The center of a Christian funeral is God, his nature, his actions throughout history, and thus his actions in the life of the deceased and in the lives of those who mourn. Also, the Christian funeral is in the context of a Christian community, a spiritual family. Jesus is our Savior, who has restored our relationship with God, our Father, and who is our Bridegroom who has gone ahead to build an eternal home for us. Therefore, even as we grieve our loss, we do so in community and with hope.

Prayer

Heavenly Father, when I reflect on preparing a funeral service, I sense my unworthiness and my frailty. May my focus shift from myself to you. Give me wisdom on what you wish me to say in each funeral service. You know the hearts of the people who will be present. May I be sensitive to your Spirit and speak your words. May the people know that I have been with you, listening to your guidance. Thank you for empowering and directing. In faith in Jesus, I pray. Amen.

Chapter Twelve
The Funeral Message

In the section, "The Essence of the Christian Funeral" in the previous chapter, it was pointed out that for a funeral to be Christian it must be rooted in the essence of the Christian faith. With this understanding, I believe the message has a critical place in a Christian funeral. The importance of the message in a funeral is not measured by its length. At times, a family will request, and might even insist, "We just want a short meditation. Keep it brief." How should a pastor respond? Why not just say a few kind words about the deceased, quote a few Bible verses, and conclude with some general comments?

The funeral message, as much as any other part of the funeral service and even the burial service, is a topic that I believe needs further attention. In short, what does a funeral sermon consist of? In the Introduction to this Guide for Pastors, I referred to my son Andrew's request

> **A funeral message should not be:**
> • A eulogy of the deceased
> • A scolding
> • A flowery description of heaven or what the deceased might be doing
> • Speculations on the eternal destiny of the deceased
> • An encouragement to just hang on

for help when he was required to plan and lead his first funeral. In our conversations (there were several as he planned his first funeral, as well as later funerals), Andrew also asked, "Dad, what is the difference between a funeral message and a regular message?" The answer to this question is critical. Death, and therefore the funeral service in which we remember a loved one who has passed away, provides a unique opportunity that no other service gives. We can and must use this opportunity to speak to the hearts of the people with the heart of the gospel. This leads to two key questions. The first is, "What do we not preach on in a funeral message?" The second question is, "What do we preach on in a funeral message?"

1. What Do We Not Preach on in a Funeral Message?

I will begin answering the question of what a funeral message should be by noting what I believe it should *not* be.

a. Not a Eulogy

The subject of the message should not be the person whose funeral we are conducting, no matter how godly the person is. Such a funeral "message" was illustrated in a memorial service I attended some years ago. Numerous family members shared memories about their father and grandfather. The eldest son concluded the service with a line that went something like this: "The message today has been the life story of our father." I shuddered as I heard that. This father was a godly Christian father and a church leader. I believe this father would certainly not have agreed with what his son had said. Undoubtedly, this father's life was meaningful, and he would be greatly missed. In fact, every life has meaning and significance. This fact is so easily forgotten in the midst of our grief. But our lives cannot be the subject of a funeral message if it is to be defined as Christian.

There is a lesson we found hard to learn as children. This lesson applies to a funeral service and specifically to a funeral message. As children, we found it hard to believe that the world did not revolve around us. At times, we realize that some adults have not learned this lesson either. No person is the center of the universe. How does this apply to a funeral? My answer is that if we are serious about planning and providing a *Christian* funeral, then the center of the service is not the deceased, but *Christ*. If we were providing a normal memorial service, there would be no problem if the center was the deceased person. But if our goal is to provide a God-honoring service, then God must be at the center and must be honored above anyone else.

Somehow, we are drawn to focus primarily on the deceased in our funeral services. This is a definite temptation when much good can be said about the deceased. The above story perfectly, yet tragically, illustrates why a memorial service is called a memorial service, because it is essentially a recounting of the memories of a person. But if a funeral is to be truly Christian, it must be more than a memorial (Rob Moll, *The Art of Dying*, 125). It must be a service where we remember what God has miraculously done in the person's life. The reason we can thank God for a person is that God, in his grace and mercy, has reached down into the life of this person. The core, or the foundation, of the funeral service must be God, not the person remembered nor our memories of him or her. If anything, the memories must be memories of God's activities reflected in the deceased person's life. A godly orientation is most critical in a funeral message. As pastors, we are often being pressured to preach about the deceased. We need to refuse this temptation, no matter how appealing and rewarding it seems and no matter how many affirmations we will receive.

Recognizing that a Christian funeral will have both words of eulogy about the deceased and words from God presented in a sermon or homily, the question presents itself, "What is the relationship between the eulogy and the sermon in a funeral service?" This question leads to two further questions: "Which will people more likely remember in a funeral service, the eulogy or the sermon?" and "Which will people look forward to more, the eulogy or the sermon, memories and reflections about the deceased or a word from God?" My answer, and I trust the answer from every pastor, is that people want and need to hear a word from God. This means that our passion and commitment should be to speak God's truth. Eulogies and memories remind us of God's faithfulness and compassion in the lives of people.

When I hear preachers share numerous memories of the person instead of speaking God's word, I am not only puzzled and disappointed, but also saddened and perplexed. Why would a preacher who has committed herself or himself to proclaim Jesus, the only hope of the world, not use the opportunity given to preach Jesus, the Resurrection and the Life?

Thomas G. Long addresses the tension between a sermon and a eulogy in the chapter, "Telling the Truth about Life and Death: Preaching at Funerals" in his book *Accompany Them with Singing*, especially pages 183-188). Long begins the section "Sermon or Eulogy?" with this: "When it comes to the idea of sermons at funerals, much confusion has raged. Is a sermon at a funeral necessary? Desirable? If so, what is it supposed to be and do? What should be its basic content and aim?" Long notes that in response to funeral sermons that were actually "rhetorically polished eulogies flattering the dead," this directive was given to preachers: "The preacher should keep it simple, not singing the praises of the deceased, but instead doing only what a sermon always should do: put the hearers 'in remembrance of their duty;' (*Directory for the Publick Worship of God* [1644])." Long also points out that the directive for the current Roman Catholic funeral mass expressly forbids eulogies. The command of the Lutheran *Manual on the Liturgy* states, "The sermon may include a recognition of the life of the deceased, but its purpose is not eulogy but a proclamation of hope and comfort in Christ." Episcopal priest Charles Hoffacker says that "a eulogy is *not* a funeral sermon....The eulogy is what happens when one hand raises the obituary notice and the other hand does not raise the Bible" (page 185).

b. Not a Scolding

I will share an illustration of the second subject we must avoid. For more than thirteen years, I was a prison chaplain in Manitoba. As a chaplain, I regularly escorted inmates on compassionate leave in order to be with close family members, especially when these family members were critically ill or when there was a funeral. On one occasion, I escorted an inmate to a funeral. All I remember is what I recall as a scolding by the preacher, confronting the audience with a call to repent and come back to church. I sensed no tone of compassion, but rather a message with one theme: "You all know the deceased. You know how he lived and why he died. Repent, or else the same will happen to you." I don't have an easy response to what I heard. But I ask, "Is a funeral service the best time to 'scare the hell out of people'?" How do we combine compassion with urging people to turn to Jesus? How best do we represent God, who is both holy and compassionate, just and forgiving?

c. Not a Speculative Description of Heaven or What the Deceased Is Doing

There is a third theme that I urge pastors not to preach on at funerals. This is to give speculative, ornate, and elaborate descriptions of what the deceased is doing. The Holy Spirit directed the Bible writers to record all that we need to know about what happens to the deceased after death and also about heaven. When Jesus promised, "I am going there to prepare a place for you, I will come and take you to be with me that you also may be where I am" (John 14:2-3), he did not answer detailed questions about the location, architecture, or geography of heaven. Nor do we find an activities program for when we are with Jesus. Yet, there are preachers who speak with authority—and a lot of creativity and imagination—on all that will happen in heaven, going into dramatic and descriptive detail to assure people that everything they enjoyed here will be there. My appeal is that we avoid these speculations. They only become distractions. Too often, those in grief will remember the fascinating and unsubstantiated descriptions of heaven, but these speculations have little to do with heaven. Regrettably, the grieving family will have heard a preacher's imaginations but will not have heard that our strength for today and our hope for tomorrow is grounded in an almighty God who carries us now and into eternity. Our God gives us hope. A preacher's speculations do not give genuine hope.

We need to be submissive to God's Word. God's Word, the Bible, limits our words to only what it says about the afterlife and heaven.

d. Not Speculations on the Destiny of the Deceased

The fourth item not to preach about is the destiny of the deceased. We need to guard our words because only God knows the human heart of the deceased. May God give us humility and wisdom to speak grace in such a sacred moment. Regarding this area, I recommend that we either avoid it or speak with extreme humility and guarded words. Here I quote from W. Ross Hastings: "There are, of course, things to say and not to say, at particular times. For example, offering a guess about the everlasting destiny of a person is probably never appropriate, given that none of us knows the human heart but God" (W. Ross Hastings, *Where Do Broken Hearts Go?*, 129).

e. Not an Encouragement to Hang On

Regarding the fifth thing not to preach on at a funeral, I will note this quote on a church sign: "When you get to the end of your rope, tie a knot and hang on." This is not what we preach, for it is not part of the Bible's response to grief, loss, and death. When life becomes too hard and we feel the intense loss of a loved one, we can't just tie a knot and hang on. This is not a proper response to any crisis, and certainly not to loss and grief.

I will give a story that illustrates how prevalent this thinking is. About a month following the death and burial service of a dear mother, a daughter wrote that she was experiencing deep grief. In her email, she wrote, "Strange how people can't seem to understand or sympathize. People think we should be over it by now. Someone actually told me that I'm not the only one who is suffering and sometimes you have to 'fake it till you make it.'"

I strongly believe that a major part of the responsibility for the widespread acceptance of this foolish "tie a knot and hang on" and "fake it till you make it" mindset firmly lies at the feet of many preachers. Too many preachers urge people to "rejoice in all circumstances" and to ignore all the lament psalms and biblical references to godly people crying out to God, confident that God would hear their prayers. Is it any wonder people do not know how to walk through grief but instead deny it and just "hang on"?

With the writer of Psalm 73, we must turn to God. Then, we must "enter the sanctuary of God." There we will "understand the final destiny of the wicked" as well as the destiny of the righteous and our final destiny (Psalm 73:17, 23-28.). We must base our lives and our preaching on the core truths of the Bible: Jesus died for our sins, Jesus arose to give us new, eternal life, Jesus ascended to heaven to prepare a place for us and to intercede for us, and Jesus is coming again to receive us to be with him forever. Only such good news gives us ultimate hope, and this is the hope we must give to those who come to us in a time of loss and grief.

2. What Do We Preach on in a Funeral Message?

Having spoken about what not to preach on at a funeral service, we come to the question: "What do we preach?" The last item introduced an answer—the focus and theme must be God.

At times, I begin by asking the family whether the deceased had any favorite Bible passages. Or I will ask questions such as: "What did Jesus mean to your mother? What qualities about God were most important? Were there special life stories where God met your mother in a significant manner? Is there a time your mother goes back to when her encounter with God changed her life and it gave her hope when all hope seemed gone?" Often, when I ask the family, or when I reflect on the person's testimony, I come to a strong conviction that the person would not want me to speak or preach about her or him. She would want me to preach only about what ultimately mattered to her, that is, God and her relationship with God. She would want me to lift up Jesus and point to Jesus, never point to herself. Therefore, my desire will be to proclaim God as experienced and seen through the eyes of a dear mother. I will ground my message on the Bible texts that grounded her life.

As you read this lofty, yet correct goal for a funeral message, you might ask, "What if this was not the central focus of this mother's life? What if she did not demonstrate a life that was pointing to Jesus?" Might I respond by stating that none of us is constantly, fervently focused on God. In fact, our lives might seldom be focused on God. We stumble and go off the path. Jesus, the kind Shepherd, draws us back. But if, in the last moments of our lives, we could articulate what we wish our life's focus was, I firmly believe this is what we would desire to be spoken about in our funeral service. This is what I believe we wish our lives had been and what we desire the lives of all our loved ones would be.

As we consider any funeral message, we will want to follow the leading of the Holy Spirit and then ask what God's word might be as it applies to the specific person whose funeral we are leading. For instance, using Psalm 73, when we enter the sanctuary of God (Psalm 73:17) and reflect on the dear mother referred to above, what might we understand? What is the word God desires the family and congregation to hear as they reflect on the life of their loved one?

I find further clarity on what to preach on in a funeral message in Thomas G. Long's chapter, "Telling the Truth about Life and Death: Preaching at Funerals" (Thomas G. Long, *Accompany Them with Singing*). Long's advice is to consider the basics of both what a Christian sermon is and what a Christian funeral is. He says that "a Christian sermon is built on the conviction that when we take what is happening in our lives and in our world to a biblical text and honestly and prayerfully listen, a word of God may be heard there." Then he writes that a Christian funeral "is a piece of drama in which the church reenacts the gospel by symbolically walking with the deceased on the pilgrim path toward resurrection, singing and praying as they go" (page 187).

This means that funeral preachers will take with them "the circumstances of the funeral—*this* death, *these* people, *this* loss, *these* needs." Then, coming from the premise that the "funeral is essentially a processional, funeral sermons are preached figuratively as the church walks to the grave. They are proclamations of what the gospel has to say about *these* people walking along *this* path carrying the body of *this* brother or sister in sorrow over *this* loss and in joyful hope of the resurrection" (page 187). Long's answer does not restrict our choice of a Bible text to any specific passages. Instead, in keeping with what I said earlier I seek to do, a funeral message will take the appropriate Bible text and apply it to the specific family and congregation to whom we are called to give God's word.

Another approach to the question "What do we preach on in a funeral message?" is to consider the larger scope, the funeral itself. Here, Thomas G. Long gives helpful direction when he presents "The Eight Purposes of a Good Funeral" (137-139) and applies these to a funeral message under the section, "The Eight Purposes of a Good Funeral Sermon" (Thomas G. Long, *Accompany Them with Singing*, 188-195). I believe it is wise to consider these eight purposes even though we may use different words or descriptive phrases.

a. The Eight Purposes of a Good Funeral Sermon

i. Kerygmatic: "In the valley of the shadow of death, you are there."

At every funeral, there are two preachers. Death—capital D Death—is proclaiming, "I win every time. I destroy all loving relationships. I shatter all community. I dash all hope. I have claimed another victim. I always win." The Christian preacher gets to shake a fist in the face of Death and must proclaim the gospel, the *kerygma*: "O death, where is your sting? Thanks be to God, who gives us the victory in Jesus Christ." Funeral sermons that spend all their time on gentle themes of comfort and pastoral care miss an opportunity to proclaim the Christian *kerygma*.

The Eight Purposes of a Good Funeral Sermon
1. Kerygmatic
2. Oblational
3. Ecclesial
4. Therapeutic
5. Eucharistic
6. Missional
7. Commemorative
8. Educational

ii. Oblational: "Bring an offering and come into God's court."

As the family or church family is carrying the body or ashes of a person, it is actually giving this person back to God. Instead of giving a normal offering, we are saying to God, "We give thee but thine own."

iii. Ecclesial: "Such is the company of those who seek God."

Death lies, deceiving us to believe that we are finally alone—the dead are abandoned, and the grief-stricken are left alone. But a Christian funeral is a reminder that we are not alone. We are with the family of God here and with the great cloud of witnesses whose rest is already won (Hebrews 12:1).

iv. Therapeutic: "In the day of my trouble, I seek the Lord."

A funeral sermon will have a goal to provide Jesus' *therapeia* (healing, restoration). Even as our goal and desire is to give understanding and compassion, we know that ultimately only Jesus can give these (Luke 9:11). There is a danger that pastors might attempt to rescue people from their grief but they are actually "using comforting words of Scripture for self-protection, to pretty up a situation whose bleakness they simply couldn't face."

v. Eucharistic: "O give thanks to the Lord."

We can give thanks for every human life as we consider it in the light of God's image and grace. From each life we have encountered, we "have learned truth, experienced growth, received gifts, and felt blessings."

vi. Missional: "That I may walk before God in the light of life."

Even as we walk to the grave, we recognize that our life does not end at the grave. We, who remain behind, return to the work of God in the world.

vii Commemorative: "Lord, you have been our dwelling place in all generations."

We tell stories about the person we carry to the grave, believing that death changes, but does not destroy, the communion with this saint. We

> **Our Hope**
> "The hope we have is in our Lord Jesus Christ who will return for us so that we will live with **him** forever. We accept that the Bible does not speak of the reunion separated family members and friends will have. Such reunions are not at the *center* of the Christian hope" (J. Todd Billings, *The End of the Christian Life*, 155). Recognizing that these reunions are neither mentioned in the Bible nor are at the *center* of our Christian hope, does this give us pause on how to refer to them?

remember the deceased because the resurrection is not a promise to raise some disembodied spirit, but the real, full person God knew, loved, and saved. We walk to the grave and we walk toward the resurrection remembering the one with whom we are traveling.

viii. Educational: "Lord, teach us to number our days."

We recognize that funeral sermons are sometimes used for crass and manipulative evangelistic goals. The gospel does not play on people's emotions or take advantage of the vulnerable. But we also need to be aware that some people at a funeral might not understand the gospel message and therefore it needs to be explained.

If there is any doubt as to what to preach at a funeral, these eight purposes of a good funeral give direction for biblical material.

b. Hope and Holiness

As I reflect further on the question, "What do we preach on in a funeral message?" I build an answer on two words: "hope" and "holiness."

A core Bible text that draws together our hope and our motivation to holiness is 1 John 3:1-3: "How great is the love the Father has lavished on us, that we should be called children of God! And that is what we are! The reason the world does not know us is that it did not know him. Dear friends, now we are children of God, and what we will be has not yet been made known. But we know that when he appears, we shall be like him, for we shall see him as he is. Everyone who has this *hope* in him *purifies* himself, just as he is pure" (italics added). As followers of Jesus, we have an unshakable confidence concerning the future, specifically that we will see Jesus and be like him, and this profound conviction and hope will have an impact on our lifestyle.

At a funeral service, we look forward to the hope we have in God. This hope is based on who God is. Therefore, as our eyes look beyond the grave to heaven, they will look up to God. This means that everything that gives us hope for the future also gives us hope for the present. The reason is that our hope is grounded in a Person, an almighty, compassionate Lord God of the Universe, our Creator, Sustainer, and Redeemer. At a funeral, we proclaim that our God is a God of the future (which gives us an unshakable hope) but he is also the God of the present (which gives us security and confidence for today).

At a funeral service we, as pastors, have before us family and friends who are walking through the valley of the shadow of death. They are facing the dark reality of loss and grief. We have the opportunity and solemn responsibility to give them a clear and compassionate word from God. Often, we will not have a lot of time to prepare and select what this word will be. We will not be able to incorporate all eight purposes that Thomas G. Long says should be in a funeral message. But, as we face a family and friends whose hope is shattered, who will need to move into tomorrow without a loved one, we want to be certain that our focus is on God.

Therefore, in summarizing an answer to the question, "What do we preach on in a funeral message?" may I urge that:
1. Our funeral messages must be grounded in a Person, our God.
2. This message should also draw out the faith and life of the loved one as a witness to Jesus.
3. This message will have a word to the grieving family, friends, and all in attendance.

3. To Whom Do We Preach?

a. The Lord God, the Primary Person in a Funeral

Here are several qualities we will want to clearly proclaim about this Person, our God:

i. Our God is compassionate. He is "the Father of compassion and the God of all comfort" (2 Corinthians 1:3).

ii. Our God is faithful. He is true to his character: "Those who know your name will trust in you, for you, LORD, have never forsaken those who seek you" (Psalm 9:10).

iii. Our God is considerate of the frail. He will look after the vulnerable.

iv. Our God is a Savior (Acts 2:36-40, 4:12, Romans 1:16-17).

v. Our God is slow to anger (Exodus 35:6, Nehemiah 9:17, Jeremiah 15:15, Joel 2:13, Jonah 4:2, Nahum 1:3).

vi. Our God is our hope. Our hope is based on God's love and power, grounded in Jesus' incarnation, death, resurrection, ascension, and coming again (1 Corinthians 15).

vii. Our God is waiting for us. Jesus is building our future home (John 14:1-6).

b. The Beloved Person Whose Funeral It Is

We might ask, "In a funeral sermon, how do we include a reference to the person whose funeral we are conducting?" Here are some answers:

i. The person was an inspiring example of faith: "Therefore, since we are surrounded by such a great cloud of witnesses, let us…" (Hebrews 12:1).

ii. The person's life and faith are a witness of his or her relationship with Jesus: "You will be my witnesses" (Acts 1:8). "When they saw the courage of Peter and John…they took note that these men had been with Jesus" (Acts 4:13).

iii. The person was not perfect, but a vessel, often broken, holding the treasure of Jesus: "But we have this treasure in jars of clay to show that this all-surpassing power is from God and not from us" (2 Corinthians 4:7).

c. The Grieving Family and the Supporting People in Attendance
i. The family: As they look ahead to a future without a loved one, they should be reminded that "God is a helper of the fatherless" and widows (Psalm 10:14, 18).

ii. Friends. These are not spectators to a performance presented by the pastor and family but are walking with the deceased in this journey to the final destination.

Reflections
I mentioned five things not to include in a funeral message:
- A eulogy of the person whose service we are conducting.
- An attempt to "scare the hell out of people."
- Imaginative speculations about what the deceased is doing and about heaven, descriptions that are not in the Bible.
- Statements about the everlasting destiny of a person.
- Encouragements to "tie a knot and hang on."

Do you agree that these are things that should be avoided in a funeral message? If not, how do we speak of these things in a way that will give compassion and hope to people, that will be consistent with the Bible, and that will ultimately glorify and honor God?

Prayer
Heavenly Father, when I reflect on preparing a funeral message, I sense my unworthiness and my frailty. May my focus shift from myself to you. Give me wisdom on what you wish me to say in each funeral message. You know the hearts of the people who will be present. May I be sensitive to your Spirit and then with wisdom, courage, and grace speak your words. Thank you for empowering and directing. May your Word bear fruit as I declare it. In faith in Jesus, I pray. Amen.

Chapter Thirteen
Difficult Funerals

The focus of this book, and specifically the preceding chapters on preparing a Christian funeral, has been primarily on funerals for elderly people who have followed God for many years. Around such funerals, there will be a combination of grief and gratitude and praise—grief by the family and loved ones that a dear mother or grandmother is no more with them, and gratitude and praise that she has finally crossed the finish line and is with Jesus. The tone of celebration and thanks to God for a saint who lived a God-honoring life will probably be more pronounced than grief, even though family members and friends will sense their loss.

However, I recognize that there are deaths that are violent, tragic, sudden, or of a nature that will result in a difficult funeral. With this in mind, I wish to express a few preliminary thoughts before I address several types of difficult funerals.

1. Preliminary Thoughts on Difficult Funerals

a. The Center of a Difficult Christian Funeral

No matter how tragic or difficult a funeral, in order for the funeral to be defined as a "Christian" funeral, the focus of the service must be the same as for every Christian funeral—our almighty and all-compassionate God. Although the circumstances might be tragic or even violent, the focus must not shift to the circumstances. Certainly, we are aware of the events leading to the funeral and even the possible ongoing challenges. Other individuals might describe the event, but, as pastors, we need to keep our purpose clear. We have the opportunity and responsibility to draw people to a compassionate and caring God, even in the midst of tragedy.

b. Grief and Love Go Together.

We might say that grief is the other side of the coin of love. When we deeply love a person who is taken away through death, then our grief will be intense as well. Further, when we deeply love a person who has died a traumatic, violent, or sudden death, our grief will be even greater.

c. All People Aren't Saints Marching Home.

We enjoy the spiritual, "When the Saints Go Marching in." The premise in this song is that there is a joyful anticipation of the time when the saints will march across the finish line to be with Jesus and we who remain will have a celebration for their victory march. The next assumption is that the funeral will be a joyous celebration. We can picture the saints, dancing and shouting, lifting their hands as high as possible, and raising their voices as loud as possible.

Yet, this does not apply to all deaths and to all funeral services. We will be called to walk with families who are certainly not celebrating that a saint has gone home. By this, I am certainly not speaking definitively about the eternal destiny of a person. That is in God's hands. But I am addressing the sense that those left behind will have.

d. At Times, It Seems We Have No Hope.

The Apostle Paul introduced the coming of the Lord for Jesus' people with the words, "We do not want you to...grieve like the rest of men, who have no hope" (1 Thessalonians 4:13). Yet there are times when our faith is tested and doubts will overwhelm us. We sit with families without answers, and we cry because the loss is beyond words. The depth of loss and grief is like a drowning tsunami that pulls us under. We can't put all the pieces of a broken family or the personal wreckage that resulted in a murder or suicide neatly back together. We certainly can't set the pain and grief aside and declare, "Yet we have hope."

This thought is a helpful corrective in our current culture where we attempt to label all funerals, no matter how tragic, as "celebrations of life." At times, we can't gather to celebrate, but rather we will gather to weep and embrace. Do we need to grasp and recognize the tragedy of the Apostle Paul's words "who have no hope"? He is acknowledging that there are people without hope when they die. Certainly, we affirm that the Lord God walks with us in our valley of death. Yet this does not provide hope when there is no hope. I invite us to give thought to how we can best embrace people in such deep grief.

e. We Don't Have All the Answers.

When Joseph's brothers feared retaliation for their acts of hatred, including selling him as a slave, he said, "Don't be afraid. Am I in the place of God? You intended to harm me, but God intended it for good" (Genesis 50:19). Somehow, Joseph knew God's intentions. But when tragedy strikes, we must accept that we do not know God's intentions. Therefore, this should keep us from making declarative statements about the reasons and purposes for disasters.

f. One Size Does Not Fit All.

Difficult funerals will often come without any warning. Therefore, we won't have advance notice to prepare for difficult funerals resulting from tragedies such as a suicide, a murder, or a drug overdose. We will likely have doubts bombard us such as: "I really do not know what to do. I've never led in such a public event. I wish I had someone who would help me decide who should be involved." May we remind ourselves that we are only responsible for what we can do in the time we are given. How we lead a difficult funeral will not be the same as another pastor would do. But, in the short available time we have to prepare, may we do our best and give ourselves grace in the difficulties.

g. Keep the People before Us.

With major tragedies, the tendency might be to shift away from the people involved to the situation itself. For example, after a mass shooting, we might focus on gun control. After a plane crash, we might focus on whether it was caused by a mechanical failure or a human error. After a drug overdose, we might focus on mental health issues. These tragedies can never be processed as mere situations. We need to remind ourselves that every crisis and every difficult funeral involves specific people. We need to draw the focus back to the people. Pastoral care can never be limited to what happens in theory or to a discussion on social issues. It is always personal.

h. Seek to See through Their Eyes.

I hesitate to mention this one, but I will because we have witnessed it too often. A pastor or a well-meaning Christian will respond to a tragedy with, "I know how you feel." These words automatically minimize or even erase the personal loss and take the focus away from the hurting person. Our goal is to see through the eyes of the grieving and feel the pain of the other, recognizing we will never be able to fully do so. Possibly, a wiser approach is to just sit with a person and weep with her or him.

I will now discuss some types of difficult funerals, with the recognition that this does not exhaust the list. There are other crisis events that lead to challenging funerals. Discussing certain difficult funerals does not mean that they are more tragic or more difficult than other funerals. Whenever there is a loss, no matter how horrific, it is a loss to the particular people involved.

2. Funerals during a Pandemic

Earlier, I noted the impact and challenges a pandemic will have on funerals as well as on issues at the end of life. I will deal with this matter in four ways: first, listing some of the restrictions imposed because of a pandemic; second, recognizing how relationships are impacted by the restrictions; third, noting the possible confusion and tension; and fourth, suggesting a way forward.

a. Restrictions

Following are some examples of restrictions imposed during a pandemic. Before a pandemic, all family members and friends are able to be with a frail or dying person. During a pandemic, often only one designated member of the family can visit a dying person. At times, even this is not permitted, and the constraints can seem unreasonable, irrational, and inconsistent. When family members come from another country to be with a dying parent or for a funeral service, they could be required to self-quarantine for a specific time, often fourteen days. The number of individuals at a funeral service or burial can be restricted. During the duration of a pandemic, this restriction will shift—from not being allowed to have a funeral service at all to having only five, ten, or fifty mourners present. Also, funeral services might be permitted in a funeral home but not in a church sanctuary. Further, the interpretations of these restrictions can vary significantly. Also, every person who is present at a funeral or burial service might need to be recorded in case someone at this event tests positive for a virus and it is necessary to determine who might have been in contact with the infected person.

b. Relationships

During a pandemic, normal social contact between people cannot occur, including during the most significant moments of life, such as the final weeks or last hours of a person's life, a funeral service, and a burial service. When a family member is permitted to be present with a loved one, this person will often be required to wear PPE (Personal Protective Equipment) items such as gloves, a gown, and a mask. It is difficult to comprehend how a dying person will feel care and compassion from a person covered with a hospital gown, a face covering, and surgical gloves. In a pandemic, individuals might often die alone, with no close family member present. Also, the representatives of a faith group—such as pastors, priests, and rabbis—will not be able to be present to give comfort and words of hope on behalf of the God a dying person believes in. In summary, core life-long relationships are disrupted precisely when these relationships are the most necessary. Individuals die alone, and restrictions are placed on family members and friends in their journey of grief.

c. Confusion, Tension, Misunderstanding

Even when adherents of a religion are committed to comply with the medical restrictions, they will likely have inner struggles on how they can be true to their commitment to each other and to their faith while complying with the restrictions. Said another way, the restrictions imposed during a pandemic will have various consequences, some minor and some major. The restrictions might result in tensions and misunderstanding between individuals. I will suggest several.

> Just as the Apostle Paul expressed joy and grace from the confines of a Roman prison, may we express comfort and peace in the confines and restrictions imposed because of a pandemic.

First, an elderly person in the beginning stage of dementia will not comprehend why her children, grandchildren, and close friends are not visiting or at the least why these visits come with restrictions that the person does not understand.

Second, since there will be various understandings and explanations of the restrictions, there will often be conflict within a family over the interpretations—some members will interpret the restrictions one way and other members another way. An example is the restrictions imposed during the COVID-19 pandemic. One segment of society (or a faith group) agreed with all the restrictions and claimed medical and scientific support for their position. Another segment of society (or of the same faith group) argued that the restrictions were unnecessary and based on a conspiracy, or at least that the restrictions were not as necessary and should not be as stringent for their group. This difference of interpretation also occurred within families.

Third, when an immediate family member, such as a daughter or son, cannot be present with a dying mother in her final moments of life, this family member will likely have feelings of guilt and anger. She/he will feel guilt for not doing what she/he hoped to do and even expected to do and anger and shame

> The mind might rationalize the restrictions, but the heart will still feel guilt and shame.

for not being able to do what she/he understands to be the right thing. When a family member is unable to be with a dying parent because of restrictions imposed for medical reasons, this will not remove the person's guilt and shame. In a daughter's or son's mind, she or he might rationalize or minimize the guilt, but in this person's heart, she or he will still deeply feel guilt and shame. Explanations do not satisfy or minimize deep commitments.

Fourth, individuals within the same religious group will differ on how to balance obeying God's authority versus obeying society's authority as represented by medical leaders.

d. A Way Forward: Extending Grace, Embracing Compassion, Trusting God

As fellow believers and as faith leaders, we are called to walk with individuals in the difficult journey of grief and loss that is made more complex because of the restrictions of a pandemic. Some religious leaders will argue that we must refuse to comply with the medical restrictions on the basis that we are commanded to obey God above all. Reference might be made to the Apostle Peter's bold statement, "We must obey God rather than men!" (Acts 5:29). During the time of a pandemic, we need to remain true to our commitment to one another. This commitment remains regardless of any restrictions. We might be upset with the restrictions. We might notice how inconsistent they appear to be and believe they are not justified or warranted. But, during a time of grief, our primary purpose is to fulfill our commitment to express God's compassion and care—and not be drawn into debilitating and unhelpful arguments about the restrictions. I believe we can fully do this while abiding by restrictions we might neither understand nor appreciate.

> May we comply with the medical guidelines, but rest in the presence of our compassionate God.

I will conclude my reflections on walking with families during the restrictions of a pandemic by noting that God graciously embraced grieving families with his compassion even as families needed to make significant adjustments. When we recognize that the primary issues during any time of grief, as well as times of joy, are our relationships with our God and with the people we love, then we will do whatever we must to express our love and compassion. The restrictions will be perceived as secondary because they do not define our deep love and compassion. I can testify that even though I was not able to lead a typical funeral service for more than two years during the COVID-19 pandemic, I witnessed many profound expressions of compassion as people opened themselves to God's love and to each other's love.

> Love and compassion will penetrate any concrete wall of separation and surmount any restrictions.

3. Funerals for Those Who Have Committed Suicide

My initial comment on how to approach the funeral of a person who has taken his or her own life is an observation in the book, *Hope Always: How to be a force for life in a culture of suicide*, by Matthew Sleeth. Sleeth states that pastors will often have thin skin when they begin in ministry, worrying about receiving criticism. He then says that a good pastor should make it a goal to grow "a tougher skin and a more tender heart" (148). Possibly there is no area where this applies more than that of walking with a family whose loved one has killed himself or herself. In the chapter, "Pastors and Suicide," Sleeth articulates what the church can do to battle the awful plague of suicide. These are key points:

- Pastors should have a clear biblical understanding on the topic of suicide.
- Pastors and churches must become engaged in the battle for the lives and souls of those who are contemplating suicide. This is of particular importance in a culture that minimizes the seriousness of suicide and also avoids the difficult root causes of suicide.
- Pastors should have funeral sermons prepared in advance for both believers and nonbelievers who have taken their own lives. This will allow the sermons to be prepared in a time of calm contemplation and prayer, guided by the Holy Spirit.
- Someone who has trust in the Lord in life but who has taken his or her own life has reason to hope for God's mercy in death.
- Pastors should not give false hope regarding those who held God in little or no regard when they were alive: "It is a sham to 'preach someone into heaven' after their death or to promise those left behind that their loved one is 'in a better place now'" (143-155).

Here, as in other areas, we pastors need to have a clear biblical and theological understanding on this topic but also have a distinct pastoral approach.

We also want to be cognizant of church history. There was a time when the act of suicide was considered a sin so grievous and damnable that a Christian funeral and burial were not allowed. Most Christian traditions have changed and have chosen to move to a more pastoral approach. Yet, two issues remain. First, there is still a stigma and shame associated with suicide. Second, some people who come to the funeral might assume that the person is condemned by God or the church or both simply because the person committed suicide.

In a funeral service, it is not helpful to invite the loved ones to rehearse the difficult details of the death. It is not that we are not interested or concerned about what happened, but we want to be very clear on why we want to know and for whose benefit we are asking the question.

Instead, it is important that we provide an atmosphere of grace and forgiveness. Suicide will certainly generate intense grief. This grief is often mixed with regret and guilt—based on what people will wish they had done as well as what they will wish they had not done. Suicide also generates anger. This anger can be directed at the person who took his own life or at close friends or family members who might or might not have been aware of the individual's tendency to depression and failed to prevent the death. Anger might even be directed towards God. How could an almighty and compassionate God permit this cruel act? A funeral is an opportunity to express difficult and deep feelings and thoughts in the context of a God who forgives and is gracious and heals.

The service should include ample congregational hymns, for these songs give the assurance of God's grace and compassion. Choose spiritual songs that point to God's love and give assurance that he cares.

I will conclude my discussion of the topic of suicide by referring to two comments by Matthew Sleeth (*Hope Always,* 145, 170-173):

1. Pastors need to speak about suicide proactively. Certainly, a pastor must speak clearly and compassionately about suicide in the funeral of a person who committed suicide. But a sermon on suicide at that time is too late, at least for the person who killed himself.

2. Sleeth offers "Twelve Ways to Help Save a Life" (that is, to help someone who is depressed before suicide becomes an option):

a. Visit.
b. Call.
c. Ask questions that are open-ended and nonjudgmental.
d. Send a passage from Scripture or an uplifting quote.
e. Make a playlist or burn a CD of uplifting songs and hymns.
f. Write a letter and send it via snail mail.
g. Share a prayer.
h. Share a meal.
i. Take a walk.
j. Sabbath together.
k. Do something fun.
l. Get help.

In this section on difficult funerals, I have included these twelve ways to help save a life for two core reasons. First, during the depressing and emotionally draining time when a suicide happens, there will seem to be no hope and no answers, at least no adequate answers. Yet, there is merit in considering specific and practical steps to take when we have any reason to suspect that someone might be contemplating suicide. Second, as people enter the last phase of life, there might be a greater sense of depression and hopelessness. A person might feel there is little reason to live. Therefore, these twelve steps, even though they are targeted specifically to a person who is feeling depressed or suicidal, are applicable for every elderly person.

4. Funerals for Those Not in the Faith

Providing a service for a person who publicly claimed no faith in God presents Issues of integrity and truthfulness. We are perhaps comfortable with providing a service for an individual who has followed God all her life and whose family and others present at the funeral have a deep awareness of her faith. But what about a person who publicly declared he chose not to believe in God or follow God? To provide a similar service for this person undermines the integrity of a Christian funeral. Yet, how Christian can a Christian funeral be about a person who publicly declared he was either an atheist or an agnostic?

Here I follow the directive of Thomas G. Long, who wrote that it can be "very clarifying theologically and pastorally for a pastor to craft a funeral service that can be employed for a person with a distant relationship to the church." He further states that the text for such a funeral can be divided into three broad categories:

1. affirmations voiced (by the church and by the Scriptures) about the meaning of life and death;

2. prayers, responses, statements, and affirmations spoken by those in attendance at the funeral; and

3. words spoken about the deceased.

The language of all three should be truthful. "But this does not mean that the categories operate at the same level of faith articulation. It is fitting, for example, to speak clearly of the church's faith in category #1 even on those occasions when such faithful language cannot be honestly spoken in category #2 or claimed for the deceased in category #3" (Thomas G. Long, *The Christian Funeral*, 199-200).

I recall providing a funeral service for a correctional officer when I was a prison chaplain. During the viewing, I prayed that God would give me clarity on the person's soul condition. I did not have a sense from God in this matter. I also knew many of the leading people in the provincial correctional system would be present at the funeral. What I sensed God saying was, "Speak my word clearly, and share it with compassion." I mention this example because it reminds me of two things. First, we are called to faithfully speak God's word as he directs us. Second, all human beings, including this officer and myself, will "stand before the living God and...will encounter there a God whose judgment, grace, mercy, and transforming love I have experienced in Jesus Christ—in short, a God who can be trusted" (Thomas G. Long, *The Christian Funeral*, 199).

W. Ross Hastings concurred with the above caution when he wrote, "Offering a guess about the everlasting destiny of a person is probably never appropriate, given that none of us knows the human heart but God" (*Where Do Broken Hearts Go?*, 129). I also wish to repeat the warning Matthew Sleeth made about "preaching into heaven" someone who had no regard for the Kingdom of God in life (Matthew Sleeth, *Hope Always*, 145).

In summary, what is our response when we are requested to provide a funeral service for a person who either did not claim faith in God or who boldly and arrogantly stated the opposite? I believe our response should include the following.

First, we should express compassion, be present, and listen to the family's pain.

Second, we should be careful with our words about the person. We should offer no false hope nor take any away.

Third, we should make sure to include congregational hymns in the funeral service. These will be an avenue for the grieving family to express their faith in God.

Fourth, as in all funeral services, we should invite the congregation into God's gracious presence, express compassion, assure those present that we are held by a Father of compassion, and trust that God's Spirit will speak through the Scripture truths what he desires to impart.

5. Funerals after a Lengthy and Often Painful Illness

You might wonder why I include this category under "Difficult Funerals." The reason is that I believe some pastors do not lead these funerals with compassion and wisdom. Therefore, these funerals have an inherent element of challenge and are thus difficult.

I will begin my comments regarding this category of funerals with an experience. A near relative had suffered weakness and frailty in the last several years of her life. The pastor's first words were, "We have come to celebrate. We have two reasons to celebrate. First, ___ is no longer suffering. Second, she is now with Jesus." When I attended that "celebration of life" service, I was beginning a series of seminars on grief. In neither the pastor's opening comments nor his message was there any reference to loss or grief. There seemed to be no awareness of the husband sitting on the front pew, surrounded by his children and grandchildren. They were missing a dear family member. They were in grief.

My concern is with how we frame the death of a person. There will always be a sense of loss and therefore grief. The simple fact that a person has suffered many years with cancer, with dementia, or with some other slow and difficult form of deterioration does not imply, by any means, that the funeral is necessarily a celebration. We automatically assume that a funeral following a sudden death—whether by an accident, violence, suicide, or even murder—will be a difficult funeral. But we cannot therefore assume that a funeral after a long, painful, and difficult illness—whether due to cancer, dementia, or Alzheimer's disease—will not also be difficult. Recognizing that all funerals have their level of difficulty, I believe that funerals conducted after a lengthy illness or disability should be in the category of "difficult funerals."

6. Funerals for Victims of Murder

This loss has elements that are often distinct from those of other deaths, and therefore this will have a bearing on the funeral of a murder victim. There are two specific scenarios to consider:

a. When the victim was targeted. In this case, there will be many unresolved issues among the people at the funeral service. Those who are grieving might be missing one more person from the family or friendship group—the person who murdered the loved one whose funeral is being held.

b. When the victim was not targeted but might be a casualty of a random shooting, for instance. There is never an "accidental death." This situation will bring up major questions directed, consciously or unconsciously, towards God.

Then there is the matter of grief. There is the immediate grief when the person is murdered, the prolonged grief in the period between the murder and the trial, and then the grief following the trial. The trial might intensify and add to the grief, but the trial will never negate or minimize the grief. Somewhere within this prolonged grief, the family will need the services provided by a pastor. Planning and leading a funeral service will require a sensitive, listening heart. Another aspect to consider is that news reporters might be present. If they are not present, they will wish to be informed of the service. This means that we need to be aware of our calling and to whom the service is directed. The service is not for the news reporters and other members of the public who are not immediately impacted by the grief.

One group we seldom consider are the loved ones, family members and close friends, of the murderer. These individuals might or might not be present at the funeral, yet they will hear what is said at the funeral or imagine what was said. Therefore, our words must be carefully chosen. Some years ago, I was informed that the mother of a murderer was a member of one of our churches. May God give us grace and wisdom in leading this type of funeral service.

7. Funerals for Children

In former centuries, the death rate of children was higher than it is today with our current medical advances. This certainly does not negate nor minimize the sense of loss. The passing of each child is always a major loss. When infant mortality is relatively rare, as it is today with our modern medical support system, this might mean that parents and grandparents feel they have been singled out by God when there is a death of an infant or child. Yet the loss is felt no less when a child dies in a famine, a pandemic, or a time of war and violence. An added component might be that the situation does not allow for an appropriate funeral and burial. This will add guilt and shame, even though the loved ones were not able to do anything about it. I note this because the loss of a child might trigger deep and unconscious memories that are suppressed and that surface later.

In planning a funeral service for a child, these are several considerations:

a. A Whole Christian Funeral

A child deserves a whole Christian funeral. However, the elements of the funeral will be adjusted as appropriate. An example is the matter of involving, or at least being aware of, the child's classmates.

b. Cruel Sentimentality

We must avoid becoming sentimental. Especially, we should not embrace the very common, yet very cruel and unbiblical thoughts that are sometimes expressed. An example is "God was looking for a flower to plant in his garden up in heaven, and he found the most beautiful flower—a little child." Regrettably, this line is included in some "sympathy" cards. If I could, I would eliminate all such "God wanted a little angel" cards. Our words should always be tender and compassionate, but we should avoid the "sweet sentimentality" that can easily slip in.

c. Biblical Texts

As noted above, a child deserves a whole Christian funeral. This means that we can draw from the whole breadth of our Christian faith. Among the many biblical texts that can be used, there are three stories that refer specifically to children.

The first is the Old Testament story in which King David appealed to God for the life of the child born to Bathsheba. When the child died, David said, "Can I bring him back again? I will go to him, but he will not return to me" (2 Samuel 12:15-23). One interpretation of this passage is that David meant that he also would die at some time and join his son in the grave. This suggests that David's words were rooted in the common view of *Sheol*, the place of the departed. In this understanding, David's words imply that the child had passed from all that was worthwhile to something that was little better than nonexistence. We might question whether the ancient Israelites accepted this dismal fate for the dead as commonly understood within other ancient cultures. It is true that the perception of the afterlife in the Old Testament was not what we have in the New Testament and certainly not what we have following the Lord's resurrection. However, I believe that David did not mean that the child had a bleak lot that he would eventually share. Rather, David's words suggest that the child was in heaven and David, as a man who followed God, would join the child in heaven. This positive view of the afterlife is given in the concluding words of Psalm 23, which was written by David: "and I will dwell in the house of the LORD forever." This does not present a dismal view of the afterlife that is essentially a nonexistence.

The other two examples are the New Testament stories where Jesus lifted children up as a model of who is the greatest in the kingdom of heaven and where Jesus blessed and welcomed children even though his disciples rebuked the parents for bringing the children to Jesus (Matthew 18:1-9, 19:13-15, Mark 9:33-37, 10:13-16, Luke 9:46-48, 18:15-17). I believe it is significant that these two stories, where Jesus affirmed and blessed children, are recorded in all three synoptic Gospels. This points to the importance of children in God's estimation.

d. Prayers

Recognizing that the needs and emotions surrounding a child's death are both specific and intense, there is value in drawing from prayers prepared for a child's funeral. Following are two prayers for funerals involving children.

i. from The Book of Common Prayer
"O God, whose beloved Son took children into his arms and blessed them: Give us grace to entrust (*name*) to your never-failing care and love, and bring us all to your heavenly kingdom; through Jesus Christ our Lord, who lives and reigns with you and the Holy Spirit, one God, now and for ever. Amen."

ii. A prayer of committal from the Book of Common Worship
"Loving God, give us faith to believe, though this child has died, that you welcome *(name)* and will care for *(name)*, until, by your mercy, we are together again in the joy of your promised kingdom; through Jesus Christ our Lord. Amen."

8. Funerals when There Are Conflicting Expectations or Desires among the Grieving Family

It seems to be an exception when all the family members agree on every aspect of a funeral and burial service. At times, the differences are minor, and then the family members will work towards harmony. But

there are times when the requests and desires are incompatible. Here are some examples:
- Some family members want a traditional burial while others prefer cremation.
- Some family members want an immediate funeral service (within a week) while others want to wait until the complete family can be present (up to three or four weeks).
- Some family members want a traditional service while others want no service at all.
- Some family members want to respect and follow the deceased's written directives while others want to ignore these directives.

These services are difficult because they call us to strive for unity in the midst of grief.

9. Requests from Outside Our Church

In most instances, we will know the person whose funeral we are conducting. This person will have been part of our church family. But, on occasion, we will be asked by a funeral director or a family member to provide a service for a person we do not know. How should we respond to these requests? There are several guidelines I follow:

1. When this request comes from a funeral director, we will want to receive this as an honor. When a funeral director selects us for this service, it indicates that she/he values our ministry. When this request comes from a family member, we will also acknowledge the request, again understanding it as an expression of respect for us.

2. Will I accept the request to serve? I take the position of W. Ross Hastings: "Refusing to offer a memorial service to a family in light of gospel hope, in the midst of such grief, is unthinkable" (W. Ross Hastings, *Where Do Broken Hearts Go?*, 129). Unless there is a significant reason, I believe we need to adjust our commitments and agree to serve by meeting this need.

3. Recognizing that this request does not directly relate to our congregation, we will want to process this request with our church leaders to ensure that we have their blessing. Normally, this will be seen as a part of the church's broader ministry.

4. We will want to meet with the grieving family and seek to learn as much as we can about the deceased. Further, we will want to involve the family in the service if they are open to this. Here we will follow all the steps that we would follow for any funeral that we provide for a person from within our church.

5. Our words must be truthful when we speak about the deceased. On one occasion, I was present at a memorial service where the person the funeral director had asked to lead the service did not know the deceased

person. Regrettably, in the speaker's attempt to be personal, he told stories of the deceased that the family and others in attendance knew were not factual. This exposed the fact that he did not know the deceased nor the family nor had he taken the time to meet the family. It also demonstrated a lack of professional integrity. The family will know that we do not know the deceased. Therefore, we do not need to make it appear as if we do.

6. We will be in prayer, seeking to say what God directs. God knows the family, and we don't. Therefore, we will want to be led by his Spirit in our speaking.

Reflections

As pastors, our focus and purpose is to remain the same no matter the nature of the death of a person whose funeral we are conducting. We have one primary responsibility—to draw those in attendance to our almighty and all-compassionate God, even in the midst of the greatest tragedy. We live in a very broken and fractured world, and the ugly expressions of this will be exposed as people feel loss and grief. May we be gracious with ourselves as we sense our inadequacy and frailty and our inability to give the answers and the hope we wish we could.

Prayer

Our heavenly Father, we rest in your compassion as we lead families in their dark valleys, at times without the hope you provide. We also fall before you, our God, who are all holy and all just. We recognize that you are a God who is aware of the hearts of those whose funeral services we are conducting as well as all the people in attendance. You know all hearts. Even in the darkest tragedy, we know you are holy, just, and compassionate. May we rightly represent you and only speak what you desire us to say. In the name of Jesus, Amen.

Chapter Fourteen
Assurance that We Will Cross the Finish Line

1. Two Attitudes and Three Commitments

This chapter is the most crucial in this book. How can I have the assurance that I will cross the finish line of life? How can I know that I will have eternal life once I cross the finish line? How can any person have full certainty on this most important matter? I want to answer these questions with what may be perceived as two contrasting attitudes: confidence and humility. Then I will offer three commitments as I give my answers.

The First Attitude: Confidence

My confidence as I answer these crucial questions is based on the authority of the Bible. I trust that the Bible speaks authoritatively to these questions. Since I base my answer on the authority of the Bible, I will have confidence.

The Second Attitude: Humility

I recognize that my understanding is limited and that I am fully dependent on the Holy Spirit's enlightenment.

I trust these two attitudes have been evident throughout this book, and my desire is that these will again be evident as I answer the question, "How can I have the assurance that I will have eternal life once I cross the finish line?"

As I present my answer, I have three commitments:

My First Commitment

My goal is that my answer will be in keeping with the Bible. In other words, I want to say no more and no less than what the Bible says.

My Second Commitment

If you belong to a Christian faith tradition that has a different understanding of the Bible than my tradition does, my desire is that you will be affirmed in your interpretation of the Bible. The key issue is that our answers are based on the Bible. Therefore, I want to be respectful of an interpretation that is different from my interpretation.

My Third Commitment

My desire is that our zeal and commitment to our God and to his Word, the Bible, will motivate all of us so that we will be fully assured that we will cross the finish line. Further, my desire is that we will be able to give clarity and hope to other people so that they will also have this assurance.

I want to return to the metaphor of the marathon, the metaphor that permeates this book. We watch with anticipation as marathon runners in the Summer Olympics approach the finish line. The 26-mile marathon race is comparable to the long marathon race of life, and we cheer in a similar fashion as individuals persevere right to the finish line.

At a funeral service, we celebrate that a loved one did not give up but, in the Apostle Paul's words, "finished the race and kept the faith." We also rejoice because the Lord, the righteous Judge, has "in store the crown of righteousness" for "all who have longed for his appearing" (2 Timothy 4:6-8). It is one thing to focus on a funeral service, giving thanks to God that a person has run the marathon of life. But it is of much greater consequence that each of us, including the person whose funeral we are celebrating, will cross the finish line. By "crossing the finish line" I do not simply mean completing life here on earth. I mean crossing the finish line to receive the crown of righteousness that the Lord will award those who have longed for his appearing.

2. Two Key Questions

Ending life successfully invites two key questions, and the second follows from the first.

Question 1: Will Everyone Cross the Finish Line?

Phrased another way, this question asks: "Will everyone be in heaven once they die?" The author of the book of Hebrews wrote, "Man is destined to die once, and after that to face judgment" (Hebrews 9:27). This judgment will have eternal consequences. Jesus spoke to this finality in his conversation with Nicodemus: "Whoever believes in him is not condemned, but whoever does not believe stands condemned already because he has not believed in the name of God's one and only Son" (John

3:18). Therefore, the answer to the first question, "Will everyone cross the finish line and be in heaven once they die?" is a serious and solemn "No." Based on Jesus' words, those who believe in him will cross the finish line and have eternal life, but those who do not believe in him will cross the line but will not enter into his presence.

Question 2: How Can We Be Assured that We Will Cross the Finish Line and Have Eternal Life?

Jesus' words give the answer: "For God so loved the world that he gave his one and only Son, that whoever believes in him shall not perish but have eternal life. For God did not send his Son into the world to condemn the world, but to save the world through him" (John 3:16-17). The core requirement for assurance is belief in Jesus. However, as we know in other situations, there are two key parts when we speak about believing in Jesus. The first is a correct understanding of what it means to believe in Jesus. The second is that a belief in Jesus is only genuine and actual when this belief is evident in a person's actions.

The angel Gabriel instructed Joseph to name his son Jesus because "he will save his people from their sins" (Matthew 1:21). When Jesus died on the cross, he died as the Lamb of God who took away the sin of the world (John 1:29).

The Apostle John emphasized that believing in Jesus as the Savior and Son of God is necessary to have eternal life: "And this is the testimony: God has given us eternal life, and this life is in his Son. He who has the Son has life; he who does not have the Son of God does not have life" (1 John 5:11-12).

Further, the Apostle John clearly stated that we can be confident we will cross the finish line and have eternal life. He wrote, "I write these things to you who believe in the name of the Son of God so that you may know that you have eternal life" (1 John 5:13).

We recognize that the most important decision we will make in our lives is to be prepared to cross the finish line and be with God for all eternity. The previous Bible verses point to this. Yet, I believe we may be limiting our understanding of the Bible, or at least the parts of the Bible we draw on, as we answer the question, "How can I be assured that I will cross the finish line and be with God?" Our answer involves more than an agreement with several theological statements, no matter how core they may be. These theological truths will include our acceptance of our sinful nature and our belief in Jesus, who died as the adequate sacrifice for our sins in order to give us eternal life. I believe it is more useful to understand these core truths of the Bible not so much as doctrinal statements but as expressions of a relationship—our relationship with God and with people.

3. Two Personal Convictions

Before I expand on the topic of our relationship with God and with people as it applies to being assured we will be with God eternally, I want to share two personal convictions. As I began this book on the topic of preparing to cross the finish line, I realized the most important issue in life was to have the assurance that we will cross from this life to eternal life with God. When I began reflecting on this most critical issue, two unsettling convictions and questions became more pronounced.

a. Lifestyle of Those who Claim to Believe

The first conviction and question was about the lifestyle of certain individuals who claimed to have the assurance that they would be with Jesus when they died. Yet these people were leaving behind a legacy of discord, abuse, non-forgiveness, and bitterness. They boldly and dogmatically claimed that they were prepared to die and had confidence they had eternal life, and they would quote numerous Bible verses supporting their claim—and yet their lifestyle betrayed their convictions.

The second conviction follows the first. The reason is that these individuals often claimed to believe one of these summaries or a variant of them.

b. The Inadequacy of Four-Point Summaries of Christian Faith

The second unsettling conviction was about some very popular summaries of what it means to become a Christian. I am familiar with these, have promoted them, and have frequently used the first four of them. I am now going to present these summaries. Then, I will make some observations and suggest some concerns with them. Finally, I will conclude with a focus on the theme of relationships. The reason I do so is that I am becoming more convinced that we will have assurance that we will cross the finish line and be with God, not when we have the ability to recite key Bible truths, but when we are in a relationship that these truths speak about.

4. Five Popular Summaries of the Core Bible Truths

I am including these five summaries of the gospel in this book for two reasons. First, these are often used to explain how a person can become a Christian. Second, individuals will often point to these summaries as a basis for their assurance that they will be with God when they cross the finish line.

The Four Spiritual Laws
(Campus Crusade for Christ, now renamed Power to Change)
1. God loves you and has a wonderful plan for your life (John 3:16, 10:10).
2. Our sin has separated us from God (Romans 3:23, 6:23).
3. Jesus is God's only provision for our salvation (John 14:6, Romans 5:8).
4. We must receive salvation by faith in Christ (John 1:12, Ephesians 2:8-9).

The Bridge to Life
(The Navigators)
1. The Bible teaches that God loves all humans and wants them to know him (Genesis 1:27, John 10:10).
2. But humans sinned against God and are separated from God, leading to death and judgment (Isaiah 59:2, Romans 3:23).
3. There is a solution: Jesus Christ died on the cross for our sins and in so doing has become the bridge between humanity and God (Romans 5:8, 1 Timothy 2:5, 1 Peter 3:18).
4. Only those who trust Christ can cross the bridge—the choice is yours (John 3:16, 5:24).

Steps to Peace with God
(Billy Graham Evangelistic Association)
Step 1. God's plan: peace and life (John 3:16, 10:10, Romans 5:1).
Step 2. Humanity's problem: separation (Isaiah 59:2, Romans 3:23, 6:23).
Step 3. God's remedy: the cross (Romans 5:8, 1 Timothy 2:5, 1 Peter 3:18).
Step 4. Human response: receive Christ (John 1:12, 5:24, Romans 10:9).

The Roman Road
1. Human need (Romans 3:23): "For all have sinned and fall short of the glory of God."
2. Sin's penalty (Romans 6:23): "For the wages of sin is death, but the gift of God is eternal life in Christ Jesus our Lord."
3. God's provision (Romans 5:8): "But God demonstrates his own love for us in this: While we were still sinners, Christ died for us."
4. Our response (Romans 10:9-10): "That if you confess with your mouth, 'Jesus is Lord,' and believe in your heart that God raised him from the dead, you will be saved. For it is with your heart that you believe and are justified, and it is with your mouth that you confess and are saved."

The First Four Chapters of Romans
Romans 1: God: God is the Creator to whom all people are accountable.
Romans 2: Man: Humans have rebelled against God.
Romans 3: Christ: God's solution to humanity's sin is the sacrificial death and resurrection of Jesus.
Romans 4: Response: Humans can be included in salvation through faith in Jesus Christ.

5. Six Cautions regarding these Five Four-Point Summaries

I will begin by recognizing the value of these summaries. They provide core Bible truths in an easily understood format. They are relatively easy to learn, easy to memorize, easy to communicate, easy to explain, and easy to understand. Yet, I want to offer several cautions on providing these presentations as the essence of the gospel. My desire is to submit these cautions with a spirit of grace.

a. Are They Too Easy?

My caution has to do with how these summaries might be used as offering too easy an assurance of salvation. At times, I sense we present them as four easy steps: A person hears them, repeats a prescribed prayer, and is told that she or he is good to go to heaven. How does this match up with what Jesus said? Did Jesus not say, "If anyone would come after me, he must deny himself and take up his cross and follow me" and "Anyone who does not carry his cross and follow me cannot be my disciple" and "Any of you who does not give up everything he has cannot be my disciple" (Matthew 16:24, Luke 14:27, 33)? Further, did Jesus not say, "Come, follow me, and I will make you fishers of men" (Matthew 4:19)? Jesus invites us into a relationship with him, to be with him, and then to be engaged in his mission.

b. Are They Faithful to the Bible?

I recognize that these doctrines are expressed very clearly and in a manner that is easy to understand. I accept that these summaries have been used numerous times by many people. But I will be so bold as to state that nowhere in the Bible are these statements provided in such a logical format as in these short summaries. If these comprise the essence of Christianity, then why are they not given together in the Bible in a similarly clear and understandable formula? Or, as we review church history, why is there no precedent for such a clear summary of Christianity until about sixty years ago? Throughout history, church leaders would gather to discern and agree on the core doctrines and creeds, but these creeds are not the same as the five four-point summaries.

c. Is Knowing Enough?

These truths are among the teachings of Christianity, but it is not sufficient to acknowledge the accuracy of them. The Apostle James warned about knowing correct doctrine yet not living it. He wrote, "You believe that there is one God. Good! Even the demons believe that—and shudder" (James 2:19). The issue is not whether we know correct doctrine, but whether we accept it and live it out.

d. What Do They Leave Out?

When we present these biblical truths in a clear and logical format, we might imply that these represent the core biblical truths. Yet what if we have omitted other equally core Bible doctrines? I will argue that these summaries have significant omissions. They focus on salvation from sin as the central message of the gospel, but there is much more to the gospel message than that.

One writer who notes the inadequacies in these summaries is J. Todd Billings. He writes, "The Spirit's word through Scripture is so much deeper and wider than the stereotypical story of Christians 'praying the sinner's prayer' and then trying to stay in God's good graces until they finally reach heaven." Billings makes reference to the sixteenth-century Protestant theologian Franciscus Junius, who taught that "all Christian theology occurs in union with Christ for the purpose of deepening our communion with God in Christ." Whereas these summaries emphasize a moment or hour of decision, Billings states that Junius's "theological reflection happens on the road of discipleship, the path of pilgrimage" (J. Todd Billings, *The End of the Christian Life*, 15-17; Franciscus Junius, *A Treatise on True Theology with the Life of Franciscus Junius*, trans. David C. Noe [Grand Rapids, Michigan: Reformation Heritage Books, 2014], 119-20).

Certainly, we need to recognize the biblical teaching of a new birth. Yet we must see this in light of a covenant relationship with God and with his people. I suggest that our familiarity with the summaries blinds us from seeing the possibility that they are an incomplete presentation of what is actually core. In other words, there are many other biblical doctrines that are not included which are very fundamental. With a fresh study of the Bible, we might recognize other doctrines as more foundational and core than those presented in these five summaries.

e. Are They Too Individualistic?

Another thing that concerns me is that these four-point summaries present Christianity as essentially an individualistic relationship with God. By this I mean that they present a Christianity in which all that matters is a person's relationship with God, apart from her or his relationship with other people. Possibly, most people who read this will respond that this is in fact what is core—a person's relationship with God. My response is that the Bible describes a person's relationship with God in the context of this person's relationship with other people—we are a body, a holy priesthood, a chosen people, a holy nation, a people belonging to God (1 Peter 2:5-9). This biblical understanding is that a follower of Jesus is in relationship with the Christian community. This interpretation is in contrast to that held by many people who believe a person can be a Christian and remain an "independent agent." Here Christianity has become "personalized, do-it-yourself, success oriented and free from outside obligations" (Fred Craddock et al., *Speaking of Dying*, 34, 82).

There are two reasons I want to stress this fifth concern.

First, these summaries present an incomplete, and therefore only a partial, perception of Christianity. They do not state that when we follow Jesus, we become part of his body, his family, his chosen people. We don't first come to Jesus and then choose whether we want to be part of his body. These come together. Rod Wilson notes that such a "privatized and individualized entry into the kingdom, with a focus on meeting needs, will set the pattern for living the same way once you are in." He further writes, "Here conversion begins and ends with the created, not the Creator" (Rod J. K. Wilson, *Counseling and Community*, 14, 13).

My second concern with presenting Christianity as an individualistic relationship with God is this. As I have reflected on the matter of people being prepared to cross the finish line, I repeatedly come across a perception in which people say, "I have decided to follow Jesus, and it does not really have anything to do with anyone else." However, when people argue, consciously or unconsciously, that they begin the Christian life independent of anyone else, they will conclude that ultimately it is only about them and God. My response is that a person's relationship with other people changes everything. I can't state it more sharply than to note that if a person claims he can be a Christian independent of any relationship with other Christians, this person is not Christian.

f. Do They Adequately Recognize Life as a Marathon?

My sixth concern about these five summaries applies specifically to the matter of comparing our lives to a marathon. In a marathon, the purpose is to start running from a starting point, remain on the prescribed track, and reach the finish line. The emphasis is on the race, and usually very little mention is made of the prize for reaching the finish line. Yet, when this metaphor is applied to our lives, the focus may be perceived as merely following some prescribed rules from birth until death, and then it is all over. But this is certainly not the case. Here is where we need to add an extra element when applying the marathon metaphor to our lives.

These five summaries might explain, albeit partially, how we begin the marathon of the Christian life. But we need to keep in mind the five cautions noted above. More is involved. We not only begin the marathon run, but the Bible repeatedly emphasizes that a prize is waiting for us only at the other side of the finish line. We are familiar with David's word of hope: "and I will dwell in the house of the LORD forever" (Psalm 23:6). Jesus is now building a room in his Father's house for us, and at the appointed time he will return and take us to be with him forever (John 14:1-4). This means we can be confident we will be fully prepared to cross the finish line only if our goal is beyond the finish line—to the prize of being with Jesus.

With this in mind, I suggest that we perceive these five summaries as partial descriptions of the moment we begin the Christian marathon. Used this way, in spite of the concerns expressed, I urge that these be used and made available. Even better, I encourage each of us who is reading this to prayerfully reflect and draw out key verses that clarify how we know we are following Jesus. For some of us, we can identify a specific event when we heard Jesus' call to follow him, responded in faith, and began our life and faith marathon with God. For others, we might have gradually turned our face toward Jesus—over a longer period of time—and then recognized that we were following Jesus. Therefore, the issue is not only the starting moment of our walk with Jesus, nor even the journey with him, but the exciting and glorious prize at the other side of the finish line—an intimate relationship forever with God. As well, as I noted in my fifth caution, the starting point, the continuous journey, and the concluding part of the Christian life are always in the company of other people. We are always in a family, in a body, in a group of believers, walking with other people. This is not evident in the five four-point summaries as I understand them.

Because of their incompleteness, there is real danger in these summaries being used to provide "assurance of salvation" or "eternal security" to individuals. I will briefly discuss this topic in the following section.

6. Assurance of Salvation?

These five summaries are often used to give a person the assurance that she or he has crossed the finish line and has eternal life. To put it bluntly, they suggest that once a person has recited the "sinner's prayer," he or she is guaranteed a place in heaven no matter what he or she says or believes or does after that. Said another way, they provide the assurance of eternal security. This leads to obvious questions: "What exactly is the doctrine of eternal security?" and "How is it applied?"

My answer to these questions is twofold. First, I do not have the space to adequately discuss this doctrine here. Second, I will share briefly how this book evolved. I initially intended to limit the scope to the topic of preparing funeral services for individuals who claimed to be Christians. However, in the course of planning and leading numerous funeral services, I became painfully aware of instances where a person claimed to be a follower of Jesus but left a legacy of broken relationships. This led to the question: "How could these individuals, who claimed to be Christians, have such a lifestyle and still affirm they were prepared to cross the finish line?"

In this book, I will not attempt to answer this question. Rather, I believe it is best if each of us reviews what is involved in having "eternal security." Therefore, I encourage the reader to do three things. First, do a personal inductive study of the Bible—and do so without the aid of any theological book. Consider themes such as following Jesus, God's compassionate care for the prodigal, and the evidence of being in Jesus. Second, study the two sides of the biblical doctrine of "eternal security"— those who claim it and those who have concerns with it. Third, carefully examine whether your life demonstrates—by word and deed—that you are taking up your cross and following Jesus.

This takes me to the topic of our relationship with God and with people as it applies to being assured that we will be with God eternally.

7. Following Jesus: An Intimate Relationship Now and Forever

In the first pages of the Bible, at the beginning of history, humankind and God were in an intimate relationship. Nothing separated God and Adam and Eve. We know the tragic story of Adam and Eve's rebellion and rejection of God, centered in pride and in deception by Satan. The design of God was broken. Then, God set in place a plan to restore what had been destroyed. These five summaries describe how the broken relationship with God is restored, albeit partially. These summaries use the metaphor of crossing the divide or chasm between God and sinful humanity. But I believe a fuller biblical understanding of what it means to become a Christian is to enter into an intimate relationship with God through Jesus and then follow him throughout our lives and into eternity.

I will offer two observations that confirm that the essence of our Christian faith is best seen as a relationship with God.

The first observation is that when we follow Jesus, this will be evident in our life. The people who know us will observe that we are following Jesus in our attitudes and actions. There will be proof that we know Jesus and Jesus knows us.

The second observation has to do with the many relationship images or metaphors that are given in the Bible to describe our union with God. The following are only a few:

i. We Are a Chosen and Redeemed People. We are called to live in a covenant with a compassionate and holy God and his people (Exodus 20:1-17, 1 Peter 2:4-10).

ii. We Are Sheep in God's Flock. We have been rescued by the Good Shepherd and are following him (Psalm 23, Psalm 80:1, Isaiah 40:10-11, Ezekiel 34:11-16, Luke 15:1-7, John 10:1-30).

iii. We Are Living Stones. We are built on a secure and solid foundation, Jesus Christ, but we are also connected with other believers, part of the same holy building (1 Corinthians 3:10-15, 1 Peter 2:4-8).

iv. We Are the Bride of Christ. We have been bought with the precious blood of Jesus, who has gone to prepare a home for us. We wait in eager anticipation for him to call us to the wedding supper (John 14:1-6, Revelation 21-22).

v. We Are a Royal Priesthood. We worship and serve with other members of the priesthood (1 Peter 2:9, Hebrews 7:26, 10:10).

vi. We Are a Holy Nation, a Chosen People. (1 Peter 2:9).

vii. We Are the Body of Christ. This body is composed of many members, interdependent on one another and fully dependent on Jesus, the Head (1 Corinthians 11).

viii. We Are Followers and Disciples of Jesus. We have been called by Jesus to follow him and to become like him, our Teacher (Mark 1:17).

ix. We Are Servants of God. We have been called to humbly serve each other, following the example of Jesus (John 13).

As we consider these relationship metaphors, I believe we can be fully assured that we will be with Jesus once we cross the finish line if we are now enjoying our relationship with God through Jesus and are anticipating the time this relationship will be even more intimate.

May we see our Christian faith through the lens of relationships. I believe the best example is a marriage relationship. In a wedding ceremony, a man and a woman will sign the legal papers, with witnesses present, to be a husband and wife. But then the focus and joy is on the intimate, passionate relationship that follows, not the legal marriage document and not the sparkling wedding rings. May we have an even more passionate relationship with Jesus.

I wish to add a concluding word to anyone who might have doubts as to her or his relationship with God. You are in good company. Before Jesus gave his disciples what we know as the Great Commission, we read these words: "When they saw him, they worshiped him, but some doubted." Then Jesus came to them and said, "All authority in heaven and on earth has been given to me. Therefore, go make disciples of all nations..." (Matthew 28:17-19). All the disciples worshiped, but among the disciples was a subgroup of doubting-worshiping disciples. Yet, Jesus gave all the disciples authority and commissioned all of them to make disciples. He included all of the disciples in this, even though some had their questions and doubted. Faith in God is not the absence of doubt. When we are in a relationship with God, we will have doubts. There are examples of several individuals in the Bible who expressed their doubts—including Job, Elijah, Jeremiah, and John the Baptist—but who are still regarded as faithful followers of God. May we keep our eyes on Jesus even as we have questions.

Before I conclude this chapter, I wish to make two things clear. I'll use a comparison to explain the first. When we have car insurance or house insurance, we insist that the coverage applies to all possible scenarios. The last thing we want is to be informed that our insurance does not cover what we thought it did. My deepest desire is that when people cross the finish line, they will be with Jesus because they accurately followed the Bible—nothing more and nothing less. Second, my further desire is that you yourself will have assurance and peace in your spirit that you are a child of God. God wants you to have assurance and feel this assurance. The Apostle Paul wrote that this is God's goal for us: "You received the Spirit of sonship. And by him we cry, 'Abba, Father.' The Spirit himself testifies with our spirit that we are God's children. Now if we are children, then we are heirs—heirs of God and co-heirs with Christ, if indeed we share in his sufferings in order that we may also share in his glory" (Romans 8:15-17).

You might still have doubts about whether you will be with God for all eternity. You have read this chapter on being assured of your relationship with God, but you are not at peace. I urge you to reread one of the summaries given earlier or find one in a Christian bookstore, online, or on a blog. Meditate on the Bible verses, and claim one or several verses for yourself. May you see these summaries as descriptions of your relationship with God through Jesus Christ. If you are unsure which verses to choose, may I suggest the following:
• *John 1:12-13*: "Yet to all who received him, to those who believed in his name, he gave the right to become children of God."
• *Matthew 4:19*: "Come, follow me, and I will make you fishers of men."
• *Romans 10:9-10*: "If you confess with your mouth, 'Jesus is Lord,' and believe in your heart that God raised him from the dead, you will be saved. For it is with your heart that you believe and are justified, and it is with your mouth that you confess and are saved."

8. Two Prayers that Provide Assurance that You Will Cross the Finish Line and Be with Jesus for All Eternity

As you consider these issues, I wish I could be with you, hearing your questions and listening to your doubts. Instead, I urge you to invite a Christian friend or church leader to sit with you and listen to your concerns. Then, give these doubts to God in a prayer. Here are two suggested prayers:

Prayer 1
Dear God:
Thank you that I can come to you with my doubts and questions. When I think of the matter of crossing the finish line of life, my desire is to have the assurance that I will be with you. In the Bible, I read that Jesus, your Son, is preparing a home, but this home is only for those who believe in him. Therefore, I accept Jesus' invitation when he says, "Come, follow me." I repent of my sins and receive Jesus as my Savior and my Lord. I confess that Jesus died for me and that you raised Jesus from the dead. Based on your Word, in faith in you, I claim that I am one of your children, I am part of your family. I want to follow Jesus, listen to him, learn from him, and do whatever he tells me. Thank you for accepting me as your child. In faith, I pray, Amen.

Prayer 2
Dear God:
I thank you that you desire a relationship with me. So often I have felt you were unknown and distant. However, it is I who have turned away. You have always sought me. I repent of rejecting you, of wanting my own way. I come back to you. As I look to you, I see your Son, Jesus, on the cross. He made a way to you possible. I know I should be punished for the wrong I have done, but Jesus paid the penalty for me. Now I believe that what Jesus did on the cross was for me. I believe in his death. I accept Jesus as the sacrifice for my sins. I come to you by faith, believing in Jesus. Based on your words in the Bible, when I believe in Jesus, I recognize that I am now a child of God. Thank you, Father, for adopting me as your son/daughter. Thank you that I now have eternal life, a life that begins here and now and continues into all eternity. With thanksgiving, I pray, Amen.

If either of these prayers represents your deepest thoughts and desires, you can be assured you will be with Jesus when you cross the finish line and that then you will be with him forever. Based upon the Bible, you are a child of God. Jesus is preparing a home for you.

Appendices

The central metaphor of this book is a marathon. The title, *Preparing to Cross the Finish Line*, emphasizes the importance of being ready for the moment we die. But, as has been emphasized throughout the book, there are specific things that can be done now to be better prepared for that time. In this appendix are various guidelines and forms that will help people in their preparation. Some of the forms will need to be adapted for the particular situation a person is at, as well as for where the person lives. Please take the time to review and, as you are able, fill in these forms or begin addressing the areas that apply to you.

Appendix A
Writing a Personal Life Story

1. Core Values in a Personal Life Story

Review the chapter on a life story (Chapter Ten: The Life Story: A Personal and Faith Legacy) and consider the following points.

- Our written life story can be perceived as our final life will. It includes the faith and the values we want to pass on to our children and the next generation.
- Our life story should begin with the basic facts of our lives but should also include times of God's miraculous intervention and restoration.
- The purpose of a life story is to bring glory and praise to God. A related purpose is that the people who read our story will receive hope and courage and encouragement for a renewed commitment to God.
- A core premise as we write our life story is that we have value. Our value is not based on what we have done, achieved, or accumulated, but on the fact that we are created in God's image.

2. Key Areas in a Personal Life Story

What are the areas you will want to include?

- **Family of Origin:** This might be perceived as establishing the roots that give us our identity. We want to note who our parents and earlier generations are. Our lives do not begin with us.
- **Childhood Events:** Here we mention special early events, both those pleasant and those painful. How were we nourished in our formative lives?
- **Milestones in Life:** Our lives are like journeys on which we encounter other people. We will begin by noting our relationships—our marriage, our children, other close family members. If we are not married or have no family, we will want to recognize other close relationships. We will also write about our education and the various areas of employment. If there has been a longer period in retirement, we will want to include special achievements or goals in our retirement.
- **Faith Encounters:** We recognize that the center of our lives is not ourselves but a caring and almighty God who has been present throughout

all the phases of our lives. We have the opportunity to write our life story so that the focus is not on ourselves but on our God. Ultimately, our lives and therefore our life story must point to God. He gives courage for each day and hope for the future. May our life stories demonstrate how God is transforming us.

Appendix B
Forms Provided by a Church

This comment is regularly made when a family is in the midst of planning a funeral: "I had no idea how many things needed to be done. Planning a funeral is almost as complicated as planning a wedding, but a family has only a few days to get it all done." Therefore, it is essential that a church will provide all the help a family needs. Every church will develop its own literature and forms that will be specific to that church.

I cannot emphasize strongly enough that we, as pastors, need to provide clear instructions and guidelines for families. We will want to be informed of all the details that are involved in planning a funeral service in our church. The family who is with us might never have planned a funeral service for a loved one before. When the family leaves our office, they might still be in shock and grief. But there is no reason they should have a sense of helplessness and uncertainty as to the steps they will need to take, at least with regard to the funeral service itself. We need to make it our priority to walk with families "in the valley of the shadow of death" so that they will have the assurance that all will go well in the funeral preparations and service.

There are many details that need to be decided in a short time. I tell the grieving family that when they come into my office, it is a "one stop" arrangement. Then I, along with the office staff, will ensure that all the contacts will be made to individuals who are responsible for areas such as food, custodial, ushering, bulletins, music, and donations. At times, the family that plans the funeral is part of our church and therefore is familiar with all the people that need to be contacted. But, in many cases, the children have moved away from the parents or the parents have moved into a new city and neighborhood in their retirement. Many times, the children are not aware of the customs in their parents' church. This is another reason it is important to be as clear and thorough as possible as we explain the guidelines in planning a funeral. The family comes to us, as pastors, to be cared for in their time of grief and loss, and we need to make it as easy as possible so that they will be assisted in their time of grief and loss. Part of caring is giving the assurance that we will walk with them in their grief.

My church has developed four forms: a master planner containing all the details, a preliminary service order, a funeral catering menu, and a price list.

A few comments are in order as you study these forms. First, every church will have its own policies, traditions, and guidelines. The forms printed here are adapted from our church's forms, but much of the information will apply to other churches and even to a service in a funeral home. I encourage elderly people to meet with me to discuss their wishes, become familiar with the funeral service, and document their plans.

1. Master Funeral Planner

I begin by explaining the "Master Funeral Planner" with the family. This is a comprehensive form that contains all the necessary information and decisions a family will need to make as far as the church is concerned. The family will need to make other decisions with the funeral home. A family might not have answers for all of the various areas when they meet for the first time, but they will know what they need to work on as they plan the funeral.

FUNERAL PLANNER

Basic Information:
Name of Deceased: _____
Date of Birth: _____
Date of Death: _____
Place of Death: _____
Family Contact: _____
Phone: _____
Email: _____
Date of Death: _____
Place of Death: _____
Funeral Home: _____
Funeral Home Phone: _____
Funeral Home Contact: _____

Viewing Public/Private:
Date and Time: _____
___ Public ___ Private
Place of viewing: _____

Funeral/Memorial Service:
Date and Time: _____
Place: _____
Minister: _____
Church Involved: _____
Church Phone: _____
Service Broadcast: Yes _____ No _____
Via Livestream: _____
TV: _____
Other: _____
Burial: Yes ___ No ___ Cremation: Yes _____ No _____

Graveside Service:
Date and Time: _____
Cemetery: _____
Minister: _____

Parts of the Service:
Favorite Scriptures: _____
_____
_____

Music: Organ: _____ Piano: _____ Other: _____
Musician: _____ Phone: _____
Congregational Hymns: _____
_____

_____
_____
Special Music: _____
By: _____ Phone: _____
Pictorial Tribute:
By: _____ Phone: _____
Life Story/Obituary:
Prepared by: _____ Phone: _____
Read by: _____
Tributes:
1. By: _____ Phone: _____
2. By: _____ Phone: _____
3. By: _____ Phone: _____
Pallbearers:
1. _____ Phone: _____
2. _____ Phone: _____
3. _____ Phone: _____
4. _____ Phone: _____
5. _____ Phone: _____
6. _____ Phone: _____
Bulletin:
Prepared and Printed by:
Church _____ Funeral Home _____ Family _____
Picture(s): _____ Number: _____
Fellowship Reception:
Location: _____
Menu Selected: _____ Size of Family: _____
Total Number of People Expected: _____
Sharing Time after Meal: _____
Led by: _____
Display:
Location: _____
Obituary:
Printed in Denominational Periodical: _____
Printed in Local Newspaper : _____
Donations in Memory of/for: _____
Recordings of Service:
Includes Sharing Time: Yes _____ No _____
Number: DVD _____ USB _____

2. Preliminary Service Order

When I meet with the family, I will say, "I am here to help you plan a funeral service for your loved ones. My desire is that you will be involved in planning this service, and I will provide help wherever you might need and request it. I also recognize that you might never have planned a memorial service. This form provides a structure on how to plan a service." While I use a standard format, I also encourage the family to suggest changes, as long as they are appropriate and fitting.

However, I also realize that in many faith traditions the leader, be it a priest, a pastor, or some other member of the clergy, will have a clearly developed and accepted structure that is fairly standard and that there will be little input from the family.

A family will often ask how long a normal funeral service should be. My response is that the part of the service that will be shorter or longer is the family part. This includes the tributes by the children and the grandchildren, as well as the spoken and pictorial life story. When there are a larger number of grandchildren, I suggest that one or two speak on behalf of all the grandchildren, sharing stories and memories from those who will not speak in the service. I also state that the pictorial life story should not include all the events from all the time periods in a long life. Having said this, I emphasize that the service will be the only one that the family will plan for their loved one. Therefore, I encourage the family to make it as special as they wish.

> **Structure of the Central Funeral Rite**
> The Gathering
> The Procession to the Front of the Church
> Service of Prayer and Word
> • Collect
> • Prayer of Confession
> • Scripture
> • Sermon or Homily
> • Naming and Witness
> • Creed
> • Prayers of Intercession
> Holy Communion
> Sending

ORDER OF SERVICE
Organ/ Piano Prelude
Procession
Welcome and Prayer
Hymn
Special Music
Family Items
• Life Story
• Tributes:
    a. Children,
    b. Grandchildren

- Visual Life Story
- Other?

Message
Music
Hymn
Closing Remarks and Benediction
Recessional

3. Funeral Catering Menu

Each church will have its own practice regarding food services at a memorial service. The family for whom the service is planned might not be a part of the church where the funeral for their parents takes place. This means that they will not be aware of the practices of the church they are dealing with. We attempt to meet specific requests from the family, such as providing gluten-free baking or providing an item that was special to the family. Each church will have its own method of providing a luncheon or refreshments. A church form should include as many details as possible. The main concern is that we be clear and open regarding the food that will be provided and the cost.

4. Price List for Memorial Services

I believe it is important to be transparent and clearly explain the costs involved. The majority of families expect there will be expenses and will be satisfied with an explanation. Each church will have its own specific arrangements. It is crucial that these are understood. These are the items on our church's "Memorial Price List":

a. Bulletins
b. Catering
c. DVD recordings
d. Facilities—itemize the various areas if necessary
e. Custodial
f. Sound technician/PA

Appendix C
Legal and Financial Matters

The following comments will best be understood using the metaphor that this book is based on—our life is a marathon that we will finish as we cross the finish line. For some people, the marathon is brief, and for other people it is longer. However, at some point, each person will cross the finish line. Each of us

> End-of-life decisions should not be made at the end of life.

has the choice—and I stress also the responsibility—to make decisions that apply both to the time before and the time after we die. Also, our choices deal with various matters. The book has dealt primarily with spiritual and relational matters. However, decisions will need to be made in other areas, including legal, financial, and medical matters. If you do not make these decisions, then other people will make them for you. Also, it is best that these decisions are made in consultation with your family members and/or close friends.

First, a word of caution: I am not a lawyer and cannot and do not provide legal advice. The contents of this section do not constitute legal advice, are not intended to be a substitute for legal advice, and should not be relied upon as such. The regulations in matters such as a power of attorney, a will, a representation agreement, and advance care planning will vary based on a person's province or state. Every effort has been made to ensure that the material is correct, but I cannot guarantee its accuracy or completeness.

Medical and health decisions will be dealt with in the next section. In this section, I will briefly discuss the legal and financial matters.

1. A Power of Attorney and a Will

A "power of attorney" is a legal document. It gives someone you trust the power to look after your property (your legal and financial affairs) if you are unable to do so. This might include paying bills, depositing or withdrawing money from your bank account, investing your money, or selling your home. There are distinctions between a "limited power of attorney" (restricting the appointed person's powers to a specific task or time period), an "enduring power of attorney" (giving the person authority which "endures" after you are mentally incapable, whether due to illness, an accident, or age-related decline), and a "springing power of attorney" (giving the person authority only after a "triggering event" such as two physicians declaring you to be mentally incapable).

The person you give this power to is called the "attorney." In this case, "attorney" does not mean "lawyer." It simply means the person you have chosen to be your decision-maker.

It is important to be aware of the differences between a power of attorney and a will. A "will" helps other people distribute your possessions after your death. A "power of attorney" helps you plan the management of your affairs during your lifetime. An "executor" is the person named in a will to carry out (execute) the instructions in the will after you have died. An "attorney" is the person responsible for your legal and financial matters during your life.

2. The Value of a Will

A will is a legal document that says what you want done with your property when you die. This property includes real estate, money, investments, and personal and household belongings. You can change your will at any time. A will has no legal effect until you die.

Every adult who owns assets or has a spouse or young children should have a will. If you don't have a will, you lose control over who gets your money and property, and when. You also give up the right to appoint a guardian for any young children you have. The costs to administer your estate will be much higher when you do not have a will.

A will doesn't deal with some types of property. A will generally doesn't cover property you don't own exclusively. For example, a joint bank account or a house owned in joint tenancy has a "right of survivorship." That means these automatically become the property of the joint survivor when you die. Also, a will does not apply to property such as life insurance, retirement savings plans and income funds, and tax-free savings accounts if you have already named a beneficiary for them.

If you pass away without having made a will, the law says how your property will get distributed and who has the right to administer your affairs.

3. Estate Planning

With estate planning, you might be able to reduce fees and taxes that your estate would otherwise pay. Consider, for example, the following strategies:

a. Joint Assets. These can include a joint bank account that two or more people own, or a home owned by two or more people as joint tenants. The owners of joint assets have a "right of survivorship." That is, the home is said to "pass outside your will" to the other joint owner.

b. Assets with a Designated Beneficiary. Registered retirement savings plans (RRSPs), registered retirement income funds (RRIFs), and tax-free savings accounts (TFSAs) all let you name a beneficiary who will get the proceeds when you die.

c. Life Insurance Policies. These let you name a beneficiary to receive money at your death. This money passes outside your will and does not go through the estate. This means the life insurance funds are not used to pay off the debts of the estate.

d. Trusts. Depending on the size of your estate, you might want to set up a trust (outside the will) to protect your estate against someone undertaking legal action to change some terms of your will (that is, making a wills variation claim).

e. Charitable Gifts. You can reduce the income tax owing from the sale of your assets on your death by making charitable gifts or bequests in your will. Here are several things to consider:
- You can reduce the income tax owing from the sale of your assets on your death by making charitable gifts in your will.
- The charitable gift might be a specific dollar amount or a percentage of the assets.
- A suggestion is to add another "child" in your will. By this I mean that if you have three children between which your estate is to be divided, then you can divide the estate into four units—each of the three children will receive one quarter, and the fourth child, your selected charities, will receive the other quarter.
- To leave a charitable bequest in your will, it is often best to use a public foundation such as Abundance Canada (www.abundance.ca).

4. The Importance of Getting It Right

There are good do-it-yourself materials available that can help you write a simple will. The will can take care of basic concerns, such as leaving a home, investments, and personal items to loved ones. However, you should be aware that there are rules and formalities that must be followed, no matter how simple the will. Otherwise, the will might not be valid.

A will is a legally binding document. Having your will prepared by an experienced estates lawyer or notary public is the safest way to avoid mistakes. Knowing your will is properly drafted can give you peace of mind. That way, you can be confident your affairs will be handled according to your wishes. To make an effective will requires a good understanding of property ownership rules and the laws about wills. The words used must be chosen carefully so that the will is clear. If the formalities are ignored or the terms of the will are unclear, there might be extra legal costs for your estate to get court orders to fix the problems—and in some cases, that might not even be possible.

Getting professional help is particularly important when there are features such as a blended family, a charitable gift, property outside the province or state in which you live, a family business, a desire to hold property in trust for someone (such as minor children), or a wish to leave certain people out of your will.

5. Choosing an Executor

When it comes to choosing an executor, you should choose someone you trust and who will likely be alive when you die. This person might be a trusted family member or friend. Often, people appoint their spouse, but if both of you are old, an adult child might be a better choice. It helps if your executor is well organized, good at keeping records, and a good communicator. Most importantly, the person must be willing to do the job as executor.

You can appoint more than one executor, and the executors can act together as co-executors. It's important to appoint an alternate executor, who can take over if the first executor can no longer act.

If you have a complex estate or investments or need someone to take over the operation of a company, you should consider naming a professional executor. This person might be a lawyer, an accountant, or another professional. Trust companies can also be the executor if the estate is big enough. Professionals and trust companies charge for their services.

6. Appointing a Guardian If you are a parent or guardian of a minor child or children (under 19 years old), the law usually lets you appoint someone to be the child's guardian in your will. It is especially important to name a guardian if you are a single parent. For separated parents, it's best to agree on the choice of a guardian if one or both of the parents dies. If that's not possible, it's important to sort out the parenting responsibilities (through a court order or separation agreement) and ensure that the other parent is included as part of appointing a guardian in your will.

Although your choice of guardian is important, the court doesn't have to follow your wishes and might appoint a different guardian if it is determined that would be in the child's best interests. The court will consider the wishes of any child twelve or older, so you should check with older children about their wishes before deciding on whom to name as guardian in our will.

The guardian's job is to look after your minor children. The guardian might in turn appoint a replacement guardian. The guardian generally doesn't have any rights to look after a minor child's property. The guardian can only receive and hold a minor child's property or money if it's worth less than $10,000. If the child's property exceeds that amount, you should appoint a trustee to manage the minor child's inheritance. The executor can be the same person as the trustee.

It is helpful to create a trust to protect a minor child's interest in an estate. Make sure your will is written so that children under 19 won't have direct access to their share until they are 19 or older. If minors are entitled to a share in an estate and the will doesn't say that their share is going to be held in trust for them, the law usually says their share has to be paid to a Public Guardian and Trustee to be held in trust for the minor until the child is 19 years old. It is best to speak to a lawyer about drafting a trust.

7. The Importance of Preparation

You can minimize legal fees by preparing well.

You should have the following information ready before you meet with a lawyer or notary public about preparing your will:

• A list of everyone in your immediate family, with their full names and contact information, their relationship to you, and the ages of all your children, including stepchildren.

• The names and addresses of any other people or organizations you want to give gifts to.

• A list of all your assets and their values, including your home, your car, your investments, and any personal items of significant monetary value.

• A description of how you own these assets (for example, alone or with someone else).

• A document that shows whose name is on the title of any real estate you own.

• Details of any insurance policies your own and, specifically, the beneficiaries under the policies.

• Details of any pensions, retirement savings plans or income funds, and tax-free savings accounts, and who the beneficiaries are.

• Information on the structure of any business you operate (for example, a company or partnership).

- Any separation agreements or court orders requiring you to make support payments or dealing with guardianship of any minor children.
- The name, address, and occupation of your executor and guardian.

8. Filing a Wills Notice

A wills notice should be filed with the wills registry of your province or state. A wills notice says who made the will and where it is kept. This is a voluntary registration and has a small filing fee. The registry does not take a copy of your will. Instead, you or your lawyer or notary will fill out an information form listing where your will is kept. After you die, a search of the wills registry is required for the court probate process to ensure the court has the last will.

9. Review the Will

It's good to review your will every three to five years to ensure that it still reflects your current wishes. You should consider changing your will whenever your financial or personal circumstances change or if your beneficiaries die or reach the age of majority. For example, if you prepared a will when your children were young and named your parents as guardian and executor, you will no longer need the guardian clause when your children become adults. You might want your adult children or a sibling to be your executor instead. You should also review your will after any change in your marital status.

It is important to realize that your will can be changed after you die. If your will does not properly provide for your spouse or children (including illegitimate and adopted children), they can request to have your will changed by a court. This is called a wills variation claim. A "spouse" includes both a married spouse and a person you have lived with in a marriage-like relationship for at least two years before your death. The law is clear that you have both a legal and a moral obligation to provide for a spouse or child in a will. If you have a disabled adult child and do not leave enough for that child, the court might order that the child receive more from your estate. A lawyer can help draft an appropriately worded trust for a disabled adult child.

10. Keep the Will Safe

A common question is: "Where should I keep my will?" The answer is that you should keep the original will with your lawyer or notary or in a safety deposit box at your bank. That way, the will is in a permanent, safe, and fireproof location. Your executor will need your original will (not a copy) to give to the probate registry. You should let your executor know where you keep your will and other important documents, so the executor will know where to get it.

Appendix D
Health Matters

In the previous section, I noted that you are able to give directions regarding your financial assets through a power of attorney and a will. But these two documents do not pertain to medical matters. The following are several ways to safeguard your beliefs, values, and wishes regarding your health care treatments.

Advance Directive: This is a legal document setting out what actions should or should not be taken in regards to your health if you are no longer able to make or communicate decisions for yourself.

Representation Agreement: A representation agreement is a legal document to help you plan for your health and personal care. A representation agreement authorizes a person or persons to assist an adult with decision making (sometimes called supported decision making) or to make decisions on the adult's behalf (sometimes called substitute decision making).

Advance Care Plan: This is a verbal or written summary of a capable adult's wishes and instructions about the kind of care the person wants or does not want in the event that the person cannot speak for himself or herself. An advance care plan can be written down or simply told to someone who is authorized to speak for the patient, such as a substitute decision maker. It can guide a substitute decision maker if that person is asked by a health care provider to make treatment decisions on behalf of the adult.

Medical Order for Scope of Treatment (MOST): This is a doctor's order based on advance care planning conversations which explore your values and goals and the range of treatments available. This is a tool to communicate medical orders to health care providers and ambulance services.

Appendix E
Necessary Information

Throughout your life, you are making decisions, some minor and some major. It is necessary and helpful to have a process of storing and finding critical documents that is both straightforward and easy. This is important at all stages of your life but especially as you approach the end of your life.

There are decisions that pertain particularly to the last years of your life. Yet it is wise if these decisions are made earlier in life. These include decisions regarding your will, organ donation, a living will, a representation agreement, and funeral plans. The option is yours: you can choose to take care of these things when you can calmly make your decisions and then inform people what these decisions are, what the important information is, and where it can be found. If you don't take care of these items now, then these decisions will be made by your children or your spouse when they are in shock and grief. Also, if your will is not made, then the government will make decisions for you.

It is wise to have conversations with your children, or whomever you assign to be responsible for your life affairs such as your medical care, finances, and funeral plans.

Family members or whomever you assign as responsible for your funeral and your estate should be able to easily locate your important information. It is necessary to review your information on a regular basis.

It is also helpful to keep a copy of this information on a computer file where it can be easily updated. However, the most reliable and accessible form of information is paper—yes, paper—because when you have entered information using some software, it is not guaranteed that your children, or whoever wishes to access it, will have the necessary software.

Professional forms with these items are available from funeral homes, insurance companies, banks, lawyers, and financial advisors.

Also, some of this information will vary depending on the jurisdiction where you live. An example is that some provinces will have standard living will and representation agreements. Therefore, when a person moves, especially in the later years of life, this needs to be clearly understood. Also, the government policy that applies where the parents live might not be the same as the policy where the children live.

Important Documents and Decisions

☐ Vital Statistics
Name: _____
Address: _____
Phone: _____
Occupation, Title: _____
Birth Certificate: _____
Medical Care Card: _____
Social Insurance Number: _____
Veteran's Serial Number: _____
Date of Birth: _____
Place of Birth: _____
Canadian Citizenship Number: _____
Father's Name: _____
Father's Birthplace: _____
Mother's Maiden Name: _____
Mother's Birthplace: _____
Spouse: _____

☐ Will:
Lawyer: _____
Company: _____
Address: _____
Phone: _____
Email: _____
Person with Copy of Will: _____
Second Person with Copy: _____

☐ Power of Attorney:
Name: _____
Address: _____
Phone: _____
Email: _____

☐ Executor:
Name: _____
Address: _____
Phone: _____
Email: _____

☐ **Living Will / Representation Agreement**
Discuss with your family and doctor.

☐ **Organ Donation**
Individual decisions each of us must make.

☐ **Life Insurance Policies**
Insurance Co. #1: _____
Policy #: _____
Name of Agency: _____
Phone: _____
Name of Insured: _____
Beneficiary: _____

Insurance Co. #2: _____
Policy #: _____
Name of Agency: _____
Phone: _____
Name of Insured: _____
Beneficiary: _____

☐ **Bank Accounts & Investments**
Checking Account #1: _____
Institution: _____
Location: _____

Checking Account #2: _____
Institution: _____
Location: _____

Savings Account #1: _____
Institution: _____
Location: _____

Savings Account #2: _____
Institution: _____
Location: _____

☐ **RRSPs, IRAs, 401(k)s**
Account #1: _____
Institution: _____
Location: _____

Account #2: _____
Institution: _____
Location: _____

☐ **RRIFs or LIFs**
RRIF or LIF #1: _____
Institution: _____
Location: _____

RRIF or LIF #2: _____
Institution: _____
Location: _____

☐ **TFSA**
TFSA #1: _____
Institution: _____
Location: _____

☐ **Other Investments:**
Type of Account: _____
Account #: _____
Institution: _____
Location: _____

Type of Account: _____
Account #: _____
Institution: _____
Location: _____

☐ **Deeds to Real Estate**
If mortgage, #: _____
Mortgage Company: _____
Location: _____

Property Type: _____
Value: _____
Location: _____

☐ **Credit Cards**
Type of card: _____
Credit Card No: _____
PIN: _____

Type of card: _____
Credit Card No: _____
PIN: _____

Type of card: _____
Credit Card No: _____
PIN: _____

❒ Income Tax Returns
Account No.: _____
Location of papers: _____

❒ Marriage License
Spouse: _____
Where Married: _____
Date of Marriage: _____
Location of Certificate: _____

❒ Funeral - Preplanned
Funeral Home: _____
Location: _____
Funeral Director: _____
Choice: Embalming: Yes___   No___
          Cremation: Yes___   No___
Cemetery: _____
Location: _____
Contact Phone: _____

❒ Funeral Service - Preplanned
Church: _____
Location: _____
Telephone: _____
Email: _____
Pastor: _____
Phone: _____

❒ Family - Names & Addresses
❒ Children
Contact #1: Son: _____ Daughter: _____
Name: _____
Address: _____

Phone: _____
Email: _____

Contact #2: Son: _____ Daughter: _____
Name: _____
Address: _____
Phone: _____
Email: _____

Contact #3: Son: _____ Daughter: _____
Name: _____
Address: _____
Phone: _____
Email: _____

Contact #4: Son: _____ Daughter: _____
Name: _____
Address: _____
Phone: _____
Email: _____

☐ **Grandchildren**
   Contact #1: Male: _____ Female: _____
   Name: _____
   Address: _____
   Phone: _____
   Email: _____

☐ **Sisters and Brothers**

☐ **Cousins**

☐ **Nieces and Nephews**

☐ **Friends - names & addresses**

Appendix F
Definitions

Burial Service: also known as a "committal service," where the body or cremains (ashes of a loved one) are committed to the ground or final resting place.

Casket: a chest or container intended for treasured items. When this word is used in the funeral context, it certainly implies that the body is treasured.

Catafalque: a wooden stand or metal support on which a coffin or casket is placed.

Coffin: comes from the Greek word *"koffinos,"* meaning a "basket." This is a long, narrow box, often tapered at both ends, in which the body of the deceased is placed.

Columbarium: an above ground structure in a cemetery where urns containing cremated remains can be placed in small compartments or "niches."

Committal service: This service has two meanings: a service in which we commit the body or the ashes to the ground as well as a service in which we commit or entrust our loved one to God.

Cortege: a solemn procession, traditionally the procession of mourners traveling on foot behind a vehicle conveying a body in a casket or coffin. The cortege will proceed from the place where the funeral ceremony was held to the place of burial.

Crematorium or Crematory: a venue for the cremation of the dead. In many countries, crematoria contain facilities for funeral ceremonies, such as a chapel.

Eulogy or Life story: The word *"eulogy"* is a compound word consisting of *"eu"* (meaning "well, good") and *"logos"* (meaning "word"). "Eulogy" and "life story" can be used interchangeably. A life story begins with the basic facts that comprise an obituary. Then, various elements are expanded upon, and personal reflections or memories are added.

Funeral Service: the traditional and accepted name for the gathering to remember a departed person.
• **Memorial Service:** a service in which we thank God for the memories of a loved one. This service will normally be without the body of the deceased.
• **Celebration of Life Service:** a service to celebrate the life of a person. When this is a Christian service, the purpose will be to celebrate God's faithfulness in the life of a loved one.

Funeral Celebrant: a person trained and certified to provide a funeral, memorial, or celebration of life service that is highly personalized to reflect the personality, lifestyle, and beliefs of the person who died.

Interment: the act of interring or burying. The English word "inter" comes from the Latin *"in"* (meaning "in") and *"terra"* (meaning "earth"). Therefore, "interment" refers to placing a body "in the earth."

Mausoleum: an above ground structure in a cemetery where caskets are placed in specially constructed compartments called "crypts."

Obituary: a short account of a person's life that includes key events. This is the brief write-up that will be used for a local newspaper or other media.

Tribute: A tribute consists of words of appreciation for the life and the achievements of a loved one. The purpose of a tribute is to share specific memories and express how the loved one left a positive impact on the life of the person giving the tribute.

Appendix G
Selected Books on Aging and the End of Life

Aging/Funerals/Dying

Billings, J. Todd. *The End of the Christian Life: How Embracing Our Mortality Frees Us to Truly Live.* Grand Rapids, Michigan: Brazos Press, 2020.

Breuhaus, Betty. *When the Sun Goes Down: A Serendipitous Guide to Planning Your Own Funeral.* New York, Lincoln, Shanghai: iUniverse Inc., 2007.

Callanan, Maggie, and Patricia Kelley. *Final Gifts: Understanding the Special Awareness, Needs, and Communications of the Dying.* New York: Simon and Schuster, 2012.

Cullen, Lisa Takeuchi. *Remember Me: A Lively Tour of the New American Way of Death.* New York: Harper Collins, 2006.

Craddock, Fred, Dale Goldsmith, and Joy V. Goldsmith. *Speaking of Dying: Recovering the Church's Voice in the Face of Death.* Grand Rapids, Michigan: Brazos Press, 2012.

Dugdale, L. S. *The Lost Art of Dying: Reviving Forgotten Wisdom.* New York: Harper One, An Imprint of HarperCollins Publishers, 2020.

Fournier, Elizabeth. *The Green Burial Guidebook: Everything You Need to Plan an Affordable, Environmentally Friendly Burial.* Novato, California: New World Library, 2018.

Gordon-Lennox, Jeltje. *Crafting Meaningful Funeral Rituals: A Practical Guide.* London and Philadelphia: Jessica Kingsley Publishers, 2020.

Habenstein, Robert W., and William M. Lamers. *Funeral Customs the World Over.* Milwaukee: Bulfin Printers, 1963.

Hauerwas, Stanley, Carole Bailey Stoneking, Keith G. Meador, and David Cloutier, eds. *Growing Old in Christ.* Grand Rapids, Michigan: William B. Eerdmans Publishing Company, 2003.

Herring, Lucinda. *Reimagining Death: Stories and Practical Wisdom for Home Funerals and Green Burials.* Berkeley, California: North Atlantic Books, 2019.

Houston, James M. *Joyful Exiles: Life in Christ on the Dangerous Edge of Things.* Downers Grove, Illinois: IVP Books, 2006.

Houston, James M., and Michael Parker. *A Vision for the Aging Church: Renewing Ministry for and by Seniors.* Downers Grove, Illinois: IVP Academic, 2011.

Lane, Annette M., and Marlette B. Reed. *Making Meaning in Older Age: Bringing Together the Pieces of Your Life.* Winnipeg, Manitoba: Word Alive Press, 2017.

Long, Thomas G. *Accompany Them with Singing: The Christian Funeral.* Louisville, Kentucky: Westminster John Knox Press, 2013.

Long, Thomas G., and Thomas Lynch. *The Good Funeral: Death, Grief, and the Community of Care.* Louisville, Kentucky: Westminster John Knox Press, 2013.

Moll, Rob. *The Art of Dying: Living Fully into the Life to Come.* Downers Grove, Illinois: InterVarsity Press, 2010.

Mitford, Jessica. *The American Way of Death.* New York: Simon and Schuster, 1978.

Nouwen, Henri J. M. *Our Greatest Gift*: A Meditation on Dying and Caring. New York: HarperCollins Publishers, 1994.

Packer, J. I. *Finishing Our Course with Joy: Guidance from God for Engaging with Our Aging.* Wheaton, Illinois: Crossway, 2014.

Perry, Tim. *Funerals: For the Care of Souls.* Bellingham, Washington: Lexham Press, 2021.

Schmidt, Alvin J. *Cremation, Embalmment, or Neither?: A Biblical/Christian Evaluation.* Bloomington, Indiana: WestBow Press, 2015.

Schmidt, Alvin J. *Dust to Dust or Ashes to Ashes? A Biblical and Christian Examination of Cremation.* Salisbury, MA: Regina Orthodox Press Inc. 2005.

Stevens, R. Paul. *Aging Matters: Finding your calling for the rest of your life.* Grand Rapids, Michigan, Cambridge, U.K.: William B. Eerdmans Publishing Company, 2016.

Swinton, John, and Richard Payne, eds. *Living Well and Dying Faithfully: Christian Practices for End-of-Life Care.* Grand Rapids, Michigan: William B. Eerdmans Publishing Company, 2009.

Verhey, Allen. *The Christian Art of Dying: Learning from Jesus.* Grand Rapids, Michigan: William B. Eerdmans Publishing Company, 2011.

Minister's Manuals and Handbooks
Biddle, Perry H. *A Funeral Manual.* Grand Rapids, Michigan: William B. Eerdmans Publishing Company, 1984.

Christensen, James L. *The Complete Handbook for Ministers.* Old Tappan, New Jersey: Fleming H. Revell Company, 1985.

Engle, Paul E., ed. *The Baker Funeral Handbook.* Grand Rapids, Michigan: Baker Books, 2017.

Erdman, Chris. *Countdown to Sunday: A Daily Guide for Those who Dare to Preach.* Grand Rapids, Michigan: Brazos Press, 2007.

Fowler, Gene. *Caring through the Funeral: A Pastor's Guide.* St. Louis, Missouri: Chalice Press, 2004.

Rempel, John, ed. *Minister's Manual.* Newton, Kansas, Winnipeg, Manitoba: Faith and Life Press; Scottdale, Pennsylvania, Waterloo, Ontario: Herald Press, 1998.

Grief and Sorrow
Billings, J. Todd. *Rejoicing in Lament: Wrestling with Incurable Cancer and Life in Christ.* Grand Rapids, Michigan: Brazos Press, 2015.

Hastings, W. Ross. *Where Do Broken Hearts Go? An Integrative, Participational Theology of Grief.* Eugene, Oregon: Cascade Books, 2016.

Manning, Doug. *Don't Take My Grief Away from Me: How to Walk Through Grief and Learn to Live Again.* Oklahoma City, Oklahoma: In-Sight Books, 2005.

Sleeth, Matthew. *Hope Always: How to be a force for life in a culture of suicide.* Carol Stream, Illinois: Tyndale Momentum, 2021.

Zylla, Phil C. *The Roots of Sorrow: A Pastoral Theology of Suffering.* Waco, Texas: Baylor University Press, 2012.

MAiD and Physician Assisted Suicide
Chamberlain, Paul. *Final Wishes: A Cautionary Tale on Death, Dignity, and Physician-Assisted Suicide,* Eugene, Oregon: WIPF and Stock Publishers, 2009.

Coleman, Gerald D. "Priests Who Minister to Patients Regarding Physician-Assisted Suicide," *Health Progress* (November December 2016): 72-76.

Euthanasia Prevention Coalition, blog maintained by Alex Schadenberg, EPC International Chair.

Evangelical Fellowship of Canada articles and posts.

Farley, Vicki. "The Chaplain's Role Where Aid in Dying is Legal," *Health Progress* (January – February 2015): 11 – 13.

Government of Canada. *Second Annual Report on Medical Assistance in Dying in Canada 2020,* June 2021.

MB Biblical Seminary, NAVIGATE, Medical Assistance in Dying (MAiD): An interactive conversation to further understanding of MAiD and our response as Mennonite Brethren, November 24, 2020, presentations by Doug Heidebrecht, Brian Cooper, and Gloria Woodland.

Simpson, Alexander I. F. "Medical Assistance in Dying and Mental Health: A Legal, Ethical, and Clinical Analysis," *Canadian Journal of Psychiatry* Vol. 62, No. 2 (February 2018): 80–84.

Woodland, Gloria. "Ministry amid Competing Values: Pastoral Care and Medical Assistance in Dying," *Direction*, A Mennonite Brethren Forum, Fall 2018, Vol. 47, No. 2: 142-153.

Woodland, Gloria. MB Biblical Seminary course, "Understand the Scope of Perspectives and Ministry in MAiD."

Financial and Medical Decisions
Abundance Canada (www.abundance.ca).

Foster, Sandra E. *You Can't Take It with You: Common-Sense Estate Planning for Canadians.* Mississauga, Ontario: John Wiley and Sons, 2007.

My Voice: Expressing My Wishes for Future Health Care Treatment. British Columbia Ministry of Health (healthlink.bc.ca), 2020.

Wark, Kevin. *The Essential Canadian Guide to Estate Planning: A Journey towards Peace of Mind,* 2017.

Restoring Relationships
Bevere, John. *The Bait of Satan: Living Free from the Deadly Trap of Offense.* Lake Mary, Florida: Charisma House, 2011.

Carlson, Dwight L. *Overcoming Hurt and Anger: Finding Freedom from Negative Emotions.* Eugene, Oregon: Harvest House Publishers, 2000.

Johnson, Richard P. *How to Honor Your Aging Parents: Principles of Caregiving.* Ligouri, Missouri: Ligouri Publications, 1999.

Kendall, R. T. *Total Forgiveness: When Everything in You Wants to Hold a Grudge, Point a Finger and Remember the Pain—God Wants You to Lay It All Aside.* Lake Mary, Florida: Charisma House, 2002.

Lederach, John Paul. *The Journey Toward Reconciliation.* Scottsdale, Pennsylvania; Waterloo, Ontario: Herald Press, 1999.

Nori, Don. *Breaking Generational Curses: Releasing God's Power in Us, Our Children, and Our Destiny.* Shippensburg, Pennsylvania: Destiny Image Publishers, 2005.

Palmer, Parker J. *A. Hidden Wholeness: The Journey Toward an Undivided Life; Welcoming the Soul and Weaving Community in a Wounded World.* San Francisco: Jossey-Bass, 2004.

Pritchard, Ray. *The Healing Power of Forgiveness.* Eugene, Oregon: Harvest House Publishers, 2005.

Seamands, David. *Healing of Damaged Emotions.* Wheaton, Illinois: Scripture Press, 1981.

Walters, Trevor. *EAS Syndrome: Healing Burnout in Adults Lacking Parental Affirmation.* Newport Beach, California: Anglican House, 2016.

Wilson, Rod J. K. *Counseling and Community: Using Church Relationships to Reinforce Counseling.* Thomas Nelson, 1995; Vancouver, British Columbia: Regent College Publishing, 2003.

Appendix H
Index

People
Auden, W. H., 82, 255
Bevere, John, 112
Billings, J. Todd, 26, 141, 160, 168, 169, 170, 264, 276, 303
Billy Graham Association, 301
Book of Common Prayer, The, 293
Breuhaus, Betty, 189, 190
Craddock, Fred, 14, 165, 261, 262, 304
Cullen, Takeuchi, 189
Fournier, Elizabeth, 189
Gordon-Lennox, Jeltje, 189
Hancock, Maxine, 142
Hastings, W. Ross, 51, 173, 177, 200, 214, 273, 289, 294
Henson, Bill, 171
Herring, Lucinda, 189
Houston, James, 82, 128, 130, 151, 165, 244
Johnson, Richard P., 84
Long, Thomas G., 30, 36, 37, 40, 43, 44, 45, 50, 52, 53, 146, 157, 160, 175, 176, 188, 191, 198, 206, 226, 243, 260, 264, 271, 274, 275, 278, 289
Lynch, Thomas, 30, 43, 44, 45, 50, 53, 175, 176, 188, 206, 260
Manning, Doug, 159, 160, 161, 189, 190
Moller, David Wendell, 156, 157
Moll, Rob, 157, 270
Navigators, 301
Phipps, William, 185
Power to Change, 301
Rempel, John, 226, 227
Schmidt, Alvin, 186, 187
Sleeth, Matthew, 287, 288, 290
Verhey, Allen, 14, 56, 157, 201
Walter, Trevor, 117, 118
Wilson, Rod J. K., p. 203, 304
Zylla, Phil C., 214

Topics
Abuse, present in people whose funeral we plan, 240
Acceptance of the present, 95
Ageism, 151
Assurance that will cross the finish line, 87, 297
    Summaries of becoming a Christian, 300
Blessing, giving and receiving, 118
Bodies (honoring our bodies), 146
Bulletins, 64, 215
Burial, 67
    Special items in a burial service, 69, 233
    Traditional versus cremation, 183
    Words spoken at burial, 219
Catafalque, 337
Celebration of life – see Funeral service
Children, 64, 215, 291
Coffins
    Selection of a coffin, 67
    Casket or coffin, 231
    Caskets, 231, 337
Columbarium, 337
Commendation, 226
Committal service, 226, 337
Community, 121
Consumerism, 174
Cortege, 337
Cremation, 183, 337
Culture – Post-Christian, 149
Death, 160 ff
    Understanding, 160
    Avoidance of, 164
Donations, 60, 208
Eulogy
    Spoken, printed, and a pictorial life story, 338
    Personal legacy, life story, 61, 79, 210, 311
    Obituary, 61, 209
    Tribute, 63, 211
    Open microphone, 163, 247
Executor, 34, 47, 48, 193, 322, 324
Family brokenness
    Recognizing brokenness, 75, 237
    Appeal for reconciliation, 36

    Conflicting expectations in funerals, 294
Flowers, 60, 70, 208, 233
Funeral home – things to consider, 43
Funeral practices, 181 ff
    Contemporary, a changing landscape 189
Forgiveness – see Restoring relationships, 116
Funeral home, partnering with, 197
Funeral service
    Naming the service, 49, 66, 199
    Need for a funeral service, 29
    Planning a funeral service, 33, 193
    Parts of a funeral service, 49, 199
    History of Christian funeral, 259
    Essence of the Christian funeral, 260
    Manuals, 261
    Structure of the central Funeral Rite, 266
Funeral message, 269
    What not to preach, 270
    What to preach, 274
    Purpose of a good funeral, 275
Difficult funerals, 281
    Pandemic – Funerals in a pandemic, 284
    For those not in the faith, 289
Health span, 162
Hope, 59, 95
Hymns, 65, 216
Grief, 57, 204, 212
Individualism, 155
Legal matters, 321
    Power of attorney, 321
    Will, 321
    Executor, 324
Life story - See also Eulogy
    Faith legacy, personal legacy, 79, 253
    Values underlying life story, 79
    Guidelines in writing a life story, 83
MAiD – Medical Assistance in Dying, 166
Mausoleum, 338
Memorial service – see Funeral service
Mentoring, 129
Message, 274
Murder – see a difficult funeral, 291
Obituary - see Eulogy, 338

Pain, avoidance of, 161
Pallbearers, 68, 232
Pastors, 243 ff
    Pastoral priorities, 243
    Clergy confidentiality, 245
    Representing God faithfully, 246
    Acknowledging brokenness and limitations, 249
Planning, 33 ff
    Considering parents, 40
    Planning reveals core values, 47
    Role of executor, 34
    When still can plan, 39
    Decisions required, 39
Personhood, 51, 200
    Greek understanding of personhood, 51
    Society's understanding of personhood, 52
    Biblical understanding of personhood, 53
Professionalism, 154
Restoring peace in relationships, 103
    Reasons to restore relationships, 104
    Classes of broken relationships, 107
    Restoring peace within a family, 115
Suicide, 83, 287
Torch, 57, 206, 268
Tributes, 63, 211, 338
Viewing, 49, 182, 200
    Reasons for viewing, 56, 202
    Reasons people chose not to have a viewing, 49.
Youth – versus inter-generational, 172

Endorsements

"Some 500 years before Christ, Heraclitus wrote, 'No man ever steps into the same river twice, for it is not the same river and he is not the same man.' In *Preparing to Cross the Finish Line*, Pastor Walter Wiens is acutely aware how very fast-moving societal shifts in our time impact all of life, including the planning of memorial services. This book is comprised of two parts, the first one addressed to families and individuals planning the memorial of a loved one, and the second one addressed to pastors presiding over funerals. Evident is the author's long experience in walking with families in their grieving while sensitively dealing with complex issues such as deciding between burial or cremation, offering comfort following suicide, dealing with the fallout from MAiD, planning a green funeral, and navigating funeral arrangements with grace when conflict has fractured a family. In addition to reflecting a rich pastoral experience, *Preparing to Cross the Finish Line* embodies wide consultation and extensive reading. Entrenched in this book is a comforting spirituality variously expressed, including a prayer at the conclusion of each chapter. Readability is enhanced by numerous insets with thought-summaries or theme-related citations. Perhaps the greatest strength of this publication is the author's continuous use of Scripture as central to planning memorials in ways that encourage both worship and healing."

– *David Giesbrecht*
Abbotsford, B.C.

"In a society that seems to reflect less on the aging process and the inevitability of each of us dying, *Preparing to Cross the Finish Line* reminds us of the reality of death and the importance of preparing for it and helping our families and others around us do the same. It does so in an engaging way as each chapter ends with thought-provoking questions and helpful next steps. The second part provides a vast resource for leaders, pastors, and officiators to understand caring for, supporting, and guiding those in grief, while also providing background for helping families prepare for a funeral. The writer's lengthy experience and passion for end-of-life issues makes it a must read for individuals and pastors alike."

– Dwayne Barkman, retired pastor,
Warman, Saskatchewan

"I have had the privilege of working with Pastor Walter Wiens as a funeral director in the Abbotsford community for many years. He and I have served together helping hundreds of families, and I have always appreciated his passion for this particular part of pastoral ministry. It is appointed unto man once to die, yet our society behaves as though we will not. Most pastors find themselves unprepared when they are first called upon to care for the grieving. Pastor Walter brings his experience to bear as he discusses the details that should be considered by the church, the clergy, and families as they prepare to honor their loved one. He has done an excellent job of covering all of the thorny issues that can come up at the time of death, including family dysfunction and leading a funeral service during a pandemic."

– Jonathan Chapman, funeral director
Abbotsford, B.C.

"A few years ago, I lost my father and father-in-law in the space of six weeks. One funeral to plan and execute, a brief reprieve, and then another one. I think we did okay, but I can see now how beneficial it would have been to have had this wisdom-packed book for guidance. Walter Wiens shows us the importance of funerals and memorial services, uncovers how funeral planning can be tricky with remaining family members, and gives us many practical checklists that will make planning more simple and meaningful. His compassionate pastor's heart shines through as he shares many stories of families who faced difficulties in the process. His chapters on recognizing family brokenness and restoring peace in relationships are very beneficial. I highly recommend this book."

– Lando Klassen, founder of House of James bookstore
Abbotsford, B.C.

"*Preparing to Cross the Finish Line* takes us on a journey through the 'end of life' concerns here on earth. Both sections of the book—for families and individuals and for pastors—are comprehensive in dealing with the subject. You might be surprised by some of the themes broached when

you thought you were only reading about how to get through a funeral. This is a sensitive and thought provoking read."
–Lorraine Dick, Care Ministry Assistant,
Clearbrook Mennonite Brethren Church, Abbotsford, B.C.

"As every pastor knows, one of the key areas of ministry is serving and caring for the dying and ministering to the families of those who have passed away. Pastor Walter Wiens has spent a lifetime in compassionate caring ministries. In *Preparing to Cross the Finish Line*, he has given those facing death, their families, and all pastors relevant essential clear guidance on death and dying. I especially appreciate his twofold focus—on those receiving care and on those giving care. I know Walter as a friend and fellow pastor and am thankful for the helpful wisdom he so willingly shares. Since death is an everyday reality for all of us, I see this as a book every family and every pastor will want to possess to guide them through those times.

– Norm Miller,
retired pastor, college president, professor, chaplain, and engineer

"As a health care worker in a care home during the COVID-19 pandemic, I spent much time with the residents, caring for them, liaising with their families, and being present at their bedsides as they passed away. In this book, the inner brokenness and unresolved issues that many of us privately carry are openly validated, affirmed, and given a voice; there is a courageous and refreshing removing of the religious veil covering up our damaged, vulnerable, grieving selves; and there is a compassionate acknowledgement of personal wounding, often resulting in deeply seated, distorted concepts of God. Yet, with humble sensitivity, an open door of hope is offered, allowing a freedom to openly express real, honest emotions and dialogue in a safe, secure environment. Ever so gently, one is drawn to a place where almost even "angels fear to tread, a place of personal encounter with a deeply compassionate, loving, caring God, a God, who knows, sees, and understands it all, a God who wants to comfort and heal our broken hearts. With much sensitivity, the urgent issue of broken relationships is clearly addressed, calling for courage to leave a legacy of reconciliation and restored peace. From the most dedicated pastor to the 'ordinary Joe,' from the completely unchurched to the aging senior, this book graciously offers a place of acceptance, recognition, and help in our common humanness and frailties. It provides a welcome rest for one's soul as we, together, 'Prepare to Cross the Finished Line.'"

– Vi Wiens
Health care worker in care homes

"The decisions and demands presented at the death of a loved one are myriad. These come when we are least able to face them. It is better to be prepared with forethought and intentional values. Pastor Walter Wiens offers us a guide which enables us to do now what we will have to do later. I encourage all readers to not only read these pages, but to also accept the wisdom and support they contain. I know Pastor Wiens to be a caring, thoughtful voice for end-of-life matters. He is effective in writing of things we tend to ignore. You will find his work to be detailed, pragmatic, and effective for the family walking through loss."
– *Scott Tolhurst, former Pastor of Clearbrook Mennonite Brethren Church, Abbotsford B.C.*

www.ingramcontent.com/pod-product-compliance
Lightning Source LLC
Chambersburg PA
CBHW080607170426
43209CB00007B/1352